SEEING OURSELVES

Exploring Ethnicity, Race and Culture

SECOND EDITION

As hard as it may be to believe,
In Canadian society, issues of race and ethnicity are often ignored.
With so little acknowledgement of our diversity,
We will remain blind to our reality.

— Kai James

SEEING OURSELVES

Exploring Ethnicity, Race and Culture

SECOND EDITION

Carl E. James
York University

THOMPSON EDUCATIONAL PUBLISHING, INC.
Toronto

Requests for permission to make copies of any part of the work should be directed to the publisher. Additional copies of the book may be obtained from the publisher.

publisher@thompsonbooks.com
www.thompsonbooks.com
Telephone: (416) 766-2763
Fax: (416) 766-0398

Canadian Cataloguing in Publication Data

James, Carl, 1952-
Seeing ourselves : exploring race, ethnicity & culture

2nd ed.
Includes bibliographical references and index.
ISBN 1-55077-103-5

1. Canada - Race relations. 2. Canada - Ethnic relations.
3. Multiculturalism - Canada. I. Title.

FC104.J35 1999 305.8'00971 C99-930426-7
F1035.A1J35 1999

Copyediting: Elizabeth Phinney
Cover Design: Elan Designs

We acknowledge the support of the Government of Canada through the Book Publishing Industry Development Program for our publishing activities.

Printed in Canada.
1 2 3 4 5 06 05 04 03 02 01 00 99

Table of Contents

Acknowledgements

That this book has been written is due to the contributions and efforts of several people to whom I owe a tremendous debt. It is appropriate that I start by acknowledging the many students (who, of course, were at the same time teachers) who participated in my classes and trusted me enough to share their experiences, thoughts, ideas and feelings during classes and through their essays. To all of them I am sincerely grateful. Their individual and collective contributions, I am sure, will further the debates and discussions of race and ethnic relations as well as anti-racism education.

I wish to acknowledge with gratitude the significant research assistance that Gordon Pon provided. His research skills, thoughtfulness, insights and commitment were critical and invaluable to my producing the manuscript and meeting the publication deadline. Gordon gave generously of his time and energy, often doing searches for me in Toronto and e-mailing materials to me in Uppsala, Sweden, where I was working in the fall of 1998. I am also grateful to Maxine Bramble, Scott Milne, Kai James and Rose Marie Patel-Fraser for their research help and support, particularly with the tedious completion tasks. Elma Thomas's computer and word processing skills as well as her general assistance were particularly invaluable in the process of preparing this manuscript. My thanks also to Fyre Jean Graveline for her illustration of the Wheel of Life.

I wish to acknowledge the superb editorial work of Elizabeth Phinney, whose revisions helped to tighten and strengthen the manuscript. I would especially like to thank the folks at Thompson Educational Publishing; particularly Keith Thompson, for his support and counsel. And to Verna Frayne, Lisa Sutcliffe and Alix Yule, who, while at Sheridan College, made possible the publication of the first edition of this book, I express my appreciation. My appreciation also goes to colleagues, especially Bengt Spowe in the Department of Teacher Training at Uppsala University, Sweden, where I was able to complete the revisions to the manuscript.

I am also indebted to my colleagues and friends, particularly Carol Geddis and Adrienne Shadd for their contribution of essays and conversations that are part of the book. Finally, a special thanks to Kai and Milderine for their constant support, of which I am always assured. In a major way, they have also contributed to this book since they have been, and will continue to be, my most significant teachers and students.

List of Tables

Preface

Since the publication of the first edition of this book in 1989, I have been fortunate in meeting and engaging in many discussions with its readers–high school, college and university students. I have also used the book in many of my own classes, and it has generated a number of questions and other very good reflective essays, some of which have been included in this new edition. From the discussions and essays, I have gained new insights and perspectives that I am also sharing. I hope that in this edition, and in the tradition of teacher as researcher, I continue to provide readers with a lens through which to view the complexity, dynamism, diversity, tensions and conflict that characterize identities and cultural relations in society, particularly in the context in which students discuss them.

In this book, the essays and comments of class participants provide critical insights into the thinking and analytical processes of "naive" or "non-expert" individuals as they reflect on issues related to ethnicity, race and culture. While I have attempted to preserve the voices of the students and the ways in which they articulate their ideas and analyses, I have used this as an occasion to dialogue with them. Therefore, while I might have a stronger presence and voice in this edition, it is not to claim a particular expertise, but to add another dimension to the debate.

I believe that effective dialogue necessarily involves the use of a familiar language or making explicit our particular meanings and/or understanding of terminologies. For this reason, I present definitions, not to underestimate the complexity of the concepts involved, but to provide a common reference. I do not pretend that there will be agreement with the definitions or with the terminologies employed. Nevertheless, I contend that they are useful tools for discussion of the issues. I am well aware that terms such as *racial minority, marginalized people, racialized Others* and so on have particular political meanings and implications, and one term might be preferred over another; so too with the terms *ethnic majority* or *dominant group*. That said, I should point out that my use of the term *racial minority* is not to indicate an inferior position but to convey the relationship of individuals or groups to the power structure of the society.

Further, on the question of complexity, it goes without saying that race, ethnicity and immigrant status do not exist independent of social class, gender, dis/ability, sexuality and other such factors. Indeed, all these factors are inter-related, and hence it is difficult to disentangle them and point to a particular factor as operating in any given situation or at one time. But the complexities and unstable relationship between the factors notwithstanding, the discussion needs to start somewhere and race or ethnicity or both are valuable points at which to enter the discussion and examine the issues.

Ultimately, any discourse that deals with anti-racism must be about preparing people to engage in social change. This means that there must be collaborative efforts, and individuals must have some knowledge about themselves and each other in order to engage in effective social action. Hopefully, the essays will provide further insight into the issues and will contribute to the discussions and dialogues in which we all must engage.

Carl E. Tonge James

INTRODUCTION

Another Look at Diversity and Difference

Racial and ethnic diversity have characterized Canada's population from the beginning. However, it has been only in recent years, with the increase in the country's racial and ethnic minority population, that we have begun to pay attention to the ways in which our political, educational, cultural and social systems meet the needs and address the issues of ethnic minorities. As Canadians, members of racial and ethnic minorities expect to have access to and participate in all of the country's activities and institutions, as well as receive all the services to which they are entitled. Given this reality, educational institutions have been initiating programs and courses to prepare students to work and live in our multiethnic, multiracial, multifaith and multicultural society.

The essays presented in this volume, gathered over a period of twelve years, contain the experiences, feelings and reactions of Ontario college and university students who participated in both compulsory and elective courses with me as they prepared to live and work in our multicultural society. The racial and ethnic mix of the students was fairly representative of the post-secondary population and program interest of students of this region; it was only because of program interests that white females were dominant in some classes, while white males were dominant in others.

What was particularly striking were the individual positions and expectations that each student brought to the course. Some wanted to hear about the Italians, West Indians, Indians, South Asians, Sikhs. As the educator and class facilitator, I was expected to teach them about these groups, since the students anticipated encountering a multiethnic work world upon leaving the post-secondary institution. Those students who were reluctant participants, and who saw diversity as a liability, asked the following questions: "Why do we have to cater to these people when they come here? After all, it was they who decided to come. Why do we have to change our way of life to please them?" And there were statements: "If I went to their country, I would have to adopt their culture. When you are in Rome, you do as the Romans do ... The immigrants are coming and taking all the jobs ... The immigrants are causing all the crimes ... The minorities are causing the racism; they cry racism for everything, especially when they don't get the jobs ... The government is just trying to please the minorities; that is why there is employment equity ... People are getting hired because of their race, not because they are qualified for the jobs." Evidently each student had a position on these issues and was attending the class for particular reasons. Encouraging them to articulate their positions and their expectations was fundamental to the pedagogical approach used in the course, for we can only engage that which is articulated, even though it may seem unacceptable (Britzman, 1991; hooks, 1988).

At the beginning of the course, participants were asked to introduce themselves only by name and the program in which they were registered (if they were in a program) or their occupation (if they were employed full time). This was followed by another round of introductions, in which participants revealed their ethnic background, race, nationality and culture to the class. As the instructor, and in order to provide an example, I usually introduced myself first. Accordingly, I identified myself as a Black African Canadian, with cultural values, habits and behaviours that reflect both my Caribbean origin and Canadian existence. I emphasized that everyone in the room was Canadian; that is, our nationality, citizenship and, to varying degrees, our culture. Therefore, unless the person were an Aboriginal, she or he must give the place (country or area) of origin of their ancestors. Caribbean participants were told that the same applied to them. Unless their ancestors were Caribs or Arawaks, they too must name their European, African or Asian origin.

Typically, participants of British origin, particularly those whose parents and grandparents were born in Canada, tended to insist that they were Canadian. When asked to recall the origins of their ancestors, they refused. Some contended that it was irrelevant and unimportant to them since their family had been here for such a long time. They practised nothing of their ancestral culture. Others would say that they would have to ask their parents for this information, because they had never talked about it at home. Frequently, some participants would say that this was the first time they had had to think about themselves in these terms and, more significantly, to articulate the word "white" as a descriptor of themselves. This exercise at times produced tension, because these "Canadian" participants felt challenged and uncomfortable. Many Black Caribbean participants, however, particularly those under twenty-two years of age and those over fifty, often insisted on identifying their ethnicity as West Indian, Caribbean, Jamaican, Trinidadian and so on, rather than African. For those Caribbean Africans, the presentation of negative images and their miseducation made them want to disassociate themselves from Africa. Some South Asians from that region would, to a lesser extent, do the same.

Some participants had trouble acknowledging the reality of racial, ethnic and cultural forces in their lives. This reflects the fact that these forces are so much a part of us that they are taken for granted. It seemed much easier, particularly for ethnic majority group members, to see these characteristics as significant to the lives and behaviours of "other" Canadians–immigrants and "multicultural" Canadians (those "with culture," such as the Italians, Chinese, Jamaicans and others).

The introductory exercise was not intended to force students to identify themselves in ethnic or racial terms or to name one as an identifier. Rather, the aim of the exercise was to have participants begin to reflect critically and examine their worldview, and to try to understand how factors such as ethnicity, race and culture help to structure the ways in which we think of ourselves and others within the context of Canadian society. It was intended to make participants begin to "paint themselves into the picture." It was meant to convey that the purpose of the course was not to study "other" Canadians–to learn about their "culture" or to study the victims of racism–but rather to have participants begin to analyze their ideas and experiences as minority and majority group Canadians, to reflect on their personal contradictions and challenges and to begin to critique the varied ways in which inequalities of power and privilege exist in our society (Dei, 1996).

The greatest challenges I faced as an instructor of this course were in persuading participants that race, ethnicity and culture are not abstract notions, but that they effect all of us personally, from how we see ourselves and others to the way the institutions in our society operate; to see the extent to which we have internalized or operate with the meanings that have been given to these factors; and to understand that culture exists and that it shapes and informs the lives of all Canadians and that it is, in turn, acted upon by all Canadians. Consequently, while assigned readings helped to create the framework for our exploration of the issues, it was the discussions, debates, reflective essays and projects that were particularly useful in the participants' process of discovery and understanding of themselves and others.

Because we were dealing with well-entrenched ideologies and deeply felt attitudes and experiences as well as with the participants' construction of reality, it was useful to present myself as both a facilitator and a learner. Therefore my presentations largely took the form of dialogue in order to facilitate students' input and to encourage them to articulate their perspectives. This was not always easy, since there were some strong oppositional or negative views that needed to be processed. However, these views were valuable, as they represent and reflect the diversity of ideas and opinion in our society. It was necessary for individuals to express them in such a way that they could be discussed in a safe and non-threatening manner.

In presenting this work, I prefer not to see my role as one of the "expert," in which I interpret or impose meaning on the participants' experiences and beliefs. Rather, I wish to present the various ways in which the

Table 1: Canadian Population by Ethnic Origin, 1996 Census (20% Sample Data)

Total population	**28,528,125**
Single origins	**18,303,625**
British Isles origins	3,267,525
French origins	2,683,840
European origins	3,742,895
Arab origins	188,430
West Asian origins	106,865
South Asian origins	590,150
East and Southeast Asian origins	1,271,450
African origins	137,315
Pacific Islands origins	5,765
Latin, Central and South American origins	118,635
Caribbean origins	305,290
Aboriginal origins	477,635
Canadian origins	5,326,995
Other origins	80,845
Multiple origins	**10,224,500**
British Isles only	1,606,445
British Isles and French	856,985
British Isles and Canadian	1,179,725
British Isles and other	2,217,370
British Isles, Canadian and other	598,635
French only	12,430
French and Canadian	597,605
French and other	435,205
French, Canadian and other	121,805
Canadian and other	579,045
British Isles, French and Canadian	280,595
British Isles, French and other	518,480
British Isles, French, Canadian and other	121,870
Other multiple origins	1,098,295

This table indicates the overall ethnic distribution of the population, based on single response categories (persons who belong to one ethnic category only) and selected multiple response categories (persons who belong to more than one ethnic category).

It also shows single response counts for all ethnic categories and multiple response counts for 14 multiple categories including British Isles, French, Canadian and other origins. Statistics Canada indicates that there is no double counting of the population in this table. Persons who provided more than one ethnic origin are included in only one of the multiple response categories. The sum of single and multiple responses is equal to the total population.

Source: Statistics Canada, 1996 Census, *Nation* tables.

participants construct themselves and others in terms of race, ethnicity and culture and to share my impressions as one who has been part of their discussions. The essays that are included were deliberately chosen to provide a picture of how anti-racism education helped, or did not help, the students to move beyond themselves to learn about each other. There may be cases with which we identify or where we see some of our own experiences reflected. Insofar as these reflections provide additional or critical insight, they might be the very catalysts that are necessary for personal growth, which in turn might compel us to engage in a process of action for social change.

Some racist or prejudiced information or positions are presented in the essays. Their inclusion is not intended to legitimize these views, but rather to engage, expose and examine them. All existing perspectives, ideas, histories and beliefs need to be included as part of this dialogue. There is a legitimate risk in doing this, for it is possible that we will merely add stereotypes, prejudices and racist information into the existing pool of misinformation, or feel that it has been validated. However, my hope is that the ideas stated in this context will help us to challenge our learned "truths" and "facts."

CHANGING THE LENS

Facilitating the study and discussion of diversity as related to race, ethnicity, culture and racism is not an easy task, for there are different schools of thought on how it should be done. There is little possibility of achieving consensus on how best to approach a teaching and learning situation in which these issues are explored. Yet, consensus is not necessary or even desirable: our social, political and emotional investment in these issues differ, and we bring our subjective viewpoints to the interpretations and understandings we hold and articulate. So what happens when we explore issues of diversity related to race and ethnicity, and give students the opportunity to talk about such issues and concerns? What will they tell us? What knowledge will be forthcoming?

I have mentioned the different perspectives that students brought to the course, the concerns expressed and the reluctance of some to appreciate the significance of exploring issues related to race and ethnic diversity. Therefore, in the tradition of "teacher as reacher," I used some classes as occasions to think through both questions of pedagogy and course content. In other words, I made a deliberate effort to consciously observe and take note of what transpired; to this end, in-class discussions and assignments were used as sources of data. As Cochran-Smith and Lytle (1993) assert, "When teachers treat classroom occurrences as data, they see discrete and

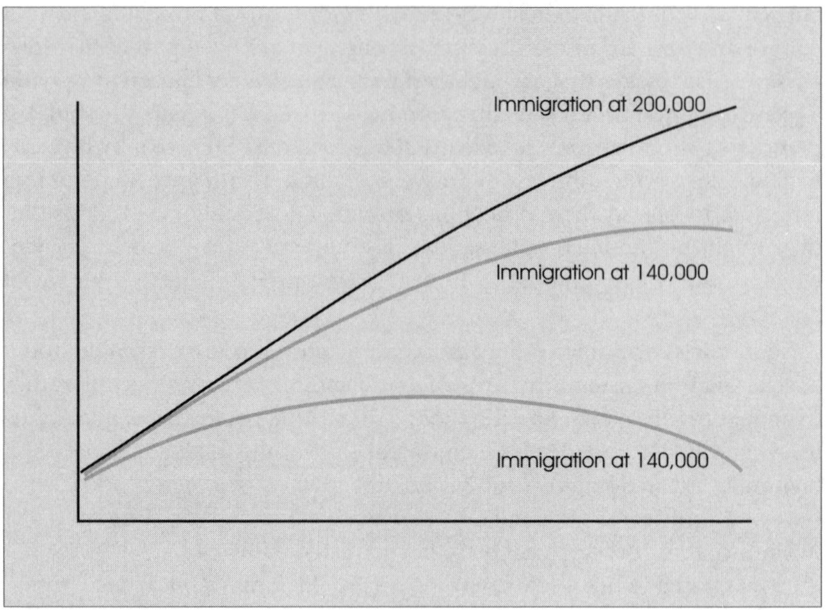

Chart 1: Immigration is critical to Canadian economic and population growth. The graph shows three "population" scenarios – high, medium and low immigration. Immigration is critical factor affecting population size. In the last decade, immigration targets have been above 200,000 per year.

Source: Statistics Canada Demographics Division.

sometimes disparate events as part of a large pattern of behaviours and interpretation" (p.48). This, I contend, enabled me to address systematically issues, concerns and problems that surfaced (see Anderson et al., 1994).

The cooperation and support of students was important to this process, for, as Cochran-Smith and Lytle (1993) also write with reference to Crouse, students and teachers construct the curriculum and "the teacher can only come to know how to teach and how to learn from teaching by being attentive to their interactions" (p.47). Consequently, it was necessary to recognize that the students and I were engaged in generating knowledge that would help us negotiate and re-negotiate our respective identities, not only as student and teacher, but also as racial and ethnic persons, and in the process affirm and/or alter our views and understandings.

The organization of this book represents the approach taken to explore the subject of diversity as related to race and ethnicity. As there is no single, universally accepted approach to presenting and analyzing the subject, what is presented here is one of many possible approaches. For the purpose of discussion and by way of establishing what might be considered a shared reference point, many of the terms are defined. As Jackson and Meadows

(1991) point out, "Individuals' definitions or conceptual frameworks ... may either hinder or facilitate an understanding of the behaviours and experiences that occur in their lives and the lives of others. Often a change in the conceptual framework can open a whole new realm of understanding of these behaviours and experiences" (p.72).

Where necessary and appropriate, complete or significant portions of the students' essays are presented to provide direct access to their words and voices and to show how they have approached, theorized, analyzed and addressed the issues and questions that relate to their own identity and those of others. While characteristics such as social class, gender, sexuality, dis/ability and geography are also inter-related and inform the understandings, interpretations and conceptualizations of racial and ethnic identities, students were expected to focus primarily on these identities as a way of beginning to appreciate the construction of self and others in these terms.

Each chapter examines the various themes around which the course was organized and those that emerged from class discussions, essays, exercises and projects. Starting with a brief review of the literature, Chapter 1 explores the issues that are often raised regarding questions of identity, race, ethnicity and culture. Chapter 2 presents class participants' constructions of their identity in racial and ethnic terms. In this process, many participants made reference to their years of growing up in Canada and trying to "fit in" socially and culturally. Accordingly, this theme forms the basis of the discussion in Chapter 3. In encouraging students to move beyond themselves with regard to how they constructed and understood their own identity and that of others, they were asked to participate in an exercise in which they interviewed someone of a different ethnic or racial background and then attempted comparison. These essays appear in Chapter 4. In Chapter 5, we discuss terms such as *race*, *ethnicity*, *prejudice*, *racism* and *discrimination*. Definitions of these terms are provided. Chapters 6, 7 and 8 respectively examine three of the major topics that emerged during class discussions. These are immigration, multiculturalism and employment equity. In Chapter 9, participants reflect on what they have learned and on how their ideas and understandings have been affirmed or changed as a result of the course.

This volume does not pretend to provide a comprehensive theoretical treatment of the subject of diversity. In fact, no single book that discusses race, ethnicity and culture can hope to present all the information, variations, complexities, puzzlements and so on that there are to explore. If this work serves to identify the many interpretations, and makes clear and explicit the related questions, issues and challenges thereby presented, and if our approach brings awareness, new insights and sensitivity to the issues, then our goal will have been achieved.

Photo: Dick Hemingway

CHAPTER 1

Culture, Diversity, Identity and Difference

> [Identity constructions] are very real. People live by them, after all–and nowadays, increasingly, they die from them. You can't get more real than that (Halperin, 1995).[1]

> Identity can be understood neither as a fixed essence nor as a vague and utterly contingent construction to be re-invented by the will and whim of aesthetes, symbolists, and language gamers. [It] is not simply a social and political category to be used or abandoned according to the extent to which the rhetoric that supports and legitimizes it is persuasive or institutionally powerful. Whatever the radical constructionalists may say, it is lived as a coherent (if not always stable) experiential sense of self. Though it is often felt to be natural and spontaneous, it remains the outcome of practical activity: language, gesture, bodily significations, desires (Gilroy, 1993: 102).

Admittedly, the discussion of the socially constructed factors of culture, diversity, difference and identity is replete with problems, particularly since they are not static but dynamic and always in process. These factors play a significant role in our everyday lives. We attribute meaning to them as individuals and as a society; and as Halperin (above) mentions, people live by them and die by them. Hence, it is important to grapple with their complex, ambiguous, contradictory, and shifting materialities. By engaging in such a process, we will likely be enabled to understand how we are implicated in their constructions, reproductions and consequences–particularly the consequences of racism, ethnocentrism, discrimination and lack of equitable educational and occupational opportunities.

In this chapter, we will seek to establish an understanding of culture and cultural identity and note some of the questions, issues and problems that are inherent in the use of these concepts. In so doing, we will: (a) explore culture as a concept with complex and varying interpretations over which there are intellectual and political struggles; (b) discuss cultural identity with the understanding that in ethnic and racial categorizing we run the risk of essentializing; (c) challenge the misguided notion of culture, race and ethnicity as something that is possessed mainly by those considered "different," typically racial and ethnic minority people; and (d) examine three

[1] Cited in Celia Haig-Brown, "Warriors Mothers: Lessons and Possibilities," *Journal for Just and Caring Education* 4, no. 1 (January 1998), 100.

students' stories of their experiences relating to their respective identities as Canadians. In concluding, we reiterate the point that, in exploring questions of cultural identities, diversity and difference in this era of talk about democracy and equity within the context of multiculturalism in Canada is both relevant and necessary.[2]

TOWARDS A CONCEPTUALIZATION OF CULTURE

In his exploration of the roots, meanings and uses of the word *culture*, Raymond Williams (1983) writes:

> Culture is one of the two or three most complicated words in the English language. This is partly because of its intricate historical development, in several European languages, but mainly because it has now come to be used for important concepts in several distinct intellectual disciplines and in several distinct and incompatible systems of thought (p.87).

In terms of its social and anthropological reference to material production, the term *culture*, as Williams emphasizes, captures the complexity of the senses and argument "about the relations between general human development and particular way of life" (p.91). Taking this complexity into consideration, and with reference to Herter's *Ideas on the Philosophy of the History of Mankind* (1784-91), Williams also makes the point that it is necessary "to speak of 'cultures' in the plural: The specific and variable cultures of different nations and periods, but also the specific and variable cultures of social and economic groups within a nation" (p.89). In this regard, then, our reference here to culture(s) is not to detract from its complexity and variations in terms of the activities, relationships and processes that the word symbolizes, but to explore its subjective and historical dimension in the way individuals have come to make sense of their lives in Canada.

In his discussion of culture, Renato Rosaldo (1993), in *Culture and Truth*, writes:

> Culture lends significance to human experience by selecting from and organizing it. It refers broadly to the forms through which people make sense of their lives, rather than more narrowly to the opera or art museums. It does not inhabit a set-aside domain, as does, for example, that of politics or economics. From the pirouettes of classical ballet to the most brute of brute facts, all human conduct is culturally mediated. Culture encompasses the everyday and the esoteric, the mundane and the elevated, the ridiculous and the sublime. Neither high or low, culture is all-pervasive (p.26).

From a social scientific perspective, "the most important part of culture," says Kallen (1995: 20), "is that it is a learned phenomenon; it is acquired, for

---

[2] We return in Chapter 7 to a discussion of culture, ethnicity and race as articulated in the Canadian policy of multiculturalism, which I contend could be read as an ideology of cultural integration.

the most part, through the ordinary processes of growing up and participating in the daily life of a particular ethnic collective."

According to this perspective, members of a particular ethnic and racial group[3] are likely to share certain patterns of living with other members who identify themselves, or might be identified, with the group. As Smolicz (1981: 18) writes, "the actions and attitudes of individual members are therefore likely to bear a 'family' resemblance to one another." Smolicz goes on to say that

> in many ethnically plural societies, a further distinction needs to be made between the ethnic group that holds the dominant position through its numbers, early settlement or impact upon the main political and economic institutions, and minority or subordinate groups that have much less influence on policy-making, and limited access to resources.... It must be recognized, however, that ethnic minority cultures have their own independent historical continuity, and although they may interact with other cultures in a plural society, this does not make them a mere facet of the dominant group's tradition" (Smolicz, 1981: 17-8).[4]

It is the case, therefore, that the culture of minority groups cannot be considered, in a reductionist way, to be a subset of the dominant culture. And even though they are members of particular ethnic and racial groups, individuals will not share in all of the beliefs and practices of the group. They should not be expected to think and act in similar ways, for social class, family composition, citizenship status, years of residency in a country and other factors all contribute to the differences among group members.

Critical theorists remind us that culture cannot be conceptualized in terms of unified systems of meanings, but rather as conflicting, contradictory, ambiguous, dynamic, and full of contending discourses, all of which are mediated by power. Paying attention to power relations, therefore, is critical to our understanding of culture. Power relations also inform individuals' struggle over meanings and the ways in which they conceive of being in the world (Spivey, 1998). And as Kondo (1990: 301) argues, some "in the world were and are more legitimate, more rewarded, more recognized than others–as anyone in a marginal or minority position will attest." Therefore, how groups and individuals construct culture will be fragmented, highly problematic and puzzling because they do so based on "contending personalities" (Spivey, 1998: 48).

---

3 The terms *ethnicity* and *race* are discussed fully in Chapter 7. Here, suffice it to say that ethnicity or ethnic group refers to a group of people who identify themselves, or are identified, as sharing a common historical and ancestral origin. *Race* or *racial group* refers to individuals who are identified by particular physical characteristics, for example, colour of skin, which come to represent socially constructed meanings and expectations that correspond to their ascribed status within the social hierarchy.

4 Smolicz also argues that each cultural group has "cores values" that characterize the group; and in "a plural society, the relationship between the core values of different groups helps to account for variations in the degree of ethnic cultural maintenance and assimilation" (p.23).

Table 2: Canadian Population by Ethnic Origin: Single and Combined Single and Multiple Origin Responses, 1996

Ethnic Origin Groups and Categories	Single Origin Responses (Descending Order)	Percent Single Origin in Total Population	Combined Single and Multiple Origin Responses	Percent of Combined Origin
Canadian	5,326,995	18.7	8,806,275	22.0
French	2,665,250	9.3	5,597,845	14.0
English	2,048,275	7.2	6,832,095	17.1
Chinese	800,470	2.8	921,585	2.3
Italian	729,455	2.6	1,207,475	3.0
German	726,145	2.5	2,757,140	6.9
Scottish	642,970	2.3	4,260,840	10.6
South Asian	590,145	2.0	723,345	1.8
Irish	504,030	1.8	3,767,610	9.4
Aboriginal	477,630	1.7	1,101,955	2.8
Ukrainian	331,680	1.2	1,026,475	2.6
Dutch	313,880	1.1	916,215	2.3
Polish	265,930	0.9	786,735	2.0
Portuguese	252,640	0.9	335,110	0.8
Philippine	198,420	0.7	242,880	0.6
Jewish	195,810	0.7	351,705	0.9
Greek	144,940	0.5	203,345	0.5
Jamaican	128,570	0.5	188,770	0.5
Hungarian	94,185	0.3	250,525	0.6
Spanish	72,470	0.3	204,360	0.5
Norwegian	47,805	0.2	346,310	0.9
Russian	46,885	0.2	272,335	0.7
Swedish	31,200	0.1	278,975	0.7
Welsh	27,915	0.1	338,905	0.8
American	22,085	0.1	211,790	0.5
Other	1,617,845	5.6	N/A	
Total Single Origin Responses	18,303,625	64.4		
Multiple Origin Responses	10,224,500	35.8		
Total Combined Origin Response			39,999,750*	100.0
Total Population	28,528,125	100.0		

* Since the number of other ethnic groups in the combined category is not available (fall 1998), this may not be an accurate figure. Since this column includes multiple origin responses, the total number does not correspond to the total Canadian population.

Source: Statistics Canada. 1998. *Census 1996*, Internet Catalogue No. 93F0026XDB96002.

CULTURAL IDENTITIES

Clearly, just as culture is complex, contradictory, unstable and organic, so too is cultural identity. Both at the individual and collective or group level, cultural identities, as Kondo (1990) contends, "resist closure and reveal complicated, shifting and multiple facets" (p.306-07). And at both levels, they are "fraught with tension and contradiction, and asserted in specific performative contexts." In discussing cultural identities, we must always pay attention to context. Stuart Hall (1995) maintains that "questions of identity are always questions about representation. They are always exercises in selective memory and they almost always involve the silencing of something in order to allow something else to speak" (p.5). Hall further writes, "Silencing as well as remembering, identity is always a question about producing in the future an account of the past, that is to say it is always about narrative, the stories which cultures tell themselves about who they are and where they came from" (p.5).

In pluralist societies, individuals commonly identify themselves in multiple ways. For example, in Canada, individuals will refer to themselves as Canadians, Jamaicans, Trinidadians, Americans, British or Caribbean, indicating their identification as citizens of or their allegiance to that nation-state, that is, "to its political institutions and economic structures" (Smolicz, 1981: 29). In contrast, identifications such as Nis-ga'a, Mohawk, French, African, Indian, or Italian are more likely to indicate individuals' ethnic ancestry, primary language and/or the cultural traditions with which they currently identify. The interchanging of these identities is possible. Understandably, these two identities are not mutually exclusive, for individuals do have multiple identities, "formed in historically specific relation to the different social spaces people inhabit over time" (Smith, 1992: 501). Furthermore, cultural identities with regard to ethnicity are hybrid, syncretic and always in process (Hall, 1995).

In addition to the question of ethnic identity is that of racial identity; for individuals or groups are not only ethnicized, but raced as well. Questions about race, as Hall (1981) argues, carry "strong emotional ideological commitments." It "is not a topic where an academic or intellectual neutrality is of much value (cited in Britzman, 1993: 27). Further echoing Hall, Britzman goes on to say that "talk about race means talk about racialized selves" for "everyone is 'raced' and so talk must include the meaning of whiteness as well as blackness" (p.27). On this point, Weis and Fine (1996: 7) state that "the project" of exploring whiteness has helped to highlight "the ways in which discourses about non-western 'other' are produced simultaneously with the production of discourse about white 'self,'" and this work is quite relevant to analyses of identities related to ethnicity and race as well as to class and gender.

Particularly significant is the relational aspect of identity. The dominant and "normalized" white cultural identity, within the context of the hegemonic relations in Western societies, can only be understood in relation to the discursively constructed "others" (Roman, 1993; Weis and Fine, 1996; Morrison, 1990). Hence, understandings of power relations are imbedded in the stories of individuals' constructions of their racial identities or "racialized selves." Accordingly, any exploration of cultural identity must take into account questions of power. However, as Lisa Delpit (1988: 282) argues, "individuals with power are frequently least aware of–or least willing to acknowledge–its existence. Those with less power are often most aware of its existence." In this regard, while racialized or minority individuals will construct and talk about themselves in racial terms, white individuals, as Rosenberg (1997), Sleeter (1993) and Phoenix (1997) found, have difficulty in doing so. Reasons offered for this difficulty include the denial of power, the general failure of whites as members of a dominant group to reflect on dominance and the lack of recognition of historical and political relations (Delpit, 1988; hooks, 1992; Giroux, 1997; Dei, 1998; McIntosh, 1995; Roman, 1993; Sleeter, 1993).

Rosenberg (1997) notes that it can be very discomforting to talk openly about whiteness and white privilege, particularly in the classroom. Referring to her work in teacher education, Rosenberg reports that pre-service teacher candidates, primarily white females, tend to "feel lost" when whiteness is broached in discussions of race, and they tend to conduct their conversations in hushed tones. With reference to her work in a similar context, Christine Sleeter (1993) contends that white people discuss whiteness and race in ideological ways that defend and justify their privileges and power accruing from structural racism. From this perspective, and on the basis of their life experiences and vested interests, white individuals construct race in terms that render them raceless or lacking in racial identification. Similarly, Phoenix (1997) found that young white people in London, England, did not see themselves as having a white identity. Rather, many insisted on "the individualism of people just being people, whatever colour they have. However, at the same time, they reinscribed essentialist accounts of black people as Other" (p.188). In these essentialist accounts, Blacks were presented as a group of people that were the "same," rather than diverse like whites.

Rosenberg (1997) also found that many "whites see whiteness as an 'empty cultural space' and their identity as white people only [takes] shape in relation to others. That is to say, they see themselves as not Japanese or not Black. Or they [will] find a personality characteristic to use for self-definition, 'I am not a generous person' etc." (p.80). This tendency to avoid seeing themselves in racial terms is possibly, as Sleeter (1993) advances, a way of suppressing the negative and stereotypical images whites have of racial minority groups. Another reason, particularly in this period of anti-racism and social justice initiatives such as employment equity, affirmative action and educational access programs,[5] might be individuals' belief in meritocracy. On this basis, they claim that education and employment are accessible to everyone irrespective of race or gender. Hence, such initiatives are discriminatory and unnecessary because they limit whites', particularly males', access to occupational and educational opportunities (Sleeter, 1993; Fish, 1993; Hill, 1997; Weis et al., 1997; also see Chapter 8 for further discussion).[6]

In light of these debates, many scholars have suggested that current discussions of racial identification are highly problematic. On the question of whiteness, Ellsworth (1997), for example, argues that it is represented, particularly in anti-racism discourses, in ways that places whites in "double binds" or no-win situations. Based on the premise that identity is heterogeneous, unstable and shifting, Ellsworth contends that "whiteness must be viewed not as a fixed, locatable identity, ethnicity or social positioning, but as a social relation that is performed." Whites, she argues, are positioned within gender, language, sexuality, class, ability, size, ethnicity and age. Thus, "at some times, and some places, those privileges and safety that come with white skin can be temporarily and problematically over-ridden or eclipsed by the oppressions and discriminations associated with queerness, Jewishness, femaleness, poverty, and homelessness" (Ellsworth, 1997: 266).

This understanding of whiteness as relational, dynamic and ever changing does not negate the fact of constructed identities related to race, ethnicity, gender, class and history, which provide meanings for individuals and upon which they act and form relationships.

Given that cultural identity is complex, relational and performative, not only with regard to whiteness but to all other racial identities, it is worthwhile to examine how certain discourses of cultural constructions and representations contribute to social formations around categories of ethnic and racial identities. While I acknowledge that it is important to avoid the risks of essentialism in the examination of cultural identities, in the interest of political mobilization for social change, "strategic essentialism" is necessary and indeed critical (Spivak, 1993; see also Dei, 1998; Henry, 1998;

[5] It must be acknowledged that while such initiatives or programs do exist, it is also the case that this is a period in which the increasing decline in neo-liberalism and corresponding rise in neo-conservatism or right-wing politics has effected the dismantling of what has been achieved as a result of social justice activism. For example, some governments, for example, that of Ontario, as well as private organizations have eliminated their employment equity and affirmative action programs.

[6] This perception of reduced opportunities caused by equity initiatives is particularly evident among young, white, unemployed, underemployed and working-class males, whose common sense understanding of race or racelessness makes them colour-blind and oblivious to the privileges they too have had over working-class men of colour (Weis et al., 1997; Hill, 1997).

Yon, 1999). Accordingly, Paul Gilroy (1993), in his discussion of the politics of authenticity as related to culture and identity, talks of the need for "anti-anti-essentialism that sees radicalized subjectivity as the product of the social practices that supposedly derive from it" (p.102). Gilroy makes the point that absolutists (those who conceptualize ethnic cultural identities in absolute terms) and pluralists (those who conceive of identity as "an open signifier," which is complex and "*internally* divided: by class, sexuality, gender, age, ethnicity, economics and political consciousness") (p.32) have become "locked in an entirely fruitless relationship of mutual interdependency" (p.100). Referring to the understanding of Blackness, Gilroy writes that the pluralist position "refers pejoratively to the [absolutist position] as racial essentialism. It moves towards a casual and arrogant deconstruction of blackness while ignoring the appeal of the [absolutist's] powerful popularist affirmation of black culture" (p.100). The pluralist position, he continues, is a "brand of elitism" that is likely to contribute to "racial conservatism" while "ignoring the undiminished power of racism itself and forsaking the mass of black people who continue to comprehend their lives particularity through what it does to them" (pp.101-02).

Similarly, June Roland Martin (1994), in encouraging feminist researchers not to become trapped in the essentialism binary, contends that anti-essentialism is at times a form of essentialism and a means of silencing. In her article "Methodological Essentialism, False Difference, and Other Dangerous Traps," she writes:

> Of course, black and white women, middle-class and working-class women, Irish and Arab women are different. But just as no two individuals and no two circumstances are alike in every respect, no two are different in every respect; the question of whether all women have one or more attributes or circumstances in common cannot be answered in advance of investigation. Supposing that similarities are found, there is of course no guarantee that they will be important. Nevertheless, as long as there might be commonalities among women–or among women such as blacks and whites who are considered to be entirely different–it is at the very least perverse to deny ourselves access to knowledge of them, and quite possibly self-defeating (Martin, 1994: 646-47).

Exploring questions and issues of cultural identity, diversity and difference, then, does not mean that we avoid categorizing or naming, nor does it mean that we eschew commonalities. Rather, it means doing so with a commitment, not to silence, but to opening up dialogue, and to gain insight into individuals' understanding of themselves and their relationships to the structures of the society and communities in which they live, go to school and develop friendships. Engaging in this process of exploration (which involves navigating around generalizations) is politically significant and should inform the ways we come to represent, appreciate and articulate cultural diversity.

WHO HAS CULTURE? ONLY SOME PEOPLE DO!

Rosaldo (1993) observes that, within nation-states, some people are seen as "having culture" while others are "without culture." What is regarded as "cultural visibility and invisibility" becomes part of the language discourse: "our" and "we" refer to the "people without culture." And, as Rosaldo explains, "by courtesy, 'we' extend this noncultural status to people who ('we' think) resemble 'us'.... Full citizens lack culture, and those most culturally endowed lack full citizenship" (p.198). Rosaldo goes on to say that "the people who have culture" tend to occupy subordinate or marginal positions within society. "Their cultural distinctiveness" is derived "from a lengthy historical process of colonial domination; [and] their quaint customs signal isolation, insulation and subordination within the nation-state" (p.199).

This understanding of culture as visible and symbolic of "foreignness" is represented in how many individuals discuss culture and their own and others' ethno-cultural identities. Those who see themselves as being without culture also regard themselves as being without race and ethnicity. They simply identify themselves as "Canadians." For these individuals, culture is identified as that which is possessed by Others, by people with particular "looks," who are often characterized by their skin colour and/or other physical features, as well as by dress (or costume), food, religious practices and other "visible" factors. These "Canadians," typically those with Anglo-Celtic backgrounds, do not perceive of themselves as having a heritage from elsewhere, while Others do. Others are perceived to have "foreign" cultural values and practices that remain static and are based largely on cultural expectations and their former experiences in other countries.[7]

This reading of cultural identities, diversity and difference is informed by Canada's multiculturalism policy. This policy not only constructs "real" Canadians as English and French and phenotypically white, but has also produced a national consciousness whereby the state is seen as being culturally neutral and therefore able to accommodate the "foreign cultures" (James, 1998; Walcott, 1997). (See Chapter 7 for a fuller discussion of this point.) Imbued with this consciousness, "real" Canadians come to think of themselves as culturally neutral and without "visible" signifiers that would constitute their culture. Moreover, as Roman (1993: 71) explains, this tendency of the multicultural discourse to "celebrate diversity" without taking into account "the power differentials among groups positioned by racial categorizations and inequalities" contributes to the notion that "white

[7] Ironically, the Canadians "without culture" will tell those "with culture" that they are in Canada now and therefore must behave "like Canadians." Are there signifiers that would indicate when someone is behaving like a Canadian? Is there a cultural pattern that is "Canadian"? We will return to this discussion in Chapter 7.

culture is the *hidden norm* against which all other racially subordinate groups' so called "differences" are measured.... [Furthermore], it can imply that whites are *colourless*, and hence without racial subjectivities, interests and privileges. Still worse, it conveys the idea that whites are free of the responsibility to challenge racism." It is not surprising, then, that the essays of many white students in this collection reveal that they construct their identities in relation to immigrants and racially and ethnically Other Canadians.

THE CONSTRUCTION OF CULTURAL IDENTITIES

In what follows, three class participants reflect on cultural identity. We will look at the significance given to ethnicity and race in their experiences. We begin with Scott's comments, in which he argues that members of the dominant racial and ethnic group avoid engaging in explorations of identity. This experience would be "traumatic," requiring them to penetrate their "protective cocoon."

> **Scott**: *"Humans often choose to remain with the familiar and forsake the butterfly-like flight into the unknown."*
>
> For better or worse, and perhaps without even actually realizing the possible consequences, most people wrap themselves in their protective cocoon of self-concept.
>
> Unlike nature's irrevocable cycle of life, however, humans often choose to remain with the familiar and forsake the butterfly-like flight into the unknown. I believe this protective cocoon of self-concept spans the racial, ethnic and cultural difference gap and is a defence mechanism that is hard to penetrate.
>
> Being asked to instigate the penetration oneself can be a traumatic experience for some. For others, it can be an uplifting and enlightening experience.
>
> For the dominant group members (and I place myself in this category), however, the racial, cultural and ethnic influence has never really come into play—in a conscious sense—in relation to values and behaviour. Therefore, it is initially rejected as a concept better left to intellectual discussion or, more to the point, left until the wells of discussion on sex and sports have run dry.
>
> When the enforced impetus of academic requirement is applied and more than the perfunctory scratching of the shell of self-concept occurs, the supposedly well-rounded individual can appreciate just who, why and what was involved in the moulding. He or she can better understand and accept the final product.

Photo: Dick Hemingway

Social research shows that as early as three years old children are able to differentiate other people by race.

That whites, such as Scott, "wrap themselves in their protective cocoon of self-concept" and do not consciously explore the extent to which race and ethnicity play a role in their experiences, values and behaviours, may indeed be considered, as Scott suggests, "a defence mechanism." But a defence against what? According to Scott, it is a defence against the "traumatic" consequences of having to deal with the "difference gap" –difference related to race, ethnicity and culture–between whites and non-whites. Seemingly, this "gap" refers to the power difference between whites and non-whites. Scott is aware of the power and privilege that accrue to him as a result of racism. Yet, his preference is to stay "with the familiar;" or, in other words, pretend ignorance (of what he refers to as the unknown). He thus maintains his privilege and avoids the trauma that might come with the acknowledgment of his role in racism.

We cannot generalize from what Scott has said, but his insightful comments are consistent with the findings and arguments of Sleeter (1993), Rosenberg (1997) and Phoenix (1997). Like them, Scott indicates that he and other "dominant group members," as he says, have difficulty in talking of themselves in racial terms. When they do so, they tend to justify and defend their privilege. We can expect, then, that the essays by white class participants in this book will reveal their avoidance of, according to Scott, "the butterfly-like flight into the unknown." As pointed out earlier, this unknown represents their understanding of the salience of race in the construction of cultural identity.

In the following essays,[8] Bina and Michelle provide perspectives on how the process of cultural identity is engaged by those who do not have the power and privilege to avoid confronting the consequences of race. Unlike Scott, Bina's and Michelle's conflict-ridden experiences are ones they would like to avoid but from which they are unable to take "flight"; racial signifiers operate, not only in terms of their own construction of cultural identity, but in how others construct them.

Bina: *"I didn't look Canadian to them, so how could I be?"*

I was born in Canada and attended an elementary school in North York. My parents both immigrated to Canada from India and England. Like most people, they came to Canada in order to make a better life for their "children." I grew up and lived in a predominantly white Anglo-Saxon community. Most of my friends were Christian, and the students in the school who were of other nationalities could probably be counted on one hand. While growing up, I never really considered myself different from the rest of the people at the school. I enjoyed my years there, from Junior Kindergarten to my Grade 6 graduation. It wasn't as if I had been moving from school to school; the whole issue in my opinion was my skin colour. I say this because it was the only visible aspect of me that caused me to be put into a different category from the rest of my class.

I honestly can't remember much that took place in the early school grades (maybe its because I have blocked it out) or maybe there isn't much to remember. However, once I began Grade 4, and until Grade 8, racial slurs and nasty comments were what I got to hear. I had great friends who, by the way, were of all nationalities. I enjoyed being with my circle of friends, but I did not like how the rest of my peers treated me. My parents never really knew about this, because it wasn't something that I discussed openly. I went to school, had a good time, and that was it. I can't really say for sure if the teachers were aware of this, but how couldn't they be? Maybe they just ignored it, because they didn't know what to say or do. I guess that is something I will never know.

After Grade 6, I went to a junior high school for two years. I can honestly say that it was here that I had my worst experiences. The guys were horrid, and the things they had to say about my ethnicity and culture were disgusting. The worst part of all this is that they didn't even know who I really was. They just assumed, and then went on from there. Some of the things people said to me were: "Where is your Paki dot?" and "Stinky Paki." They even used to sing songs: "Circle, circle, dot, dot / Now I've got my Paki dot." Of course, I didn't have a "dot" and, to top it all off, I wasn't a "Paki." Experiences like these led me to ignore and retaliate against my own religion and culture.

---

[8] As mentioned in the introduction, here and in many other cases throughout this book, the students' essays are presented in length. This not only preserves the voice of the writers, but also reveals the process in which they engaged the issues.

> I am not an immigrant to Canada and I was born in Canada, yet I could never make people understand I was "Canadian." I didn't look "Canadian" to them, so how could I be? I began to deny my ties with any other ethnic group. My response was always, "I'm Canadian, a Christian. I celebrate Christmas, and I don't speak any languages other than English." Of course it was all a lie, except for being Canadian. My name was also a dead give-away. Bina Patel; a Christian? After a while, I thought I had successfully convinced everyone. Even at home, I tried to distance myself as much as possible from my cultural roots. I wouldn't watch movies in which Hindi was spoken, and I wouldn't dress up in my cultural clothes.
>
> As a member of a minority group, I was forced to conform to the existing cultural norms of the white majority group. It wasn't that they forced me directly; it was all the things they said to me and the teasing that I couldn't stand. I disassociated myself from India and any links I might have had with it.
>
> It wasn't until high school that my perceptions changed. High school was a completely new experience for me. I met many people who belonged to the same ethnic group as I. I had a great time learning different things about my religion and culture. As I had avoided learning anything about it in the past, it was neat to have friends who knew so much. I started to identify myself as both South Asian and Canadian and had no problems with either one. I had always enjoyed school, but it was the treatment and comments that I was subjected to while growing up that made me hate everything about my culture. However, at high school, I came to accept my difference.

What comes through quite prominently in Bina's narrative is the extent to which, within the school context, particularly junior high, racism and sexism intersected to make those years her "worst."[9] She states that the males "were horrid," referring to their racist and sexist comments that made her feel like an outsider. In response, Bina tried to "disassociate herself from India" and signifiers such as religion, language, and the little red "dot," and establish her identity as a "Canadian." But, as she states, her "skin colour" and name–those "visible aspects" of her–remained in how others constructed and essentialized her. She was not only an "Indian," a foreigner, but she was also a young Indian woman with strange habits. Essentially she was different, a "difference" that she would later come to "accept" in high school.

What about cases where racial identity is not so clear? Michelle's narrative about racial ambiguity is not ambiguous after all. She is not white, so she is an Other. But which Other? Here is how Michelle remembers her early life and the process of identity construction.

---

[9] Note that Bina did not tell her parents what was happening to her at school. This is likely a result of what she perceived to be her parents' cultural and educational expectations of her; and of their capacity to assist her. And while Bina states that she is not sure if her teachers were aware of what was happening to her, in her question, "How couldn't they?", she implies that they likely did know but did nothing because they were unsure of how to respond. This reflects the responsibility or lack thereof of the teachers in helping students deal with issues of identity and difference.

Michelle: *"This name reminds me of who I am and where I come from."*

My name is Michelle Green. I am the daughter of a Jamaican man and a First Nations woman. My name itself tells the story of slavery and massacre. Green, I believe, was my slavemaster's name, and Michelle reflects the influence the French had on the Cree nations of Saskatchewan. Nonetheless, I take great pride in this name, as it reminds me of who I am and where I come from. My people (both Black and Native) have come a long way, and to this very day "we" struggle for equal opportunity and equal justice. Many would like to believe that we live in a just world and really feel that multiculturalism is bringing us closer together. The truth is that we have been socialized to see and judge "difference," and there is still a long way to go until we truly see one another as equals. In this essay, I will discuss who I am in relation to others and explain how this has affected my identity.

I began school in Toronto, where my family and I lived for a short period of time. I can remember when I first started. I remember being excited and eager to go. I can recall playing in the sandbox, colouring, finger painting and sitting in circles singing "frolicsome" songs. I remember the teachers and students and how playful we were allowed to be. Those initial days in school, it seems, brought no real problems to my life. In fact, I do not think I could even comprehend what a problem was at that time, or perhaps I just do not remember much about my feelings back then.

When we moved to Brampton [a suburb west of Toronto], I had to make quite an adjustment. I began to realize that there were very few "coloured" people in the world. In Toronto, there had been all kinds of people; people with yellow skin, people with black skin, people with white skin. There had even been those with red skin. I remembered the candy store and the Chinese man behind the counter. He always smiled at me and my step-brother and was always happy to see us. He even knew our names. Brampton was very different from this. It seemed like a whole new world. For the first time, I think, I began to feel different—I felt isolated.

This new community (environment) my family and I became a part of was predominantly European and/or Anglo-Saxon and consisted mostly of middle-class people. These factors alone affected my perception of the world. Coming as I had from a poor, working-class environment where we had been surrounded by government housing and high-rise buildings, I was just not ready for my new "habitat." Unlike the friendly, warm community that I had been forced to leave behind, the people of Brampton were very private, and they all seemed to share an agenda that was in many respects different from those in my old community. I was immersed in a totally different cultural setting. I remember wondering where all the various colours had gone. What had happened to the "rainbow" of people that had given me a sense of security and a feeling of belonging? I missed the Chinese man at the corner store and his friendly smile—I missed home.

In Toronto (in the neighbourhood at Jane and Finch), there had been different people with their own unique way of "being," but everyone in Brampton "appeared" to be the same. They shared a common language/dialect, they acted the same, they even began to look the same! I could not figure out where exactly I fit in. Thus, I yearned to be just like "them." My desire to become a part of this community was so great that I became two different people. At home I lived through cultural expressions that had been "handed down" to me from my parents. However, when I was outside of my home I expressed the adopted culture that was dominant in my community. I saw that my parents were also doing this. For example, at home my father spoke with a very strong Jamaican accent, but when dealing with people on the "outside," his language became "distorted" (it sounded strange, unreal). He tried very hard to sound "proper." In fact, several times he commented on my own "broken" English. "Speak properly!", he demanded.

I slowly got used to things in the public school I attended, and I even made new friends. My closest friend was an Irish girl named Susan, whom I admired greatly. I loved her curly blonde hair, her white skin and her perfect family—I loved everything about her. In fact, I can even remember wishing that we could trade places. Just about everyone and everything at school was representative of all the things Susan was and I was not. All my teachers, whom I liked very much, were European and/or Anglo-Saxon; all the people in the story books I enjoyed reading were European and/or Anglo-Saxon; all the pictures hung around the school were of people who were of European and/or Anglo-Saxon decent. For goodness sake! Columbus was European, and he discovered Canada—or so I was told. The dominant culture that was taught and displayed in my school played an increasingly significant role in the formation of my identity. Tell me, what person in their right mind would not want also to be white? After all, whites seemed to be like the most important people in the universe. I realize now that the relationships I had with Susan and "others" (teachers, friends, mentors) undoubtedly caused me to question who I was, as I was not satisfied with just being me. I would have been a lot more content being a "pretty little white girl" with a nice family.

My feelings of difference and isolation, I believe, compelled me to form an identity that was untruthful. In fact, this identity became very real for me. When my peers asked me why my skin was so much lighter than other Black people's skin, I would tell them that I was a "half-breed" (a stereotypical name for a person who is of mixed Black and white lineage). This somehow placed me closer to "them" (Anglo-Saxon people). Well, at least I thought it did. I thought that maybe if they believed I had some of the "good" colour in me, they would like and accept me more. However, I was wrong. Instead they called me "oreo-cookie," "caramel" and even "Nigger."

I was an ignorant child. As I grew up living separate from my mother, I did not really understood where she was from. I visited her only two times a year, and when I saw her, she appeared white to me. My father would tell me that she was a Métis Indian and that the reason she was so light in complexion was because her father was French. All this Indian "stuff" made no sense to me. I dared not admit that my mother was Indian; it was bad enough that I was Black. I was not even sure what an Indian was. Was she the Indian that I saw in the old western movies? Or was she the Indian that so many made fun of at school and called such names as "Paki" and "Coolie"? I did not really care which Indian she was. I decided that she looked white, and that is what I told everyone.

For many years I was happy with this story. Some people actually thought I was special and/or unique—or so I believed. I recall one of my elementary school teachers saying, "We don't have many of your kind around here." To this day I wonder if she was being nice or if she was being rude about my "difference." I have learned that whites often use the term *your kind* to mean that you are separate and inferior to them.

Every day in school I listened to the lessons. I believed what the teachers taught, and I abided by their rules. I was a "good" student. Unconsciously, I was proud to have assimilated so successfully as it made "them" happy, and it also made me acceptable. It did not bother me at all that my culture(s) was not represented in the school curriculum. Never once did I say I was bored with their Euro-centric material. Never once did I think that something was wrong with what I was being taught. I never consciously noticed that every "good" person we talked about was European and/or Anglo-Saxon. In fact, I was never taught to think critically about my "place" in school. I was learning to be content with being a part of the "norm."

It was not until my later years in high school, in Grades 12 and 13, that I began to realize who I really was. My friends and one particular teacher opened my eyes to "Black-Native" consciousness. I began to understand my "real place" in society, and for the first time, I began to tell people that my mother was Native. Still, I was ignorant about many things, and the learning process seemed to begin all over again.

University has provided me with the opportunity to learn more about myself. As I am majoring in history, I have made it my personal goal to find out more about "my people." As I was raised in a Caribbean social environment, I seem to have taken on more of my Black identity than my Native. This is not to say that my Native identity is less important to me (in fact, this year I am taking a Native history course), I am only saying that I can more easily identify with the culture entailed by being Black. I do not, however, disregard the Native in me, as its spirit has shown me good things about the way one should live. Most importantly, though, I struggled with my identity, and it took me years to figure out where I belong.

Michelle's narrative illustrates the multiple, shifting, conflicting and relational aspects of identity and the significance of history and contexts (e.g., physical or geographic and educational space) in its construction. Michelle is not only "both Black and Native"; at times she identified herself as "Black" and as "half-breed." She did not "choose" to identify herself in these ways, but did so because of her schooling and community experiences. Interestingly, while Michelle claims that the Anglo-Saxon culture to which she was subjected in school "successfully assimilated" her through the Euro-centric curriculum, it was also in this very context that she was made to question her identity. It seems, then, that while this assimilation process of which she speaks did work to bring her to an appreciation of, and at times identification with, European values and habits, it did nothing to erase her "difference." Her race, as her teachers and peers perceived it, remained a signifier of that difference.

Michelle recounts how she came to recognize her difference in relation to the community in which she lived. She was able to fit into a working-class community of Toronto because of its racial diversity and the "warm and friendly" people with whom she interacted. But, in the "predominantly European and/or Anglo-Saxon" middle-class community of Brampton, she was an outsider, not only because of race, but also because of social class and language. Further, this "move into difference," as Haig-Brown (in press) would say, and how Michelle eventually understood and engaged with her difference, is connected to her experiences (with, for example, name-calling), as well as her desire and need to feel a sense of "security" and "belonging"–the need to feel at "home."

Like Bina, Michelle worked hard to distance herself from the essentialist notions of her "difference"–"I dared not admit that my mother was Indian; it was bad enough that I was Black." And while she acknowledges that she is not only Black and Indian (she is part French as well), that European or white self she once claimed seems to have vanished in her later construction of identity. Eventually, recognizing who she "really was" and understanding her "real place" in society, she re-constructs a self that is based on her learned colonial constructions. She talks of "my people" and "we," referring to the struggles, histories, and goals of Black and Indian people. She also talks of having "taken on more of my Black identity than my Native," and identifying with "Black culture." Michelle talks of these things as if they were unitary, static and uncomplicated, when her own story reflects the complexities, contradictions and ongoing process of identity construction.

Is it possible to get around the essentialist construction of identities? It is likely that the cultural identities that both Bina and Michelle construct and articulate are reflections of, as Gilroy (1993) states, the power of racism, which has informed how they and others see them fitting into this diverse

Canadian society. Indeed, it is individuals' realities, their everyday lived experiences, as they interpret and articulate them, that are particularly significant in our understanding of identities.

SUMMARY

Notwithstanding the politics, subjectivity and problems of definition and categorization, we have sought in this chapter to delineate the ways in which culture and cultural identities are understood, used, referenced and articulated by individuals and the society as a whole. Anthropologically speaking, culture is a concept that refers to the ways in which people, individually and collectively (as members of a group, community or society), understand, organize and respond to the environment around them; and it is informed by the unequal power relations that are found in societies. Culture is a product of both group and individual struggle over meanings, legitimacy, recognition and rewards. Hence, as we have demonstrated, not only is culture complex, contradictory, ambiguous and dynamic, it is also fraught with tensions as it is shaped and re-shaped in response to the hegemonic power relations between groups. And contrary to the claims that some people might make, culture is all pervasive; no one is culture-free.

We also explored cultural identity in terms of how individuals see themselves, how others see them and how they negotiate and navigate the challenges of living and surviving in a society that is mediated by unequal relations of power and attendant constructions of varying social group members. While individuals exercise agency in terms of their construction of identities, which in turn renders identity as multiple, ambiguous and performative, we have argued that the problem of naming and categorizing individuals does not detract from the fact that categorizations do occur and individuals identify themselves or are identified as members of particular ethnic and racial groups. Critics have argued that a major problem of categorizing is that of essentialism. However, we have observed that in making sense of their own and others' complex, ambiguous, contradictory and paradoxical existence, individuals resort to categorizing. In doing so, particular signifiers are employed. The problem, therefore, seems not so much to be categorization or essentialism or that individuals employ signifiers such as skin colour, race, ethnicity or physical appearance to construct themselves or others as different. Rather, the problem seems to be what individuals do with the signifiers and "difference."

While writing this conclusion, I talked with a friend who identifies herself as a Black Caribbean woman. I wanted to hear how she would respond to the suggestion that this is being essentialist. She acknowledged that she has been called essentialist. However, while her construction of herself might seem "unitary and fixed," she hoped that it would be understood that "this identity does not capture all of who I am, nor does it foreclose the contradictions and omissions that are intrinsic to any kind of categorization." There are, as she stated, other factors, such as being working class, immigrant, educated and so on, that are part of who she is. However, she has chosen to name herself in ways that she feels capture her "essence," her "way of knowing and way of being" in the Canadian society.

The narratives of these students illustrate that identities are multiple, conflicting, contradictory, relational and always in process; and that they embody both possibilities and limitations on how individuals understand themselves and each other and ultimately on how lives are lived. For instance, while identities might contribute to stereotyping, exclusions and oppressive experiences, they also make possible unions among people with perceived commonalities. Notwithstanding the politics and problems of identities, ethnic and racial categorization are prevalent in a society such as ours. In discussions on culture, identity and diversity, they are inescapable.

In sum, we have attempted to establish a context for examining students' experiences, their understanding of culture, their construction of identity (of both themselves and others) and the ways in which they comprehend and respond to diversity when issues such as social justice, equity and anti-racism are being taken up in our classrooms. But as our discussion indicates, the discourse around such issues is highly problematic, especially when we take into account the varying individual investment in the issues. Nevertheless, it is important that we engage the issues if social change is to come about. To this end, and with reference to students' narratives,[10] we seek to show how individuals *see* themselves in relation to the power structures of the society in which they live, and their consequent commitment to either maintaining the status quo or engaging in systemic changes.

SUGGESTIONS FOR DISCUSSION

1. Discuss what accounts for the claim by some Canadians that they have no culture?
2. If we acknowledge that Canada is ethnically and racially diverse society, are we less likely to see "difference" as foreign and exotic?
3. Is naming identities necessary for organizing around equity issues?

[10] As has been pointed out, it is important to remember that these are individual accounts and therefore cannot be generalized to others, not even to those of similar ethnic and racial background.

Photo: Dick Hemingway

CHAPTER 2

Race, Ethnicity and Cultural Identity

> Within any human society, in any historical era, the social construction of the concepts of race and ethnicity reflect the ideological, political, economic and cultural biases of the ruling authority of the society. Those with the power to rule inevitably have the power to define. Populations defined in terms of the social constructs of race and ethnicity are not merely categorized or classified in a statistical sense; they are evaluation in terms of the values and standards established by majority authorities as the norms for all members of the society. It follows, then, that the social constructs of race and ethnicity are not in any way neutral or scientific clarifications.... When social constructs of race and/or ethnicity are used by majority authorities to rationalize differential treatment of populations so classified, socially-created "race" becomes translated into the social realty of racism (Kallen, 1995: 18).

In this chapter, we explore race and ethnicity as characteristics by which individuals are identified in our society, around which selves are constructed, privileges are ascribed and mediated and consequences are experienced. The term *cultural identity* is used to refer to the collective self-awareness that a given group embodies and reflects (e.g., racial, ethnic, gender groups) and the "identity of the individual in relation to his or her culture" (Adler, 1977: 26). It is the latter aspect that is important to us here. We will explore the dimensions of cultural identity as "a functioning aspect of individual personality and a fundamental symbol of a person's existence" (Adler, 1977: 26).

Figure 1 illustrates some of the factors that contribute to the development of individual cultural identity. The construction of cultural identity is a complex process. Nevertheless, the chart is an attempt, not only to show its complexity, but to illustrate that, while individuals are primarily exploring how race and ethnicity feature in their cultural identities or the selves they construct, other factors play equally significant roles. These factors change over time, with individuals' changing awareness of self, others and the social system, through interactions and in response to social change. Apple (1993) contends that identity "is not necessarily a stable, permanent, united centre that gives consistent meaning to our lives. It too is socially and historically constructed, and subject to political tensions and contradictions" (p.vii).

Social characteristics such as gender, race, ethnicity, ability, age and sexual orientation, together with factors such as education, citizenship status, political affiliation and so on influence a person's attitudes, perception,

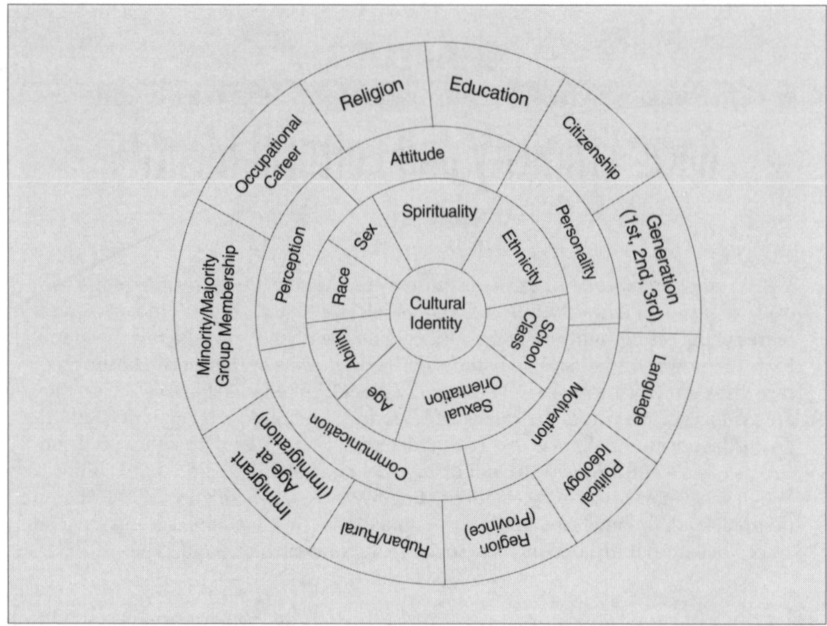

Figure 1: Identity Diagram–Factors contributing to an individual's cultural identity (starting from inner circle). (1) Individual's personal cultural identity determines lifestyle and behaviour. (2) Personal factors (social), mostly ascribed. (3) Psychological factors. Some are based on innate sources; all interact with the personal and social factors. (4) Social factors that are shared by group members. Many of these are institutions through which socialization takes place, culture is transmitted, or behaviour is determined. (Spirituality here refers to that which is an integral part of a person's life. In some cases it is referred to as religion.)

personality and motivation. Socializing agents such as the family, teachers, peers, mentors, coaches, significant others and the society in which the individual lives play a significant role in the influence of these factors and the way in which they find expression. When combined, these inter-related factors play a role in the socialization process, in the nature of the culture that is transmitted and constructed by the individual and ultimately in the behaviour of that individual.

Individual stories indicate that ethnicity, race, religion and nationality do not influence each person in the same way or to the same degree. The influence of each characteristic varies according to the individual and his or her experiences. National origin or place of birth of the individual or his or her parents may be more significant if the person is an immigrant, or if his or her parents are recent immigrants. In some instances, religion may be of stronger influence than race, language or ethnicity. For some, there are links between ethnicity and religion; in many cases it is difficult to separate them, and it is therefore important to understand the inherent dynamic relationships.

RACE AND THE SOCIAL CONSTRUCTION OF IDENTITY

Race is an arbitrary and therefore problematic term that is employed in the classification of human beings. Over the years it has been used to refer to (a) lineage (groups of people connected by common descent or origin); (b) subspecies (populations of people with distinct genotypes); (c) ethnic groups (e.g., Anglo-Saxons, Italians); (f) religions (e.g., Jews); (g) nationalities (e.g., Irish, Chinese); (h) minority language groups (e.g., French Canadians); (i) blood groups (e.g., Blacks; South East Asians); and (j) people from particular geographic regions (e.g., Mediterranean, European) (Elliot and Fleras, 1992: 28; Li, 1990: 6). Such varied usage has resulted in race being seen as an objective biological and/or social fact that operates through independent characteristics (Omi and Winant, 1993). Further, there is the accompanying belief that there are personalities based on racial characteristics; and that inherited biological or physical characteristics are the most important individual and group traits.

Obviously, the meaning of the term *race* is not "fixed" but is dependent on historical period and context. The problem is this: who really belongs in these categories? Many persons don't fit into any of the five colour-based racial categories (brown, black, red, yellow, white) in use today.[1] Where would we, for example, place Arabs or persons from the Middle East or those with a combined racial background? A list of all such exceptions would be quite long, but one thing is evident–there is no clear, indisputable definition of race. Does this then mean that our reference to different racial groups or identities is merely a means of manipulating and creating division among people? Do racial characteristics play a role in people's lives? Omi and Winant (1993) argue that "the concept of race operates neither as a signifier of comprehensive identity, nor of fundamental difference, both of which are patently absurd, but rather as a marker of the infinity of variations we humans hold as a common heritage and hope for the future" (p.9).

For the purpose of our discussion, *race* will refer to the socially constructed classification of human beings based on the historical and geographic context of individual experience. An individual's race is determined socially and psychologically, rather than biologically. It is often the basis upon which groups are formed, agency is attained, social roles are assigned and status is conferred. Consequently, individual and group identities and behaviours are a product of these factors.

It is clear that race affects how individuals identify themselves, interact with others and understand their place in society. Race is significant as long

[1] It is only in recent times that we have begun to use the term Brown, particularly in Toronto, to refer to people of South Asian origin. In England, South Asians are referred to as Black; and in the United States, in Los Angeles, for example, Brown refers to Latin Americans.

as groups are determined by their physical traits and attributes are assigned as a result of these traits. It is significant as long as groups and individuals suffer consequences because of race. The social meaning of race is well understood by all members of society, even though it is racialized Others who often name race as a force within their lives.

Leo Driedger (1986), in writing about ethnic and minority relations, notes that Northern Europeans, the dominant population in Canada, tend to be very conscious of skin colour and often classify people accordingly (p.284). Yet when asked to describe themselves, members of the dominant population tend to omit race as one of their characteristics, while minority group members, particularly Blacks, tend to identify race as a significant characteristic. As the dominant racial group, whites tend to see their colour as the norm while identifying non-whites in terms of colour. In fact, race is a part of everyone's identity.

The assumption that the term *race* refers mainly to racial minorities was revealed in one classroom discussion when students were asked to talk about themselves in racial, ethnic and cultural terms. One white participant insisted that he was Canadian, and therefore his racial and ethnic identities were irrelevant. When asked how he would feel if a Chinese person and a Black person both insisted that they were Canadian and therefore refused to identify themselves by their ethnicity, the participant responded by saying he would not be satisfied with their answers because, to him, Canadians are people who look like him: "Chinese and Blacks are immigrants–they do not look Canadian." Another participant said to me, "I feel when you mention race you're talking about people of different ethnicities and countries."

Another common tendency is to equate talking about or naming race with a display of prejudice or racism. Hence, when asked to talk about race as it relates to their identity and behaviour, white participants tended to become defensive. They responded: "I never see race ... I see the person, not her race ... I don't feel uncomfortable with Black people"; or "Every time I've talked about race, it's been about stereotyping or prejudice." Others wrote the following:

> **Greg**: As for my race, I am white, but I never really had to think about it before. I don't feel that it ever affected the people with whom I associated or talked to. My two best friends are Black and (Canadian) Indian. I was brought up in a family that didn't believe in prejudice and I'm proud of that. If I don't like a person, it is because of their personality, not their race or heritage.

> **Henry**: Concerning my race, which is Caucasian, I really don't believe that it has contributed enormously to my identity or behaviour. I feel this way because my culture is basically all Canadian.

Laurie: I ... cannot see how my race influences or affects me. I have always been aware of how my ethnicity influences my ideals, morals, values and beliefs, and these personal elements have not changed. For me to say that race affects me would either show that I feel inferior or superior to other races, and this is incorrect.

Why have Greg, Henry and Laurie given so little or no thought to their race or "whiteness?" How can they claim that their race has not contributed "enormously" to their identity, values, beliefs and behaviours? Is it really because their culture is, as Henry claims, "basically all Canadian"? And what does it mean to be "Canadian" when one is white? Is their denial of race an attempt, as Laurie hints, not to "show" their feelings of superiority to other races? Is it likely that those who identify themselves racially are people who "feel inferior or superior"? And what about when someone like Greg, who does not think of himself in racial terms, identifies others, such as his "two best friends," by their race or ethnicity? Is he re-inscribing their inferior and his superior status (Kallen, 1995)? In a way, Greg is indicating that he is the "norm" (Sleeter, 1994; Roman, 1993). The norm is understood by all and therefore need not be made explicit. And in identifying the race and ethnicity of his friends, Greg is socially constructing them as racialized Others, as different from his white self. In essence, the comments by Greg, Henry and Laurie indicate their attempts to avoid naming their whiteness, for to do so would require them to also acknowledge their race privilege (that "invisible package of unearned assets," as Peggy McIntosh [1995] puts it) and surrender the myth of the racial neutrality of Canadian society.

Ruth Frankenberg (1993: 6) argues that speaking of the social construction of whiteness reveals locations, discourses and material relations to which the term *whiteness* applies. She further points out that whiteness is related to "a set of locations that are historically, socially, politically and culturally produced." This set of locations is linked to relations of domination (cited in Weis and Fine, 1996). This idea of domination and construction of whiteness dates back to early colonial times. European scientists ranked "the 'races' of the world in hierarchical order of innate inferiority and superiority ranging from primitive to highly civilized," and "at the pinnacle of the hierarchy" were the "'white' Euro-Christian 'races'" (Kallen, 1995: 24).[2] Compare this hierarchical interpretation of human

[2] Todorov (1993) notes that François Bernier of France was one of those who in 1684, "first used the word 'race' in its modern sense" (p.96). But it was Linnaeus, who in his work *Systema Naturae* (1740), classified human beings in terms of Europaeus albus (white), Americanus rubescens (red), Asiaticus fuscus (yellow), and Africans niger (black). Later, in the nineteenth century, LeBon, "a partisan of polygenesis" equated the human races to animal species using "anatomical characteristics such as the colour of the skin, and the shape and volume of the skull" (Todorov, 1993: 107). Based on "civilization" and "culture," European being the norm, LeBon also placed human beings in a hierarchy in the order of White, Yellow, Black and Red (Todorov, 1993). (See also Satzewich's (1998) discussion of "race, racism and racialisation.")

Figure 2: Fyre Jean Graveline illustrates that everything around us is interrelated. It is important to note that this is not a linear depiction of traits or attributes of any particular group of people, but rather a metaphor of the equal inclusion of all races of peoples within the wheel of life.

differences with the teachings of the Medicine Wheel of Aboriginal peoples (Figure 2).

It seems likely then that when white participants attempt to deflect discussion about their whiteness or refuse to make their own racial selves or identities explicit (as in the case of Greg, Henry and Laurie), they are attempting to hide their knowledge of their location and the ways in which they socially, culturally and politically produce relations of domination.

In the essay excerpt that follows, Carol explores her identity as a Black woman who has immigrated from the Caribbean. Her words reveal that her understanding of racial superiority and inferiority and her relationship to white people must be understood within a global context of colonialism. This legacy of colonialism, more specifically, the legacy of colonial discourse, write Lois Weis and Michelle Fine (1996; with reference to Moharty and Zoderfer), operates to construct whiteness as the norm against which all other communities are judged. It helps to produce knowledge that constantly inscribes the marginalization of people of colour. So, in Trinidad as well as Toronto, the colonial discourse operates to influence Carol's sense of self, her values and behaviour.

Carol: *"I grew up thinking that whites were superior ..."*

Sixteen years ago I immigrated to Canada. It was in the early 1970s, when there was an influx of immigrants to Canada, especially from the Caribbean. I was born in the Caribbean island of Trinidad to parents of West Indian nationality. My father's and mother's ethnicity is African.

Racially I am Black. I have lived half of my life in Trinidad, where the majority of the population is of African descent and the second major group is of East Indian descent, interspersed with Chinese and whites. Living there, where the majority of people were Black, I felt no threat to my self-esteem because of prejudice or racial discrimination. However, from a very early age, I learned that to be white or fair-skinned with long hair was much better than being Black. I grew up thinking that whites were superior, prettier, richer and never did menial jobs, because that's what I saw of the whites I came into contact with in Trinidad.

This belief was inculcated in me by my parents, who always spoke highly of whites, showed great respect for them and made remarks and comparisons that made them appear superior. As I grew older and learned about the history of my race, I realized that the attitude my parents had towards the white race is a legacy that was passed on to my generation, and dates back to slavery and colonialism.

Immigrating to Canada has been an eye-opening experience for me, because it has helped to change my beliefs and my concepts of white people. It has also made me more conscious of my race because I am now in the minority, and I am reminded of it daily. For example, when I listen to the news and read the headlines in the newspapers, if there is something negative about a Black person, I feel as though I am a part of it. I feel as though everyone is looking at me and thinking about me in the same negative light as that person who committed the crime. I feel as though I am on stage. Similarly, if there is something positive or good, I feel proud.

To an extent my race does influence my values and attitudes, because as a member of a visible minority living in Canada, I feel that achieving success in anything means extremely hard work and struggle. As a result, I place a very high value on education, which I feel is one of the main tools to success. I am passing on this value of education to my children because I realize that, without it, their chance of success is almost nil. In addition, I am trying to instil in my children the value of being proud of their Black heritage. I am also trying to develop in them a self-esteem that would counteract the darts of racism, prejudice and discrimination that they will definitely have to face in this society. I am also making them aware of the fact that, even though they are Canadians, their success and achievements can be attained only through working twice as much as their fellow white Canadians.

However, as I reflect on my values, behaviours, morals and attitudes towards life, I must also note that, whereas culture, ethnicity and race are significant, I am to a large extent strongly influenced by my religion. As a

Christian, I try to apply the principle of love to my fellow men, by using the golden rule: "Always treat others as you would have them treat you." Practising this rule sometimes becomes difficult when I am faced with racial discrimination, prejudice or racial slurs. For example, I remember walking home from the bus stop one day when some young men passing by in a car shouted, "You ... Nigger!" A mixed feeling of anger, devastation and prejudice came over me. I had to quickly console myself by thinking that they were just ignorant strangers who didn't know me, so I should ignore this remark. There were other incidents, like when my husband and I were looking for an apartment. We were told on the phone that an apartment was available. We made an appointment to see it and went there. The superintendent took a white couple to see the apartment and left us waiting in the lobby, then returned and told us it was taken. We were living just across the street, so we walked home, phoned the same building and inquired, and were told by the same superintendent that the apartment was available. We got the message and started to look elsewhere. These and other incidents while job hunting, and even things at school, make it difficult for me sometimes to practise this principle of "love your fellow man" and the golden rule. But over the years, I have learned to cope by practising this rule and ignoring derogatory slangs hurled at me or racial discrimination and prejudice. Now, I do not feel the sting of racial prejudice as much as when I first arrived here.

In my daily life I try not to see people first through their colour or race, but as individual human beings. In spite of cultural differences, ethnicity, race or religion, we all share a common heritage as members of the human race, and we have the same basic human needs; therefore we should not make ourselves feel superior or inferior to others.

Being a Black Canadian who is a part of a minority group, I am aware that my ethnicity and race will always play a role in influencing my values and attitudes in life. However, because my religion is a way of life for me, it determines how much of society's values, behaviours and attitudes I assimilate. It, therefore, affects my main outlook on life.

NAMING: CONFUSION AND CONTRADICTIONS

In the following essay excerpt, Lorraine draws attention to the problem of naming based on what we have come to accept as racial classification. Most notably, Lorraine shows us how the category of race, particularly in the ways in which she experiences and conceptualizes it, is related to context and relationships. She says that, for her, "race has always been an unstable" identity, which changes according to family, peers, partner relationships and maturity. Also significant is the role that individuals and the media have played in forcing her to identify herself in racial terms. Lorraine's essay makes explicit the contextual and relational nature of racial identity and simultaneously shows her own contradictions, conflicts and ambivalence with being categorized. Nevertheless, she gestures to, if not claims, a Black identity. Is this argument only that of a "bi-racial" person? Is the same "instability" or "fluidity" evident in others who are not of "mixed" racial origin?

Lorraine: *"I am not a typical 'half-breed' ..."*

In the field of social science, classification by "hypo-descent" refers to affiliating with a subordinate rather than a superordinate racial group. This system of racial classification not only averts the ambiguity of intermediate identities, but it also ensures that the white race maintains its purity. Within North America, where the principles of hypo-descent have been an institution since slavery, no formal distinctions have ever been made between one's *genotype* and *phenotype*. In general, the term *genotype* refers to one's total, absolute genetic inheritance, whereas the term *phenotype* refers to any aspects of one's genotype that are expressed. Due to the fact that systems of classification are arbitrary in nature, it is only logical to assume that race as a concept is a social construction. Individuals with varying amounts of "non-white blood running through their veins" are at risk of satisfying countless different racial classifications across the globe. The criteria is not universal; hence, race as we know it is a product of social engineering.

Although I technically subscribe to the end results of hypo-descent, I am vehemently opposed to the principles behind it. My racial identity is not based on a need to identify with a subordinate, intermediate or superordinate race; each of those terms denotes a hierarchy that I am not at all comfortable with. My conception of race has always been unstable; it has changed in light of my family allegiances, peer groups, mates and maturity. During my adolescence, I saw no need to draw a distinction between the concepts of phenotypes and genotypes in regard to racial classification. It all seemed so straightforward: Your outer appearance affected the way in which others perceived you. Hence, if others perceived you as Black, you were Black. However, if your skin colour, hair and features could "pass" as white, then for all intents and purposes you were "white." It wasn't until my final year in high school that I realized just how faulty my thinking was. This epiphany didn't come from an insightful text book or seminar; ironically, it came while watching an episode of *Oprah*. The topic was about "Children of mixed race and how they identify." The "expert" panelist essentially confirmed each and every one of my naïve beliefs about racial classification. She (a white female) dominated the discussion until a male in the audience stood up to pose a question. He stated that he was of mixed racial parentage. His mother was Vietnamese and his father was a Black American soldier, but he looked Latino, so how should he identify based on her previous definitions? She was stumped! I was stumped! His unique dilemma caused me to question the straightforwardness of my initial argument.

Soon after, another audience member stood up to make a comment. This blonde female's statement also demonstrated why such a difference exists between one's phenotype and genotype. She stated that her mother was white and that her father was a mulatto. However, she bore no "negroidal" demarcation whatsoever. Although her genetic disposition made her one-quarter Black, her external features failed to express it in any way.

At that moment I realized that, if I were ever to procreate with a white male, I would risk creating a further discrepancy between my child's genotype and phenotype. When I visualize my future children, they all have black skin, dark brown eyes and textured hair. However, even if I do choose to safeguard against having a white partner, the chance still exists that my father's recessive genes (white skin, blue eyes and straight hair) could re-assert themselves in the next generation.

I'm not a typical "half-breed," to appropriate a derogatory term formerly used to describe mixed-race Indians. I unequivocally look Black; I could never even think of "passing" based on my skin colour alone. My nose is extremely straight and pointy, my eyes, dark brown, my lips, moderate in size and my hair, thick and curly. Strangers know I'm mixed with something, but they are always curious to find out what. They frequently ask, "Where are you from?", in order to ascertain the nationality of my *other* parent. By default, I always answer, "Canada." I know I am only frustrating the person asking me, because that answer reveals nothing about my parentage. This line of questioning will only desist when I eventually reveal that my mother is a Black women from Jamaica and that my father is a white male from Quebec.

Genetically speaking, I am in fact bi-racial; my mother is Black and my father is white, but if ever given a census form with a "bi-racial," "multiracial" or "other" option to fill out, I would quickly tick off the box labelled "Black." Although my complexion and features may have been diluted to the outside world, I still represent some form of Blackness. Though it may be muted to many, for others it is just as threatening, just as unattractive and just as unemployable.

The reason that I can collapse my bi-racial identity into an all-encompassing Black one is due to the fact that I make no distinction between the two. My self-concept is inevitably shaped by the actions of other Blacks (bi-racial or otherwise). When I watch an awards show, and I see a person being acknowledged for their good deeds or contributions to society, it gives me a warm feeling inside; seeing that that person is Black makes me internalize their achievement all the more. On the same hand, when watching the news and hearing of a violent, unspeakable act, it upsets me and enrages me. If the culprit happens to be Black, it succeeds in making my heart sink just that much more.

Maybe the distinction is easier for me because my phenotype is a genuine expression of my genotype, or maybe its because there is more than just a "drop of Negro blood" in me. Whichever the case, I will go on "passing" as a Black female until they revoke my membership.

ETHNICITY AS PART OF SOCIAL IDENTITY

The terms *ethnic population*, *ethnic food*, and *ethnic music* are used often in Canada. In some cases, *ethnic* is used to describe Italians, Portuguese, Ukrainians and others. It is also used as a stereotype. The term *ethnic* is sometimes used interchangeably with *race* and *immigrant* and *culture* to try to socially define or locate people.

> **Leslie**:*"I have thought of myself only as Canadian ..."*
>
> To me, ethnicity was something that belonged to people who differed from the so-called average white Canadian—differing perhaps because of language, accent or skin colour. Thus, I believed ethnicity was something noticeable or visible. I believe my ignorance regarding my ethnicity is because I belong to the dominant group in Canada. Because I am white, English speaking and have British ancestry, I have thought of myself only as a Canadian. In essence, I didn't realize I had ethnicity, because I did not differ from the stereotypical image of an average Canadian.

The common notion among many Canadians is that ethnicity is based on how people choose to identify themselves and is presumably of no concern to society in general. But ethnicity is not simply a matter of individual choice: members of society play a role in defining ethnicity. For example, class participant Jackie Stewart writes that, when she tells people her name, some respond by saying "Grrrrrrreat day for motorcar racing!"

> **Jackie**: I must hear that line at least once a day. People tend to associate my name with the once-great racing car driver, Jackie Stewart. The last name, Stewart, is a dead giveaway that I am of Scottish origin or ethnicity. People generally don't ask my parents where they are from, because they recognize their Scottish accent. However, when I mention that I too was born in Scotland, they look at me questioningly, and ask me why I do not have an accent. Or they ask me why I do not have freckles, or pale skin with rosy cheeks. How am I to know?

Ethnicity gives individuals a sense of identity and belonging based, not only on their perception of being different, but also on the knowledge that they are recognized by others as being different. Isajiw (1977) notes that, in terms of ethnic cultural practices, individuals go through "a process of selecting items, however few, from the cultural past–pieces of ethnic folk art, folk dances, music, a partial use of language, knowledge of some aspects of the group's history–which become symbols of ethnic identity" (p.36).

Another student participant recalled how he struggled with his identity.

Stefan: *"I saw my ethnicity as an advantage and disadvantage ..."*

My ethnic identity is Polish. My parents were born in Poland and came to Canada in 1967. I was born in Toronto, Ontario, a couple of years later. I saw my ethnicity as an advantage and a disadvantage during my lifetime. When I was younger, I didn't want to admit that I was Polish. Even though I was born here, I felt that admitting my ethnicity would be a barrier to joining the "in-crowd" or the "cool group" at school. I even skipped the Polish language classes my parents sent me to after school. As I became older, I realized I couldn't change my ethnicity. I was who I was. I became more proud of my Polish background. It felt good to be part of a Polish community where I was able to participate in ceremonies and activities based on my Polish background. It gave me a sense of belonging to a group, a sense of identity, a sense of security.

Individuals with several ethnic identities are free to identify with all of them. However, individuals often identify most strongly with the one that forms the basis of their socialization at home or with their peers, the one that seems most acceptable by the dominant group in society or the one by which others identify them.

Some years ago, while facilitating a group discussion with Grade 6 students in Toronto, one blonde boy identified himself as Italian (they were all asked to identity their ethnicity). Members of the group doubted that he was Italian: they noted that his last name was "not Italian" and he did not "look" Italian. In fact, his mother was Italian and his father was Irish. He pointed out that he lived in an Italian neighbourhood and spoke Italian. On another occasion, I was chatting with a young man who looked to me to be Black and possibly of mixed race. In our conversation, he revealed that he was Italian. He had grown up in an Italian community and spoke Italian fluently. He further said that people often doubted his Italian heritage. However, it was the only one he knew, since he grew up with his Italian mother and did not have much interaction with his father.

Ethnicity, like race, is socially, politically and historically constructed and is subject to the ambiguities and contradictions that are found in societies.[3]

> It is dynamic. Its meanings change over time. Nevertheless, ethnicity serves to establish status allocation, role expectations and group membership. Marger and Obermiller write that ethnicity is "a form of social organization, the boundaries of which are flexible in various social contexts. Cultural features are only symbolic and serve to mark out particular group boundaries" (cited in Elliot and Fleras, 1992: 134).

[3] In Canada, one of the ways in which ethnicity is constructed involves the "official" notions of "bilingualism and multiculturalism."

In the following essay excerpts, individuals explore their understanding of ethnicity.

> **Damian**: "*My roots are very much embedded in the Slovenian way of life.*"
>
> My cultural and ethnic backgrounds are very much Slovenian. More specifically, they originated in a northern province called Slovenia [in the former Yugoslavia]. My parents immigrated from there twenty-two years ago and I was born here in Canada.
>
> My parents brought with them all of their beliefs, values and traditions. A big part of their life was, and is, a dedication to hard work and their religious faith. Throughout my life I have been taught to respect those values and accept those religious beliefs.
>
> With regard to ethnicity, its influence ranges from the way I dress to the type of food I eat. For example, my parents hate to see me in torn clothing. When I was a child, and even now, their ethnic values made them feel that I should be well groomed all the time. I feel that now, in my early adult years, I carry a lot of those early impressions with me.
>
> The work ethic is very important to me. I feel that I always make an attempt to do things well and with enthusiasm. This is one of the main cultural differences. Canadian culture dictates a more relaxed attitude towards work. One of the strange things that I tend to do is slack off when in an environment of long-time Canadians, simply because of this attitude. In a predominantly Yugoslavian environment, I tend to work faster and a lot harder. In this way, I am more Slovenian than Canadian.
>
> A central focus in my life is my religious faith. My parents and most who live in the province they come from are Roman Catholic. My faith has always been a basis for my attitudes, actions and beliefs. With respect to sex and morality, the church dictates a lot in my life. This causes many nagging conflicts. Popular Canadian values and beliefs with which I sympathize come in direct conflict with the teachings of the church. I must, many times, reach some sort of compromise. Abortion is a great example of such a conflict. While the church strictly rejects the idea, I am not sure as to where I stand on the subject. I am, I feel, a little more open-minded than many of the older-generation Slovenians in my community. That is part of their general character, which comes from that deep-rooted faith they grew up with. The fact that I grew up with the many different viewpoints of my friends and their respective backgrounds means that I have a broader outlook. In conclusion, I can say that while I was born here in Canada, my roots are very much embedded in the Slovenian way of life.

It is common to find that religion or religious affiliation is an integral part of a person's ethnic identity, values and behaviour. In such cases, ethnic culture and religious culture are inseparable. For example, as Damian points out, his Slovenian ethnicity influences his values and behaviour, but his faith is also central to his life. Religion or spirituality is more important to some ethnic groups than others, particularly those of orthodox affiliation. However, with the increase in secularization and religious diversity in today's society, the influence of religion is diminishing. In the following essay, Mark, a Jewish Canadian, explains the role of religion in his life.

Mark: *"I believe it is important to keep the Jewish faith alive..."*

"Yes, I am Jewish. Is there anything wrong with that?" I cannot remember how many times I have said that sentence, but I know it has been far too often. I believe this problem arises because too many people classify others into groups based on their ethnic backgrounds. When people are classified into different groups, each develops its own set of values, beliefs and attitudes.

I would not consider myself a religious individual, nor would I consider my family religious. As the generations progress, the emphasis on religion decreases. When I was young, I was given the opportunity to learn about my ancestors, my heritage and my religion. My parents provided me with the guidance to learn what being Jewish is all about. I must admit I am glad to know my background, yet I feel I place little emphasis on it.

Although I am not a religious person, nor do I come from a religious family, some attitudes and values remain of great importance to me. The one that stands out above the rest is to continue the Jewish religion by marrying within my own ethnic group. Even though my religion may not be of great importance to me, I believe it is important to keep the Jewish faith alive so that following generations may learn of their heritage as I did. By providing children with a definite religion at birth, they are able to know and understand where their ancestors came from. It is through this understanding that people are given a certain sense of belonging and are pointed in one direction. Because I am of the Jewish religion, that is the direction I hope my family will maintain, although I do not feel that my methods are superior to those of others.

HYPHENATED CANADIANS

There are some Canadians, largely ethnic and racial minorities and immigrants, who identify themselves in terms of both their ethnic origin (e.g., French, Irish, Dutch) and their citizenship or nationality (i.e., Canadian). For these Canadians, their identity is hyphenated–they are neither more nor less one or the other. This sentiment is articulated by Katie in the following essay (see also Moran's story in Chapter 3).

Katie: *"I consider myself to be a hyphenated Canadian ..."*

Racially, I am white. My ethnic background is Ukrainian. Three of my grandparents were born in the Ukraine. They immigrated to Canada in the years prior to World War I. My maternal grandmother was born in the United States, and her parents were born in the Ukraine. They moved to Canada from the United States at the turn of this century and were part of the group of Ukrainians involved in opening up the Canadian West.

Culturally, I consider myself to be a hyphenated Canadian: Ukrainian-Canadian. My parents and my brother and I were all born and raised in Canada. We practise Ukrainian culture as it was passed on by my grandparents. In Canada, when someone asks me what ethnic group I belong to, I say Ukrainian. However, when outside of Canada, I consider myself a Canadian.

How have these backgrounds affected me? I take my white colour for granted since we live in a predominantly white society. I am only conscious of it if I am with a group of Blacks or Asians and I would be if I were to travel to a part of the world where there are few whites (e.g., Zaire) or where it is an issue (e.g., South Africa.)

Canadian culture is more deeply ingrained in me as evidenced by the clothes I wear, the language I speak (English) and the everyday Canadian foods I eat. I have been influenced by the Canadian rat race for affluence and success and the possession of various material goods that are part of the "good Canadian life," such as a television, a VCR, a car and furniture and so on.

I use my Ukrainian culture as a reference point from which I can observe other cultures and look for similarities. I notice this every year when I go to Toronto's Caravan festival and visit the various pavilions.

As a second-generation Ukrainian born in Canada, my family and I have assimilated well into Canadian society and, fortunately, no longer experience the discrimination that our great-grandparents did upon first arriving here. However, I can empathize with other ethnic groups who are under Soviet rule (e.g., Estonians, Lithuanians, Afghans) and feel their dislike of the Russians. I can also feel for those who are being persecuted for expressing their wish to be self-governing or for speaking out against human rights violations. Ukrainians have long experienced domination, which is the reason why so many are in Canada today and continue to preserve their language and culture. Thus, I can better understand political prisoners around the world. On the other hand, I have some understanding of Russians, as both they and Ukrainians share the same devotion to tradition and, unfortunately, long speeches!

In the past year, I have become more interested in my Ukrainian heritage, and I am currently studying the language since I was unable to learn it well as a child.

I did not know until recently how much my Ukrainian Orthodox background influenced me. We did not attend church regularly except for Easter, and I left the Orthodox church during my teen years. After attending different Protestant churches over the years, I decided to adopt the Anglican Church. Its liturgy more resembles that of the Orthodox church, and it feels more like "home" to me. It was interesting to discover how much even my small church involvement in childhood influenced my current religious practices in an almost unconscious way. I celebrate our Ukrainian Christmas as well as December 25, and Ukrainian Easter with my family every year. There are many other Ukrainian influences, such as music, crafts, foods and other religious practices.

My cultural influences have made me more open to the differences in other cultures, especially European. I can feel more a part of them and assimilate a little more easily into Polish or Greek cultures, for example, whereas my "WASP" friends feel more awkward and different in comparison. However, I do feel different when exposed to non-European cultures, such as Hindu or Central African and so on. I can understand why so many have immigrated to this country, especially when it has been for political and religious reasons.

DOMINANT GROUP MEMBERSHIP

The history of a society provides indicators as to the dominant-minority status of its different ethnic and racial groups. Kinloch (1974) points out that minority groups are characterized by their having experienced oppression at some time in the country's development. Burnet (1981) further points out that minority groups tend to be vulnerable and subject to discrimination. Physical and social attributes, such as race and ethnicity, then determine social interaction and involvement within the society. In Canada, the dominant ethnic group is Anglo-Celtic, and the dominant racial group is white. The remaining racial and ethnic groups can therefore be classed as minorities. Ng (1993) writes about the power of the dominant group and how that power is normalized. She points out that, in Canadian society,

> European men, especially those of British and French descent, are seen to be superior to women and to people from other racial and ethnic origins. Systems of ideas and practices have been developed over time to justify and support their notion of superiority. These ideas become the premise on which societal norms and values are based, and the practices become the "normal" way of doing things (p.52).

Insofar as race and ethnicity are a part of identity, so too is dominant-minority group status. Through socialization, "the lifelong learning process through which individuals develop selfhood and acquire the knowledge, skills and motivation required to participate in social life" (Mackie, 1986: 64), individuals acquire a sense of identity as members of the dominant or minority group. Those who belong to a group that strongly identifies with the dominant or minority group will ultimately come to think of themselves as dominant or minority group members respectively. Individuals' cultural identities become linked with their historical experiences, values, ways of life and the social patterns that are part of their group life.

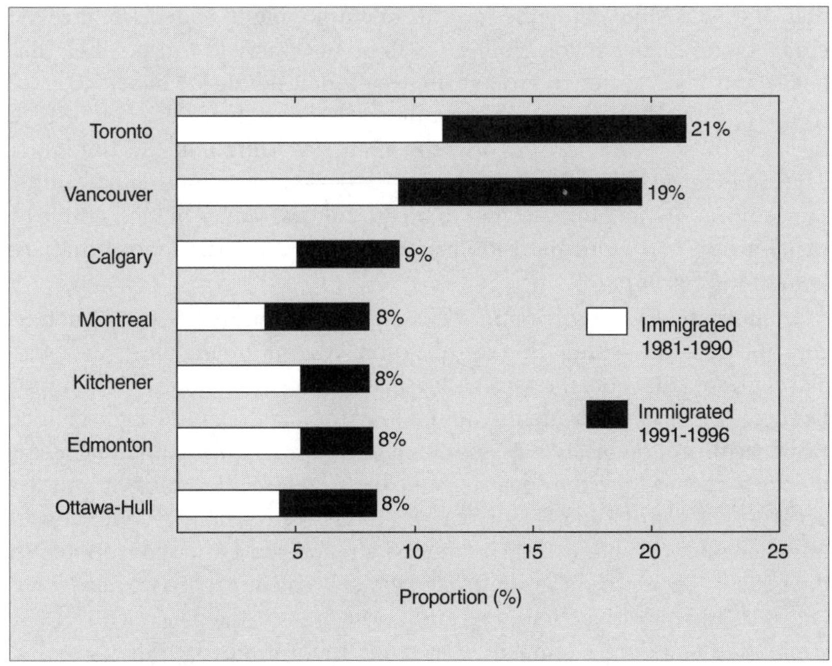

Immigrants who arrived in Canada since 1981 as a percentage of selected Census Metropolitan Areas.

Source: The Nation series (Statistics Canada Catalogue No. 93F0023XDB96000).

Acquiring an ethnic and racial identity and a dominant-minority identification, however, is not simple in our contemporary, pluralistic, Canadian society. Individuals are influenced by many factors outside of their home and their immediate ethnic and racial groups. They are influenced by schools, churches, workplaces, media and other major institutions. Sometimes it is in encounters with these institutions that individuals come to recognize the privileges they have as racial and ethnic group members. Dominant group members may come to realize that they have a privileged and prestigious position in society, and, as a result, access to all the social, political and economic institutions within that society. They might even come to realize that they can "get ahead" without compromising their identity. Peggy McIntosh (1995) explores this notion of privilege in her essay "White Privilege and Male Privilege: A Personal Account of Coming To See Correspondences through Work in Women Studies." She writes that the phenomenon of white privilege is "denied and protected, but alive and real in its effects."

Minority group members, on the other hand, may come to realize that to get ahead they may have to compromise their ethnic identity. They learn that "if they wish to enjoy the rewards of employment, education or social contact with higher-status groups, it will be necessary to forsake their language and many other cultural attributes of their ethnic [or racial] groups" (Agocs, 1987: 170). This could also mean denying their ethnicity or race because these characteristics identify them as "different" or "inferior." They may reject their ethno-racial group experiences or, alternatively, they may embrace what they consider to be the cultural values of their ethnic or racial group and work hard to change the negative perceptions that are held of their group.

In short, the dominant or minority status of an ethnic or racial group mirrors its position within the stratification system of the larger society. Through socialization, individuals learn about their position. This in turn is likely to influence their identity and behaviour. In the following accounts, when writing of themselves as dominant (or majority) group members, participants reveal how they learn about their status, internalize it and act accordingly. Carol told her story earlier, in the section on race. She showed how her minority status or her status as a racialized Other contributed to the issues with which she is confronted while living in a society where privilege is linked to colour. Here, Lyn and Lorne express that it is not only their white race and Anglo ethnicity that make them the people they are, but also the privilege that comes with being part of the white, dominant group. Interestingly, these Canadians tend not to refer to themselves in hyphenated terms. They are, as Henry claims, "all Canadian," and some go so far as to say that they have no ethnicity, just as they are not raced.

Lyn: "I am a member of a majority group that has a great deal of power."

As a white English Canadian, my values, behaviour and attitudes are influenced by my origins in direct relation to the fact that I am a member of the single largest group, racially, ethnically, and to a large extent, culturally. In this short essay, I would like to focus on how these racial and ethnic cultures reinforce each other and how, when combined together, they can mask a number of assumptions I have about my relationship to the society I live in and my acceptance of that society's norms. In essence, I want to show how the values, attitudes and behaviours of the cultures I belong to fit into a system of thought and action that perpetuates those cultures and the power they hold.

I would like to take discrimination as an example. My experience of the class system in Britain has made me aware of how differences in origin, in this case most noticeably defined by accent (in speech), have a direct relationship to the position a person may hold in society in terms of economic power, political influence and control over day-to-day life. What I learned as a teenager in the 1960s in North America, when issues of civil rights and discrimination were in the news, the subject of popular books, and certainly regularly discussed in classrooms, reinforced my awareness of what influences a person's ability to be accepted in society—to succeed in the terms laid down by that society and also in terms of personal freedom.

But I am a member of a majority [i.e., dominant] group that has a great deal of power. So, for example, being racially white, I may have an awareness of these issues, and I may condemn my society for its inherent racism, but it is white culture that I experience day to day, and the very fact that discrimination is rarely an issue for me personally results in my own racial identity becoming an invisible thing. The powerful people within my experience, directly or indirectly—the politician, the employer, the teacher, the social worker—are invariably white. I know that my race will not be an issue with most of the people I must deal with, as I know we will have a commonality from the start. Being in the majority in all three origins, there is also a good chance that either culturally, ethnically or both, our backgrounds will be similar. Neither will I expect my values or behaviour to be an issue because I fit into the "norm."

It is in the idea of the "norm" that racial and ethnic cultures mesh to form a powerful image of what is accepted or expected. I see myself reflected not only in the powerful people I am in contact with but in the books I read in school, the movies I see, the people I read about in newspapers. My day-to-day experience of life reinforces all that I have learned—the language and behaviour I have been taught; the values I have been told are the most important; the attitudes, inevitably, of which I am or am not conscious. As a result, I begin to see no other, and I then begin to measure other cultures by the standards of my own without being aware that I am doing so.

It is this lack of awareness, this assumption of the norm, that has the strongest ability to perpetuate all the other behaviours, values and attitudes of my group, because it dictates what I do and do not perceive. It blocks my ability, then, to understand and appreciate other values, other cultures and to question my own. I see what is different, but I don't analyze the difference. And it isn't crucial that I do so because I do not have to adapt myself. My group has the power, and I don't have to attune myself to any other way of living unless I choose to. And choice versus necessity has a strong impact on what I see and learn.

So my group, being dominant, has the power to define what is acceptable, what is most valuable in me and, in doing so, to define the attitudes of which I am and am not conscious. If I cannot see myself, I cannot see others clearly; and if I cannot see others clearly, seeing myself becomes more and more difficult. The mask is never removed. In this way, the power of the majority group is maintained, as their values, behaviours and attitudes become self-perpetuating.

Lorne: *"I was conscious of belonging to the 'privileged' class ..."*

I am a male, born to white Anglo-Saxon parents and raised in a small town north of Toronto. The European heritage of our family is obscure. We assumed we were British, but there may be some German background as well. My mother has recently done some genealogical research into our origins. She found that both her ancestors and those of my father immigrated to Canada from the United States shortly after the Revolutionary War of 1776 and had lived in the United States for a considerable time before that. We have been in North America for nearly 300 years and in Canada since before it was an independent country, so our connections with Europe can be considered unimportant.

I spent most of my teenage years rebelling against what I perceived as the confines of my cultural heritage. I was conscious of belonging to the (supposedly non-existent) "privileged" class, and was deeply embarrassed about it. I saw smugness and complacency everywhere and was determined never to be a part of it. Like many others my age, I grew my hair long, not simply in an effort to appear different, but to mark myself as being outside of my parents' culture. This was far from rare, but I still consider it an important phenomenon. It was less a case of fashion than a conscious attempt by the youth of the day to define their own culture as visibly different as possible from the one into which they had been born.

I rebelled against both the church (of which my parents were esteemed and active members) and the public school system. I felt that the interest of the church lay more in making its members feel comfortably secure in their own goodness than in spiritual exploration. At school, I refused to be part of what I perceived as training for hypocrisy, and my marks fell as I decided to educate myself as I chose. I was interested in politics and read avidly of the struggles and revolutions of oppressed peoples. Lenin, Castro and especially Che Guevara were my heroes. I wished that I had a struggle as important as theirs, something solid to fight against, a cause that belonged to me. I realize now that many of the things I thought at that time had a lot to do with my own search for identity. I felt that belonging to the majority was a barrier to my individuality, that I had no real traditions or culture of my own.

I have changed since that time. I am no longer embarrassed about belonging to the majority. I have found enough individuality within myself to assure me that, yes, after all I'm not just like everybody else. Through experimentation in different religions, both Eastern and Western, and associations with people from different backgrounds and cultures, I have come to believe in the power of individuals to define themselves as outside of cultural boundaries and to re-shape their beliefs in the light of experience. This belief has its own drawbacks, however, as I shall discuss shortly.

Since I have ceased to struggle so adamantly against my culture, I have often been surprised to find attitudes and ideas that could not have come from anywhere else. I am speaking primarily of unconscious prejudices and assumptions that surface when I least expect them to.

For example, I take many things for granted as natural rights. I am comfortable in society; I feel that there is nowhere that I am not allowed to go if I wish, and nothing that is not prohibited by law that I cannot do. I don't fear the police. I am not in danger of being the victim of racially inspired violence. The only barriers to work or accommodation are my own qualifications and my financial situation. To illustrate the unconsciousness of this assumption of safety, I will tell a little story.

When I was living in Vancouver, I decided to take a walk at dusk along the beaches near the university. It was early spring and still quite cool, so the beaches were deserted. I walked about five miles, enjoyed a magnificent sunset and returned home after dark. Some friends were there and naturally I told them all about my stroll. One of my friends, a female, said that she felt very jealous that I was able to do something like that. At first I didn't know exactly what she meant. Surely she was healthy enough to go for a walk if she felt like it. Then I understood that she was speaking about fear. Momentarily I felt defensive, as if she were blowing something out of proportion and making it partially my fault. Then I understood that she was perfectly right. She perceived something as simple as going for a walk alone after dark as a privilege that I enjoyed and that she did not.

Another result of my heritage, and one that stems directly from the feeling of safety that I have spoken of, is the belief that I talked about earlier—that the individual is the author of his or her own destiny, that we make ourselves. This implies another lot of assumptions. Basically, it assumes that the only limits to our choices are of our own making. It does not take into account how individuals may be forced or coerced into situations they would not otherwise have become involved in. It does not take into account how institutionalized racism and violence might hinder the growth of self-esteem. And it does not take into account how living with violence and hatred changes everyone.

Despite this, I still find my little creed valuable to me. For while others may have valid reasons for not being able to overcome the negative influences in their lives, I have no such excuse. It is up to me to make myself the better person I know I can be.

RECOGNIZING PRIVILEGE

I often hear people ask how it is that some people (I would contend that social class would influence the situation) who live in a diverse community like Toronto know so little about other or minority Canadians and have had very little interaction with them. When they do, they report that they become "awakened to the reality of others." Some even express fear and nervousness, particularly when their encounters with racial minority group members place them in a minority position. Kallen (1995) tells us that the most common response of whites when confronted with racially diverse environments is to withdraw.

Insofar as Kallen's assertion is true, this reaction of some white Canadians should not be surprising. As Sleeter (1994) points out, "people need affective bonds with each other, and given the segregation of society, the strongest bonds are usually with members of our own race" (p.36). She further points out that the isolationist tendencies of whites, even those living in diverse societies, are part of the passive way in which racist ideas are reproduced. From the perspective of a white, she writes:

> In general, whites stick together on common definitions of issues that involve race relations, and behave accordingly. We live largely with other whites, socialize mainly with whites, consume media, vote for whites, etc. Although, today, most whites profess colour blindness and support for equal opportunity, in fact we behave in a very race-conscious manner (Sleeter 1994: 33).

This in part might explain the following experiences as reported by John, Mike, Kendra and Janet.

John: *"I tended to ignore non-WASP problems and cultures ..."*

Upon meeting Virginia and Bill, both native Canadian Indians, and listening to their opinions, comments, ideas and insights as to why others react to them as they do, I realized that although I had preconceived notions concerning the Indians, I was more ashamed of the fact that I tended to ignore non-WASP problems and cultures than of the fact that I did have some biases towards others.

I recognized, and they helped to point out that, as a white male in Canada, I didn't have to be interested or concerned with the plight of others; my heritage almost guaranteed me success in whatever I set out to accomplish. They, conversely, were always aware of who they were and of the treatment this afforded them. All along I had taken my heritage for granted while others were not allowed to do so and were reminded of this fact daily. I think more than anything else this fact awakened me to a new reality.

Mike: *"A feeling of uncertainty came over me ..."*

I felt that I had no prejudice towards any other person. I later learned that the bias I had towards people of other races was in fact prejudice. I could see that I was more relaxed around people of the same colour and race as me.

The following incident occurred in mid-October while I was studying in the library in Bramalea. I was seated completely alone at a large table. A group of young Blacks came and entered what I felt was "my space." I can't remember their exact names, but they chose to sit all around me. A feeling of uncertainty came over me, and I began to feel very nervous. I had never in my life experienced anything like it before. They could sense that I was nervous, and they seemed not to be really concerned about what was going on. I don't know, maybe they were used to integration with whites, but I sure wasn't used to being around Blacks, not alone anyway. I then realized how the members of a minority group must feel when they are surrounded by people who are different from themselves. It would have been easy for me to leave the situation I found myself in, but I wanted to feel the real feeling that I thought members of minority groups experience all the time.

Later that day I talked to one of the Black guys I work with. I asked him if this was how he felt when in that same situation. He said that he only felt hostility towards the majority group when he was singled out and put down, because at such times he had no backing from people of his own race. I then could see what prejudice was. After I left the library, everything returned to normal. I was once again in my own environment. It was possible for me to return to the average white class I was so used to. For just a few brief hours out of the twenty years I have been alive, I feel I experienced something new.

It seems that in every situation we Canadians find ourselves, prejudice will always be present. It is a fact that the society we live in has to become more aware of prejudice and racism. I found myself in a situation and was able to relate somewhat to how members of minority groups must feel. This could never be done fully because I will always be white, but learning of others has opened my eyes to how racism and prejudice act as barriers to interaction between people of different races. I trust that, from this learning experience, I will become a better person, more sensitive and understanding.

Kendra: *"It was a rude awakening for me ..."*

The research I did on Blacks was a real learning experience for me. As I had never been exposed to the Black community before, I expected them to be much like how they are portrayed on television. Although I knew that everything on television has to be taken "with a grain of salt," I was still not sure what to expect. The trip to the community was very scary for me. As I am white and had never been in a minority situation or experienced discrimination, going to a place where I was clearly in the minority made me very uncomfortable. I had never given my colour much thought until I was in a situation where it slapped me in the face. It was a rude awakening for me. I never stopped feeling uncomfortable, but I realized how wrong my perception of Blacks had been. They were friendly, helpful people, no different from the people I grew up with. I know that our cultures make us different, but if we look past those differences, we are all human beings. It was a very rewarding experience for me.

Janet: *"I could not imagine how our society could treat them like they have ..."*

When I think about the word *Indian*, I think of my Grade 8 history class. We were studying the War of 1812. I will always remember how the Indians helped Canada win the war at the battle of Queenston Heights. They seemed so proud and determined ... and now they look defeated. I have always wondered what they must be thinking and feeling about the way most of their people are living.

As I got older I heard about their living conditions—the cramped shacks they lived in, no plumbing and so on. I was horrified. How could anybody be so cruel? I had also heard that many Indians used alcohol to escape from the reality of their lives. I did not want to believe these stories and thought that, if they were true, the number of Indians was exaggerated. I could not bear to think that these once proud and strong-willed persons might be alcoholics, nor did I want to face the facts about some of the reasons why they might be drinking. I wanted to believe that most people care about each other.

I was glad to have the opportunity to investigate the Indians. I could learn the truth and see some of the reality that the Indians face. The day I went to an Indian Centre, I had mixed feelings. The Centre was located in a slum area, and we had to walk about eight blocks to get there. I had dressed up for the occasion, believing that the Centre was a place where Indians came together to practise their culture and spiritual beliefs and to feast.

Once I arrived at the Centre I learned that it served as a shelter for the Indians to come and talk and have a meal with friends. Unfortunately, my worst thoughts about how these people live were true. I did not know what to think. I could not imagine how our society could treat them as we have. On the other hand, what happened to their will to be strong and to control their own destiny?

My feelings for the Indians have not changed greatly, but the research definitely opened my eyes to how some of the people in my own country live. I still believe the Indians have the power to change their lives, to stay together as they once were. This will all happen with time. I do not think any less of them because of their alcoholism or poverty, but I am ashamed that as Canadians we let it happen and subject them to it.

SUMMARY

In this chapter we have examined how race and ethnicity contribute to the social, political and cultural construction of individual cultural identities. We have tried to demonstrate that race, ethnicity and cultural identity are complex concepts that are historically, socially and contextually based. These social relations are dynamic; their meanings change over time. Apple (1993) refers to them as "place markers," operating in a complex political and social arena. The social meanings given to racial and ethnic identity are directly related to the dominant and minority variable, and also to many other variables. Social, cultural and political institutions, as well as individuals, help give meaning to these social factors, which in turn determine how individuals act upon these meanings.

In writing about the relationship between identity and culture in his essay "Beyond Cultural Identity," Adler affirms that

> the psychological, psychosocial, and psycho-philosophical realities of an individual are knit together by the culture which operates through sanctions and rewards, totems and taboos, prohibitions and myths. The unity and integration of society, nature, and the cosmos is reflected in the total image of the self and in the day-to-day awareness and consciousness of the individual. This synthesis is modulated by the larger dynamics of the culture itself. In the concept of cultural identity, then, we see a synthesis of the operant culture reflected by the deepest images held by the individual (1977: 28).

Indeed, Adler demonstrates the significance of culture in establishing individuals' sense of identity. Their ethnic and racial cultures serve as a means of providing stability and comfort, mediating the ways in which the dominant Canadian culture constructs the group's cultural identity. The degree to which individuals identify with their group culture varies depending on place of birth, social class, abilities, education and occupational expectations and achievements, interaction with members and non-members of their group and their willingness to adapt to the main cultural norms.

Ethnicity plays an equally important role in the formulation of cultural identity for the members of the dominant cultural group. However, this group's situation contrasts with that of minority groups. Smith (1991) argues that, while the ethnic identity development of the majority group individual is continually being validated and reinforced by both his membership group and by the structure of the society's institutions, such is not the case for members of many ethnic minority groups. Positive reinforcement frees the majority individual to focus on aspects of his or her life other than ethnicity (p.183).

Finally, the participants' essays illustrate the complexity, tension and contradictions inherent in any attempt to identify persons mainly by their race and/or ethnicity. The essays also indicate the similarities and the differences among the members of the various racial and ethnic groups, and the degree to which their sense of cultural identity and their social interactions are influenced by ethnicity and race. The social meanings are very much related to the mechanisms of cultural control, which we will explore in Chapter 5.

SUGGESTIONS FOR DISCUSSION

1. What is ethnicity? How does is differ from nationality and race?
2. Compare and contrast the different ways in which race has been constructed in Canada, both historically and currently.
3. What impact would Canadian culture have on the identity formation of a newcomer to Canada?

Photo: Dick Hemingway

CHAPTER 3

Negotiating Identity

The early years of formation or the "growing-up" years are particularly significant in setting the framework for the development of cultural identities. Of particular relevance are the communities or neighbourhoods in which individuals are raised, their family situation, the schools they attend, the peer groups with which they socialize. In essence, then, the social, economic, cultural, political and educational contexts in which individuals have lived their early lives speak, to a considerable degree, to what they have become, to the social selves that emerge and to the identity they construct. When class participants were asked to write about how ethnic and racial identities might explain their values, ideas, aspirations and sense of place (or "belonging," in terms of identifying with Canada as "home"), they therefore wrote about their years of growing up in Canada.

In the essay excerpts in the first part of this chapter, participants write about their "growing-up" years. In the second part, participants share their experiences of trying to "fit in" during these years, and beyond. For some, these experiences were attempts to fit into a society that continually constructed them as Outsiders while demanding that they adapt, integrate and become Canadian. For others, these experiences meant "fitting in" in order to take advantage of available opportunities.

GROWING UP: FAMILY, COMMUNITY AND IDENTITY

In the following essay excerpts, all of the writers identity where they were born (not specifically requested) and then proceed to explore the significance of their early neighbourhoods in their understanding of themselves as racial and ethnic persons. They talk about their family lives and values, their parents' aspirations for them and how their parents attempted to pass on their cultural values. Evident in their stories are the issues, tensions and conflicts with which they struggled in coming to recognize their raced and ethnic selves and the corresponding privileges or lack thereof. Missing from their accounts is the role that schooling played in helping them to understand their respective situations and deal with their struggles. It seems regrettably true, as Peggy McIntosh (1995) has pointed out, that these young people did not receive schooling that would aid them in making sense of their own and others' privileges or, alternatively, their own oppressive experiences and those of others.

In this first section, all of the participants except John tend to write directly about themselves and how their race and/or ethnicity have informed their lives. Sarah, Barbara and Naomi tell how being Jewish was understood and acted upon by their respective families and the people with whom they interacted. It is instructive to note that, for Barbara, who declares that "my ethnic background was a major part of my early years," the historical and social situation of her parents contributed to their belief that "a good command of English and a good education" for her was of paramount importance. This was her parents' attempt to ensure that she "fit" into the Canadian society and succeeded. (This will be discussed more fully in the next section.) Nadine relates what it meant to be a Guyanese, South Asian, Hindu immigrant child in Canada, who was torn between two cultures. And both Vanessa and Hillary write about their struggle to "fit in" as Black children in their respective communities and in society generally.

John, on the other hand, merely mentions the birth place and ethnicity of his parents and the fact that he has "a love and respect for the monarchy and the Commonwealth." He speaks little of how his race and ethnicity influence his life. When he does so, it is in relation to others; for example, to the Black and Japanese families in his neighbourhood. He mentions being "the only non-African" at a party and recounts an occasion when he "was asked the time by two young Black men on a deserted street." This illustrates the extent to which John's identity as a white person is tied to that of racialized Others or racial minorities (Weis and Fine, 1996; Rosenberg, 1977). It appears that it is only through these encounters that John is able to talk of a racial identity; but, as he concludes, his heritage is "merely one of many." Might this be an attempt to retreat to his "raceless" cocoon, so that he does not "see" his privileges? (see Phoenix, 1997, Rosenberg, 1997; Sleeter, 1993).

John: *"I was the only non-African attending, and I felt like I glowed in the dark."*

I was born in Toronto, Ontario, to a mother of English nationality and a father of Canadian nationality. Both of my parents were born prior to World War II and were raised in conservative, white-dominated communities. My mother's ethnicity is English. My father is of Scottish and Irish heritage, so my roots are completely centred in the British Isles. These roots and the values, ideas, thoughts and beliefs passed on to me from my ancestors have helped to shape me into the person that I am now. It is these origins, ethnic and cultural, as well as race, that have helped to influence my attitudes and behaviours.

I, like my parents, was raised in a predominantly white neighbourhood. There was one Japanese family and one Black family, but they were both "Canadianized" and were considered to be merely different-coloured white families. Both families spoke English without a trace of accent, were involved in all the community affairs and functions, and therefore did not pose a threat to the conservative, upper-middle-class lifestyle. Had they spoken differently or exposed their racial or ethnic rituals publicly, I believe that they would not have been so readily accepted.

When I was about twelve, a Black family moved to our street and immediately the neighbours and my parents lamented, "There goes the neighbourhood." It was firmly believed that more Black families would soon follow, and the area would be considered undesirable. Although my parents were raising me to believe that God loves everyone, that racial minorities had suffered great hardships and that we must try to understand them, it still wasn't right that they were moving into our neighbourhood.

About three years later, I met a young South African boy at school who soon became my best friend. We were inseparable. Although his skin was much darker than mine, I never really realized he wasn't white until I went to a family party of his. I was the only non-African attending, and I felt like I glowed in the dark. Suddenly all the jokes about Negroes I had heard (and told) in school, all the prejudices I had acquired from family cocktail parties and all the snide remarks I had heard about "undesirables" came crashing down and confronted me. These people were friendly, polite, funny and, most of all, caring. I enjoyed their company and they enjoyed mine. It was really the first time I broke out of the beliefs and values instilled in me by my parents and established my own.

I have lived and attended school in the United States as well as in Canada, and have seen quite a difference in the two cultures of these countries. I would say that I am influenced by both. When out of one country, I sorely miss its unique way of life. I know a lot of individuals who, when they think of the United States, think of loud and brash people, crime, commercialism and money. These elements can be found within the American culture, but I tend to notice the more subtle aspects. I think one aspect of the U.S. culture that has profoundly influenced me is patriotism. I don't mean parades and fireworks, but the feeling inside that you are proud of the country in which you live and of all the good things it has offered you and millions of others. I like the idea of the "melting pot." Although multiculturalism can be found in abundance in the U.S., I like the notion of people from all over forming one unified blend from hundreds of different "spices." I also like the credo of "the land of opportunity," which I feel is at the core of American culture. The belief that, "with enough hard work and sweat and a little bit of luck, you can realize your dreams" seems to be woven into the fabric of the American culture, and it is truly something which I apply in my life.

Through my parents' traditions and my early schooling, I retain a love and respect for the monarchy and the Commonwealth. I feel a kinship with other Commonwealth countries like Australia and a special unity with the people who reside there. I am glad that they form part of my Canadian culture.

Although I am now twenty-five years old and have experienced many varied people and places, values and beliefs, I still find myself occasionally thrown back to my upbringing and the ideas to which I was exposed when I was young. One example is the night in Los Angeles when I broke into a cold sweat after I was asked the time by two young Black men on a deserted street. My old stereotypes came racing back, and I had to deal with them instantaneously. Another example is the time I knew I had won a job only because I was white, male and of British heritage. I felt a certain smugness in feeling that I belonged, rather than that I deserved the job. This situation again illustrated to me how deeply I had been influenced by my racial and ethnic origins and how, although my heritage is important to me, it is not necessarily the best but merely one of many.

I am proud of who I am and where I came from. Most importantly, however, I am proud of the person I am striving to be and of the diverse groups who continue to shape and improve me.

Sarah: *"As a white person in Canada I feel confident and comfortable."*

I was born in Montreal, Quebec. My parents were also born in Montreal, to immigrant parents who arrived in Canada as young teenagers. They came from Russia, Poland and Romania. The cultures of these particular countries did not play a large role in my life. Until the age of thirteen I was surrounded by my grandparents and two sets of great grandparents. Yiddish was spoken at their homes. I did not learn how to speak Yiddish, but I did learn to understand some of it. This allowed me to understand quite a bit of the Yiddish humour, which was an important part of my life. This knowledge was also a bond with the older members of my family, as they did not speak English.

In Montreal I was also exposed to the French language and culture. In the 1950s the French were expected to speak English, even though Montreal was predominantly inhabited by French-speaking people. As English-speaking children, we did not go to the same schools as the French children in our neighbourhood, nor did we play together. I regret that I lost the opportunity to learn another language and another culture first hand.

Racially, I am white, like the majority of Canadians. Being white, I am easily accepted and not subjected to prejudicial stereotyping (although once my name is mentioned this attitude often changes). As a white person in Canada, I feel confident and comfortable.

As a child I was raised in a predominantly white, non-Jewish neighbourhood. There was one Black child in my class, and we were often drawn together, possibly because we were both in the minority. I remember when I was twelve, my father and I were browsing through a bookstore, and I found the book *Black Like Me*. It instantly intrigued me and my father encouraged me to read it. The book told of the experiences of a white man who changed his colour to Black and lived in the southern United States.

I can still remember the strong impact this book had on me. Being a naïve pre-teen, I could not believe that the Blacks were not allowed to drink from the same water fountains, use the same washrooms, or sit in the same sections of the bus as the whites did. I will always be grateful that my father and I were able to discuss this book and reach a better understanding and respect for another race. I am pleased that my children attend a multiracial school and have had the opportunity to learn about other races and also share information about their own.

My ethnicity is Jewish, and this plays a very strong and important role in my life. Family ties have always been strong. I was brought up in a large extended family. This is also my children's experience. Perhaps this bond is the result of the years of persecution in other lands, which forced Jews to realize that the only real thing that mattered was the family. We could lose our homes and possessions—they could be replaced. But our families couldn't be replaced.

The Ten Commandments tell us to honour our parents, and the Torah guides us towards maintaining a strong family unit. Children are most precious, and I personally do not approve of abortion unless it is necessary to save the mother's life. This is consistent with the laws of Judaism, which put the life of the mother first.

Charity or *tzdakah* is an obligation of every Jew. It is a mitzvah or duty to give money, clothes, food or time to those who need it. I belong to a women's organization that raises money for Arab and Jewish women and children in Israel. I also help the Canadian Cancer Society.

I value the State of Israel, and I appreciate its existence. I have never visited Israel, but I have a strong bond with it. During my parents' generation, Israel did not exist; perhaps if it had, my mother's grandparents, aunts, uncles and cousins would not have perished in the Holocaust. Israel gives me a sense of security. Israel was the only country to come to the aid of the prisoners of the hijacked plane in Entebbe. During their forty-year history, the Israelis have welcomed Jews who have been expelled from Arab lands, fought to free Soviet Jews and rescued the Jews of Ethiopia.

Synagogue is a central part of my life. All major events are tied to our *shul*—birth, bar mitzvahs, marriage and death. We observe the Sabbath and all the Jewish holidays. As a child, I attended Hebrew school and Girl Guides, which both met at the *shul*.

As a Jew, I have had to live with anti-Semitism. I must face the incomprehensible fact that six million Jews were slaughtered by Hitler simply because they were Jewish. Fear, to a certain degree, surrounds me. There is always the fear that one day I might be forced to witness my children and family systematically being killed. This does not mean that I constantly live in fear in Canada. But I must remember that the Jews in Europe felt very secure in their belief that they truly belonged in their respective countries. When I was nine, I remember being punched in the stomach by an older boy I often played with. He yelled that I had killed Christ. I did not understand why he had suddenly turned on me. This caused me to feel fearful and suspicious of others. For the longest time when placed in a new situation, I did not mention the fact that I was Jewish. Years and maturity have made me confident in my Judaism.

While living in Kingston, Ontario, our family met many young people who had never met a Jewish person before. We opened our home to them, and soon we were on very friendly terms. One evening, while working in a restaurant with two of my new friends, I was shocked to hear them say that they had been "Jewed." They explained that they had been short-changed on a bill. I then explained the origin of the remark. Both women seemed shocked to learn it was a slanderous remark against Jews. This led to many more discussions on Judaism. We remained friends for many years, and I feel this integration helped build a greater understanding of our different ethnic backgrounds.

My behaviour is also greatly affected by Judaism. I celebrate all Jewish holidays. I believe this is a link to the past and to the future. I choose to live in a racially and ethnically mixed neighbourhood that also includes other Jewish families. I want my children to appreciate Canada's multiculturalism while still holding on to their Jewish identity. We belong to a Jewish community centre and Jewish service clubs. My children attend Hebrew school after their regular public school. While we do not keep kosher, we do not mix meat and milk, nor do we eat pork. I tend to dress modestly. Strict Jewish law would dictate that I wear a wig and that my arms and shoulders be covered at all times, but I choose to dress more in the Canadian style. Friday, our Sabbath, is a time for family. We eat a traditional meal and often share it with visitors. We follow the rituals of lighting the Sabbath candles and saying the blessings over the challah and the wine. I love to read and Judaism has always encouraged the quest for knowledge.

My cultural background is Canadian. As a Canadian, I value my freedom. I can choose which neighbourhood I live in, which school I attend and where I work. I am also free to practise my religion. As I have previously stated, there are discrimination and prejudices in Canada, but we have a legal system to protect us.

I consider myself to be a very proud Canadian but one who will always treasure my unique ethnicity.

Barbara: *"My ethnic background was a major part of my early years ..."*

I am a Canadian Jew. I was born in Toronto in 1935 and have lived in Canada all my life. In this essay I shall try to explain how my racial, ethnic and national origins have shaped my attitudes and behaviour.

Both my parents were Polish Jews who immigrated to Canada in the early 1930s. They left Poland because they believed that they could lead richer and fuller lives in Canada. Apart from the fact that they spoke Polish, there was nothing Polish about them. They felt little warmth or affection for the country that had treated its Jews so badly.

I grew up in the College-Bathurst area [of Toronto], which, at that time, had a large Jewish population. Practically all my friends and classmates were Jewish. At the high school that I attended, 90 percent of the students were Jewish. Most of my parents' friends and relatives lived in the same area, and there was a great deal of visiting among them. There were four synagogues in the block where we lived, one of which my parents attended on religious holidays. The majority of stores in our neighbourhood were owned and operated by Jewish merchants. This environment made me very aware, at an early age, of my Jewishness.

While my parents were not deeply religious, they were certainly practising Jews. We observed the dietary laws in our home, and we celebrated the Sabbath and all the other major religious holidays.

While both my parents spoke Polish and Yiddish with each other and with their friends and relatives, they made no effort to teach me either language. Unlike most Jewish children of my generation, I did not even attend Hebrew school. To my parents it was of paramount importance that I acquire a good command of English and that I do well in school.

The war years were very difficult for my mother. She was the only member of her immediate family to immigrate to Canada; all the others remained in Poland. Unfortunately, she lost them all: her parents, her six sisters and brothers and their spouses and children. I believe that the enormity of my mother's loss instilled in me a deep and abiding prejudice along with the firm conviction that it must be resisted. I learned very early how evil, ugly and destructive prejudice can be.

I think that my experience as a member of an ethnic minority has also made me more sympathetic to the feelings and the problems of new Canadians. I realize that non-white Canadians, unlike myself, encounter even more prejudice and discrimination. I can still remember when there was a good deal of accepted prejudice within Canada. Only thirty years ago, our political, social and economic institutions were under the virtually complete domination of the traditional white, Anglo-Saxon male population. In Ontario it was not until the 1950s that legislation was passed to give minority groups some protection from discrimination in housing, education and employment.

Partly because of my lack of religious conviction and partly because of my lack of formal Jewish education, I am not a practising Jew. Although I maintain close contact with my relatives and my Jewish friends, I do not observe the dietary laws in my home, and I attend synagogue only on ceremonial occasions.

Obviously my ethnic background was a very major part of my early years and I have always had a strong sense of being Jewish. However, while I am a Jew, I am also a Canadian. In contrast, my sense of identity as a Canadian did not emerge until I was an adult.

When I attended school during the 1940s and 1950s, the British influence was still very strong. We concentrated on studying English history and English literature. In common with Canadians everywhere, we sang "God Save the Queen" and flew the Union Jack.

Since then, my growing awareness of being a Canadian has reflected Canada's own growing awareness of itself as a separate and distinct nation. In the intervening years I have become more familiar with Canadian history and Canadian literature. I have travelled widely in Canada and have developed a deep affection for all its varied regions and people.

In the early years of my marriage we lived in Saskatchewan. This gave me perspective on a very different part of Canada and intensified my sense of being a Canadian.

During the past eighteen years I have lived with my family in an area with significant racial, ethnic and cultural diversity. My children attended schools with young people from all over the world. I believe that this has been a positive experience for them; they learned at an early age not to think in racial or ethnic stereotypes.

As in earlier years, these changes have been achieved in a peaceful and democratic manner. In Canada, social change has been accompanied by relatively little violence and a respect for law and order. It is precisely this ability to solve problems in a healthy and constructive manner that I find to be quintessentially Canadian. This legacy of non-violent change has made Canada such an attractive country for so many people. It is this very quality that makes me optimistic for this country's future.

Naomi: *"I have yet to understand what it means to 'look Jewish' ..."*

I was born in Toronto, Ontario. Both my parents are Polish Jews, who immigrated to Canada in the early 1950s. The culture from Poland did not play a large role in my life.

My father is a survivor of a concentration camp. Unfortunately, he lost his whole family: his parents, eight sisters and three brothers. My father lost his family in the horrifying war, and as a result, I never knew my aunts, uncles and grandparents. My father felt it was important to share with his children his religious roots and his experience in a concentration camp. I think it is important to remember the Holocaust so that future generations will not forget it and will prevent such a catastrophe from occurring again. At a very young age I learned how evil and destructive prejudice can be. The message my father instilled in me was "Do not hate! Do not harm, and share with others less fortunate." So much of what I aspire to be as a person I learned from my wonderful father. To my father, establishing a new life and developing a family was of significant importance.

I was raised in a predominantly Jewish neighbourhood. Yiddish is spoken in my home. As a child, I remember asking what each word meant and now I can fully understand it but I cannot speak it as well. The humour in the language is great and to this day I appreciate it.

My parents are not deeply religious, but we celebrate the major religious holidays. We do not keep kosher in the house. My home is more traditional, rather than religious. Friday, our Sabbath, is time for family. My father says the blessing over the challah and wine, and my mother says the blessing over the candles. We eat a traditional meal, often shared with family and friends. My parents have a strong sense of family and community. They have passed this down to me, and I hope I do the same.

I do meet up with prejudice. People whom I meet frequently ask, "What are you?", as a way of determining my racial background. I then proceed to tell them that I am Canadian. They then ask me, "Where are your parents from?" I tell them Poland, and they then look confused and say things such as "You are not fair and blonde" (stereotypes of a Polish person). When they learn I am Jewish, their response always amazes me. People express surprise and say, "You are Jewish!" As if it were a disease or something. And some people think they are paying me a compliment by saying, "We do not think of you as Jewish; you are different than most Jewish people we know." This is an outright insult of my ethnicity of which I am proud. Another typical comment is that I "do not look Jewish." To this day I do not understand what it means to "look Jewish," considering there are Jewish people from all parts of the world.

I believe that my experience as a member of an ethnic minority has made me empathetic to the problems faced by new Canadians. I am aware that non-white Canadians face more prejudice and discrimination than I do. However, my cultural influences have made me more open to the differences in other cultures.

Finally, having been born and raised in Toronto, I have had the privilege of access to a good education. I value my freedom. I am able to choose which school I attend, where I live and where I work. I am proud of who I am and the person I am continually striving to be and of the diverse individuals and groups who continue to shape and enlighten me. I believe that children should be taught the differences and similarities of various cultures at a very young age. As a result, we as individuals would understand each other more and realize that there are more similarities than differences among cultures, and our country would be a better place to live in.

Nadine: *"Being a ten-year-old and coming to this country was horrible."*

I was born in Guyana, South America, as were my parents. And, as far as I know, so were four generations before them. Therefore, my nationality is Guyanese, while my ethnicity is East Indian. My ancestors came from India. My original language is English.

Life in Guyana was very simple. I realized this when my family moved to Canada. I was ten years old when we came here, and the differences were clear to me right away. Where I had been used to having Mom at home, now she was working. Women back home did not work as much as here. I noticed that both my parents were very uptight all the time, which is something I never saw back home. Life over here was all work. They were always worried about house payments and all kinds of bills. They never owed anyone money in Guyana.

Being a ten-year-old and coming to this country was horrible. First of all I came half way through the school year, in the midst of winter. Not only was it hard to adjust to school, but also to the weather, my new friends and speaking English the Canadian way.

It took me a long time to get used to all of this. At home I was Guyanese, in that I still spoke the same way and ate the same foods. But at school I tried very much to be Canadian. Somewhere along the way I decided I did not want to be Guyanese any more. I was going to try the hardest I could to be Canadian, like my new-found friends, and disregard my Guyanese heritage. For a long time I wished I was white. Life just seemed simpler—you didn't have to lie or make excuses or even apologize if your skin colour was white. I really envied white people.

I did meet up with prejudice. I can remember taking the long way to school just to avoid running into people who would call me racial names. However, there were people who would say to me, "Well, you are white in the way you think and act." I used to take it as a compliment, but as I grew older I started to understand that there's not a more terrible thing a person could say to me. I think it's adding insult to injury when someone says that.

My mom and dad brought us up by Guyanese standards—very, very strict. The emphasis was on getting a good education and eventually getting a good career—absolutely no socializing. That was when I started rebelling. I wanted to go out just like all my friends did, but I wasn't allowed. I was torn between the two cultures. By day I was at school, being very much Canadian in the way I acted. I used to get very depressed and hurt over this, because my parents couldn't understand what I was going through. It was only when I was nineteen that my parents started to let me go out. I felt a lot of resentment and hate for a long time towards my parents for this, but my four older sisters seemed to be better able to accept it.

My parents are both very hardworking people, who always wanted the best for us. As my father has said to us so many times, "You can do anything or be anything you want in this country." That's why he brought us here—for a better life—and I really do believe that. I live my life today by those words.

We were never religious. By tradition we are Hindu, as most Indian people take on that religion, but my parents never practised it. Therefore any religious beliefs I have are only from what I've learned over the years, and I do have a very strong belief in God.

Although Canada is multicultural, at times I am still very self-conscious of my colour. Mom and Dad have always taught us to be objective and to think about other people's feelings—to take people for who they are, not what they look like. So I can honestly feel for all other minorities in this country, and not only because of skin colour. I can feel for anyone who is discriminated against for whatever reason. And from being in a minority, I've learned to appreciate all people, regardless of race, creed and ethnicity because I have been on the receiving end of it. Therefore my skin colour, coupled with my parents' influence, has made me a better person.

I've adapted to Canadian culture very well, but I still have Guyanese in me. I think I'm a bit of both. I dress Canadian; I eat Guyanese foods; my friends are both Canadian and Guyanese.

The places I go to are very much Canadian—the bars I go to or the events I participate in socially. I've only gone out with white guys, and this is a preference and maybe a prejudice. I can't explain it other than by saying I've never been attracted to any other guys except whites...

I now feel a great admiration for my parents for coming to a new country and starting all over again, and for being extremely successful in doing so. I now realize it was just as hard for them to adjust as it was for me. If anything, I feel ashamed for all the problems I caused them. I know I'm a better person for all they've taught me. There's a lot of love and respect for them on my part. I don't deny myself my Guyanese heritage anymore; as a matter of fact, I am very proud of it.

In conclusion, I would like to say that I feel very privileged and lucky to be able to have two cultures. Although it was a struggle in the beginning, now it's a blessing. I have been given the opportunity to take what I like best from both.

Vanessa: *"Is it possible to be Canadian as long as you look like me?"*

I came to Canada from the Caribbean when I was two and one-half years old. All of my education has been in Canada. In light of this fact, being recognized as a Canadian should not be an issue for me. However, other groups have influenced me. In addition to my educational socialization, my membership in a cultural youth group as well as my Black West Indian family were significant in determining the rate at which and the extent to which I would be identified as Canadian.

Growing up in a Caribbean household, I learned the ways and customs of the old country. Without effort, I developed an authentic "Trini" accent by the time I was ready for Grade 1. However, my teacher never really appreciated this sweet sound and enrolled me in speech classes. I learned to speak, dare I say, "proper English" as my teacher would have it. But rather than completely abandoning this accent, I kept it and mastered how and when to turn it off and on at will.

In the evenings at a cultural centre, I became familiar with the traditional dances of the Caribbean and Africa. There, I became acquainted with the arts and crafts as well as the folk tales of my ancestors. In the day-

Photo: Dick Hemingway

Schools provide structured opportunities for social interaction and for becoming better acquainted with others and, ultimately, with ourselves.

time, I studied about the Group of Seven, Sir John A. Macdonald, Peter Rabbit and the Brothers Grimm. In the evenings, I read about Anansi the Spider, Toussaint L'Ouverture and Sam Sharpe. Clearly, I had the best of both worlds growing up—I was a Canadian Black with knowledge of her ancestral past.

So why is it that this Canadian, who is often seen eating fries and hamburgers and wearing jeans and a T-shirt, continues to shock white people when she answers "Canadian" to their question, "What are you?" After I respond, I hear, "No, I mean originally." It seems that if you are non-white, regardless of how long you has lived here or indeed even if you were born here, white society never fully accepts you as Canadian. The assumption is always that you are from somewhere else. Yet, a white person from Scotland, who has lived in Canada for as long as I have, would not get a raised eyebrow if she or he answered "Canadian" to the question, "What are you?"

It appears that only when you reach the height of national or international fame is your ancestry ignored and you become Canadian. I think of Oscar Peterson, the jazz pianist; Lincoln Alexander, the Lieutenant-Governor of Ontario; and, dare I say, Ben Johnson, the athlete.

These Black men seem to be accepted by white Canada as being Canadian. Unfortunately for Ben Johnson, we witnessed him fall from being a Canadian to a Jamaican-Canadian in the space of one weekend. This incident causes one to question how permanent and secure that title of "Canadian" really is. And, indeed, is it truly possible to become one as long as you look like me?

Hillary: *"Nor did I ever want to be white in order to fit in ..."*

To my knowledge, I was born in Montreal, Canada, and was adopted by a white couple while I was an infant. As far back as I can recall, I noticed the difference between my family and myself. I was Black, they were white—it was an obvious difference.

In our neighbourhood, which was white and French, it was a setback to be English, and having a Black child living among a white family, willingly, was a major strike. There was no worse a household could do, it seemed. My family endured black cats in our swimming pool, broken windows and many ignorant comments and questions, such as, "Does she eat at the table with you?", from ignorant people who had trouble seeing a human being behind skin colour.

I also encountered many racial slurs, but learned to be thick skinned and quick mouthed. I also realized that only an uneducated person voiced such ignorant and foolish things. Therefore, I ignored them. This was another trait I developed; ignoring people quickly and easily. My brother also taught me how to defend myself. He said he didn't want me coming home beaten up because someone didn't like the colour of my skin.

After many years we were finally accepted, since we posed no visible threat to the community. But by that time we had had enough and were ready to move. We moved to Ottawa when I was twelve years old. There weren't any Blacks in the neighbourhood, so obviously I hung out with white individuals in my age group. But I always knew and was proud to be Black. I was never ashamed of the colour of my skin, my heritage or my cultural background. Nor did I ever want to be white in order to fit in better with my family. If anything, I wished that they were Black.

Growing up in a white family has been in a sense a growing experience, as well as a strange and difficult experience for me. People ask me frequently, "What is it like, growing up with whites?" How can I answer that? I've never known anything else. Growing up among whites has taught me to be open-minded. It has taught me about cultural diversity and about trust. Yet it has also taught me to distrust many whites after individuals have proved themselves trustworthy.

As a youth, most of my friends were white, and I developed a broad interest in music. Now most, if not all, of my friends are Black, and my interest is centred on traditional "Black" music, such as R&B, hip-hop, rap, reggae, soca, jazz and the like. I have tried to know and understand all aspects of my culture.

At times I wished that I knew and lived with my natural family so that I could be enveloped by people that I could compare myself to inside and out (I went through a very difficult transitional period in my teens because I was slim, and I wished I knew my family to see if it was genetic, to hear advice and so on.), and relate to culturally. But I didn't. My family is white, and I love them.

The preceding essays demonstrate the extent to which, at a very young age, these individuals actively engaged in constructing their identities. Family and community played a significant role in shaping their cultural identities, but ultimately it was the meaning and understanding that they gained through their life experiences that were most crucial. It is they who understood their experiences; it is they who had to negotiate and navigate within the society and communities in which they must live and survive. As one person puts it, "I have to search deep into my background and culture, by childhood and upbringing, my old and new surroundings, in order to find reasons for my behaviour and to search for answers."

FITTING IN: CONTENDING WITH DIFFERENCE

> **Avinder**: *"I try to fit in with other groups.... All I would like is the same respect back."*
>
> I am seen by others as a minority. Some people tend to see me differently because I am of a different race. But what they do not know is that I am not so different from them. I speak the same language, eat the same food and do the same activities. Just because I am of a different race they think that I do different things. I try to fit in with other groups and try appreciably to learn what others can teach me. All I would like is the same respect back. Religion is important to me and also very important to my parents. This does not mean that everywhere I go I take my religion with me, because this is not so. Since I was brought to this country, I try to do what others do, and I practise my religion in my own home. I believe that my family and I carry out our responsibilities as Canadian ought to. We should have our religion inside us somewhere, but practise it on your own time.

In the above essay excerpt, Avinder indicates that he is seen by others as a "minority" living in Canada. Contributing to this construction are his perceived religious beliefs, which he states are important to him and his family. But this, he contends, should not result in the disrespect he experiences. Evident in his comments, and in the comments of many whose essays appear in this section, is the distress they experience as they try to "fit" into their peer groups, their schools, their communities and Canadian society. This distress persists despite their concerted efforts to negotiate their identities and their presence as responsible Canadian citizens. For the most part, many seem to accept their "difference"–be it race, ethnicity, language, immigrant status–but wish, are indeed determined, to retain that which is important to their cultural identity or self. Like Avinder, a number of the writers articulate the lengths to which they have gone to fit in and de-emphasize their "difference." In fact, what emerges is their emphasis on "sameness." As Avinder notes, "I speak the same language, eat the same food and do the same activities." Seemingly exasperated, he goes on to say, "Just because I am of a different race they think that I do different things."

In other words, he is asking, Have I not done enough to show that I am the same? Shouldn't this be enough to "fit in" and receive the "same respect" that others do?

While Avinder and others, such as Moran, did engage in the cultural integration or acculturation process (Kallen, 1995: 154)–a process of learning those cultural ways of the dominant Canadian "ethnic collectivity" to which they do not belong–they were doing so within an established system of ethnic stratification. So while they were taking on the norms, values and patterns of the dominant group in society and also attaining some level of proficiency in utilizing these cultural attributes for effective participation in the public institutions of the society at large (Kallen, 1995: 154), they remained, as many of them so painfully admit, different, minorities, foreigners, outsiders, immigrant, individuals with accents, non-English speaking, half-breeds, bi-racial. Comparatively, white participants, particularly James, the Scottish-born Canadian, understood that race and ethnic privilege would help them to get by in the society.

Moran: *"It has been hard for me to fit into the Canadian culture and/or be accepted by other Chinese."*

I am a twenty-five-year-old, second-generation Chinese-Canadian female. My name means "Admired Lotus Lily." I was born in Belleville, Ontario. My parents are naturalized Canadian citizens originally from The People's Republic (of China) who met in Hong Kong. Because we re-located to Toronto when I was approximately two years old, I remember little of small-town Ontario. Practically my entire life has been spent in the big city; I have never left North America. And luckily for me, there is a stable community of my own ethnic background. I take great comfort in this.

The term *Chinese-Canadian*, in my opinion, describes a person of Chinese descent living in the Western society of Canada. It has been difficult for me and I am sure for many others of my culture to assimilate into some of the dominant Canadian values. Take, for example, the family. My family is very important to me but no one actually realizes the obligations that I take on happily. Few of my friends and co-workers who are not Chinese-Canadian know that I am expected to support my parents in old age (and definitely not put them in an old age home!). It is a time in my career when moving out of Toronto may be advantageous, but I could never move out. Some people think it's because I am insecure, but they just don't understand. I worry about my parents a great deal and moving out is not culturally encouraged for reasons other than that of marriage (if that!). But before I finish making my point, it should be noted that I take on these duties and responsibilities willingly. I would feel tremendous guilt and pressure if I upset everyone in my family.

I can hardly communicate to my parents in their native tongue, and I am not literate in Chinese. I do not see this as a liability but my mother does. She is concerned about the preservation of the Chinese culture. For this reason, she also frowns on inter-marriage. My mother still complains that my third cousin married a white Jewish male. She argues that it is because the culture will be lost within a generation, but I do not see the difference between me and my third cousin's children. I must disappoint her greatly.

It has been hard for me to fit into the Canadian culture and/or be accepted by other Chinese. I sometimes become paranoid and think that my cultural peers perceive me as a "wacko." This is probably because they may think of me as overassimilated and assertive beyond their comfort zone. I don't fit the stereotype of the submissive East Asian woman. My dress and accent do not give me away. In fact, I am probably not living my culture in many ways because I have assimilated much more than first-generation immigrants. On the other hand, even though I do not readily mesh with my own culture, I do not possess the privileges that many Canadians of European descent possess. They can mix right into the predominantly white culture at their whim; I will always have my skin colour and physical characteristics to set me apart. Metaphorically I sit on a fence and cannot be categorized or ordered into any group. First-generation, lower-income immigrants naturally assume that I am totally Westernized, and whites think that I am totally Chinese in my ways of thinking. In some ways, both points of view have grains of truth. But where do I fit? And where do I belong?

For a substantial part of my life I grew up in a predominantly European Catholic neighbourhood. It was hard to make friends because I was different, specifically because I was from a different race. That was the first time that I experienced racism. Not only was it among students from school who sadly picked it up from their parents but also from neighbours who did not like Chinese people. You see, our family was one of the first non-white families to move into the lower-middle-class white neighbourhood. Many of those families have moved to the suburbs now. In fact, my neighbourhood is quite "yuppie-ized" and has a greater East and South Asian population now, but I will never forget the feelings of ostracization and isolation that I felt then.

As a law student (yes, there are Chinese law students!), I experienced a more subtle racism. During my articling interviews, many potential employers asked me if I could speak Cantonese, because they had many commercial law clients from Hong Kong. At a Bar Admission presentation, I was told that I had an accent. In fact it was another woman who had the accent, but who incidentally was white, and I was the only visible minority present. After the seminar, a fellow law student noted that I did not have a Chinese accent, and that it was in fact a distinctly "Toronto" accent.

Often people will ask me "What are you?" or "Are you Filipino?" It really bothers me. I guess you could rationalize that I get mad because people are prejudging me. But it goes deeper than that. Much deeper. I get angry because I expect people to know that I am Chinese and not Filipino. The differences are vast and I perceive myself as more culturally Chinese.

Sometimes I reflect and wonder what kind of Chinese I am. Am I a good person? Am I a bad person because I do not have the burning desire to go back and visit the lands of my ancestors? A lot of friends want to do this, but I do not need to see "Mecca." Am I in denial about my ethnic roots? I often did and still do have problems telling people what professions my parents were in. My mother used to be a garment worker around the Spadina Avenue area in Toronto. It might be a mixture of shame of being from a lower-class family. It could be the fact that I don't want people to stereotype my parents or people of my race as people who work only at low-paying, back-breaking work. The image of the immigrant garment worker and immigrant restaurant worker are classic Canadian stereotypes. It could be because I want to disassociate myself and leap into a better class and I think that knowledge of my family background would hinder my chances. So many East Asians are ghettoized and fall into a vicious cycle.

James: *"My identity is never questioned. People automatically assume that I am Canadian, born and raised here."*

The often-asked philosophical question "What is the meaning of life?" is very difficult to answer, but I believe that in order to answer it we must first know who we are—our identity. For if we do not know ourselves, how can we begin to understand the meaning of our existence? To know ourselves is to be able to define our identity, who we are and the factors that contribute to our being the person that we are.

I don't think of myself as having a "colour," and I guess that is because society does not highlight or stress this message to me every waking moment as it does to a person whose skin is not white. The message sent by our First World society is that the "civilized world" is white; I can't imagine how that impacts on a person who is not white. The formation of a person's identity is surely influenced by colour, and in the case of a person who is not white, this can cause a great deal of confusion (which might be termed an identity crisis).

I am an immigrant. I was born in Glasgow, Scotland, and my family immigrated to Canada when I was four. This would be my ethnicity, but I have no specific, conscious attachment to the culture of my place of birth. Coming to Canada at a young age, I had not fully absorbed the culture of Scotland, and so it was not very difficult for me to assimilate into Canadian culture. I did not have to suffer the potentially painful effects of acculturation, because Canada was, and continues to be, in many respects very similar to Scotland. The neighbourhood that I first lived in consisted of white, working-class families, and I can't recall any people of different cultural backgrounds who lived there.

While I was never bombarded as a child with messages of my Scottish ethnicity, I was still very much socialized into that culture. The friends of my parents were mostly Scottish (i.e., first generation here in Canada) and all were white. And I grew up conscious of some of the negative perceptions that were associated with being Scottish, such as being cheap, wearing a kilt, eating porridge and speaking with an accent. There were occasions when I was a young person that I would not acknowledge my ethnicity because of the stereotypes associated with being Scottish (Certainly the impact of what I perceived to be negative characteristics pales in comparison with stereotypes that people of other cultures are subjected to.).

In high school, starting in Grade 10, I played basketball with guys who were mostly from the Caribbean. While I did spend a great deal of time with the guys on the team, I maintained other friends. This in part may have been due to the fact that none of the guys I played basketball with were in any of my classes (This was because they were taking trade classes, and their regular classes were not at the advanced level.). I spent about four years with the same guys from the basketball team. We would go to parties together on the weekend, which I also did with my group of mainstream friends. I went to all the school dances and liked the music that was being played. This kind of music was recognized or associated with Black people.

The way I dressed was "mainstream." I did not try to dress like the guys I played basketball with. There were very specific styles that were associated with particular cultural groups. I had developed two distinct circles of friends and felt comfortable in either circle. The two circles of friends were those who I played sports with (who were predominantly Caribbean) and those that I knew from grade school (who were mostly white). In high school I never used pejorative language, and I distanced myself from friends that did.

During high school I was not conscious of my behaviour until, during a conversation, a friend (who is Black), mentioned that I "acted Black." This struck me as a very strange comment, and my response to him was that I was not acting in any particular way but just being myself. I inquired further as to what it was that he thought I was doing that had led him to his conclusion. He could offer no specific answer as to the specific Black behaviour(s) that I exhibited.

The next time I heard a similar comment it was from my college basketball coach, who said I played basketball like a Black guy. This was easier for me to relate to, because I could actually picture the meaning of what he was saying. Now, I did not make a conscious effort to play basketball like a Black guy, I just played the way I had learned. This learning had taken place with the guys who were Black. I actually considered the statement the coach made as a compliment, because Black guys were some of the best basketball players around.

My identity is never questioned. People automatically assume that I am Canadian, born and raised here. I am almost never asked where I was born; in fact, many people are often surprised when I tell them I was born in Scotland. I am also never asked what kind of an accent I have, although when I visit Scotland I am often asked if I am American (at which I take great offence).

As a white person, I am never asked to be the spokesperson for all white people, a position that many minority people can easily find themselves in. I guess this is because most white people know that all white people do not think alike; but those same white people assume that people of other racial groups think alike.

Have I had privileges because of the fact that I am white? Well, because I understand how society works, I would have to say "yes." A more difficult question to answer is: What were those privileges that I received, aside from not being followed around in stores by a sales clerks, or receiving better service in a restaurant? I don't know. Did I ever get a job because I am white? I don't know. Perhaps this is the crux of the problem that whites have in accepting equity programs. It is that we honestly don't believe that we have ever had any special privileges purely because we are white. This demonstrates the urgent need for societal re-education.

Joe: *"We began to distinguish ourselves as ... Anglocized Italians ..."*

My parents emigrated from Italy in the early 1950s. They were married in Hamilton, and that's were the family was raised. I am the youngest of four children.

I grew up in a decidedly non-Italian neighbourhood. The kids in the neighbourhood were a mix of Canadians, i.e., second-, third- and fourth-generation British, Scottish and Irish descendants; first-generation Eastern Europeans; and perhaps one or two first-generation Italians. This ethnic profile was, however, simplified according to the distinctions we used at the time. As far as my parents were concerned, the populace was divided into two: English and Italian. Anyone who didn't fit into either one of these categories (say, for instance, my Lithuanian friend) was viewed as innocently irrelevant to the basic societal dichotomy of English and Italian.

The ethnic mix became somewhat more complicated in elementary school, because the school was at a distance from our immediate neighbourhood. Ethnic origins and ratios had been altered. It became a little more problematic to cram all those non-Italians into the English camp, but it was even easier to entrench ourselves into the Italian camp because we were readily identified as such by both the school administration and other students. We were perceived as Italians. The predominant authority of the school was Irish and Catholic. The nuns and priests were Irish and Catholic, and we were the rather difficult but redeemable Italian Catholics. Belonging to such an identified and identifiable group gave rise to varied perceptions of identity. My "Italian-ness" could be causing me to suffer silent embarrassment one moment and defiant satisfaction the next. One thing was abundantly clear: I was outside the cultural norm.

The tables were turned rather dramatically in high school. The elementary school had been in a predominantly non-Italian area, but the high school was in an area where many Italians lived. Many of the students were from immigrant Italian families. It seems that the old English or Italian distinction wasn't quite relevant any more. It was time to start making much finer distinctions. We, my immediate clique and I, chose to carve out a new, unique identity for ourselves. We began to distinguish ourselves as the more advanced, sophisticated, Anglocized Italians. Our group tended to deride the excesses of our less genteel compatriots while at the same time negotiating diplomatic relations with the English. The negotiations were fruitful, and permanent relations were established with a number of English cliques.

It is rather facile to proclaim that I always sensed something was wrong with this perception of who I was in relation to my world. During high school, however, I did develop a distinct dislike at being categorized as Italian or anything else. University was a welcome relief. Few of my peers went to university, and though I still lived in the same city, I lived in a different world. I consciously avoided anyone who dragged me back to the English or Italian characterization of my identity. I sought refuge in the company of foreign visa students. They knew nothing of this, or did they? I suppose my friends from Singapore had their own notions of what it was to live in a former British colony.

At present, I choose to verify my "Italian-ness" against my parents. It's become a very personal, individual identification. The connection is a specific one.

My ethnicity has been a significant factor in shaping my notion of self. Societal pressure has imposed its interpretation of who I am from the outside, and unexamined internal acceptance has reinforced this view. But all this is water under the bridge, isn't it? Surely this nonsense is buried in the past.

I have found that the insidiousness and subtle harm of ethnic and racial categorization is persistent. I can still feel the ghosts of "silent embarrassment" when British people reminisce about times gone by. Do they know that I feel uncomfortable? Are they conscious of the institutional baggage of their dominant position?

Until very recently, I denied this whole issue and held to the opinion that all of it was, in fact, buried in the past. I rejected my own unease and dismissed suspicion of the cause of this unease.

As an ESL (English as a Second Language) instructor, my association with recent immigrants has been instrumental in re-awakening my sensitivities to the issue. I can see the same type of ethnic and racial categorization being applied to the learners in my classroom. I can see them being constantly reminded that they are somehow inadequate in their present form. If they don't change, they'll never move from within the periphery of society. I am white and, despite any "Mediterranean" features, can do a pretty good job of disguising myself as part of the dominant group. I can fit; I can move in closer than the periphery. What, then, is a "more visible" visible minority to do? Will a Black African or Southeast Asian ever be adequate? Will they ever fit in enough to move closer to the centre of society?

I do what I can to assure the learners in my classes that, ethnically, racially and religiously, they are adequate. I try to be a sympathetic listener who sees their frustrations as justified. I also try to use my membership in the administrative mainstream, albeit probationary, to act as a liaison.

Ethnic identification can be a psychological touchstone; ethnic categorization can be an unwelcome burden.

Anthony: *"I didn't want to be called an immigrant."*

I was born here in Canada. I am white, and have no trace of any accent. The language that is spoken in my home is English, and my family does not practice any religious customs other than status quo Christianity. Yet I think I can still empathize with the way in which many new, non-Anglo Canadians must certainly feel during this latest craze of immigrant bashing.

My mother emigrated from Poland at a young age. My father, although born here, is Italian and was socialized in Toronto's large Italian community, which thus preserved many cultural traits. My name is obviously Italian, and my physical features seem to make it easy for everyone I meet to assume that I am Italian, a fact that brought me much grief while I was growing up.

I was very aware of the stigma attached to the word *immigrant* while growing up in Toronto. Although the word simply means a person who was born in one country and has moved to another one, it carried other connotations as well. I didn't want to be called an immigrant; I perceived it to be an insult. Although I was somewhat aware that the stereotypes of immigrants who were racial minorities were much more harmful and negative, the stereotypes of Eastern and Southern Europeans were still very much present. While playing down my Italian background as much as possible, I flat out denied being Polish.

Most Italian and Polish people I have known have been very proud of their heritage. Yet, as a youngster I did not feel this way. There was no one single incident that brought these feelings on. I was never singled out in front of a large group in order to have my ethnicity ridiculed. I was not taught to hate myself the way native Indians or Africans were. I had never known first hand the dehumanizing racism that people of colour must go through everyday. But, as far back as I can remember, I thought that the word *immigrant* meant stupid, unclean, strange, outsider.

I remember the first day of many school years. The teacher would call my name and ask if I were Italian. The word instantly conjured up images of the greasy, over-sexed, uneducated "Wop" that seemed so prevalent on television. I was young; I wanted to be like everyone else, not an unwanted immigrant. I often answered "no" to the teacher's question. However, I was even more embarrassed to be Polish. After hearing years of Polish jokes, I actually began to wonder if Polish people were really inherently unintelligent.

I can remember when my grandmother dealt with the neighbourhood people; they were also immigrants. She was friendly and warm; she felt quite comfortable in her dealings with them. They appeared to me to be people who were just like us and not people to be intimidated by. When she had dealings with authority figures—they were exclusively Anglo, native-born Canadians—she became immediately apprehensive, telling me always to watch what I said around those people, to make sure never to insult them. Many of these people were polite, but I remember the ones who were rude and insulting towards her. She was just another dumb immigrant who couldn't speak English.

Besides learning to be intimidated by authority figures, these situations reinforced for me the idea that immigrants were second-class citizens and that native-born Anglos were the ideal Canadians, who were to be revered and respected. To me, being other than Anglo meant being an immigrant. It meant being a janitor or cleaning woman. It meant dressing in strange attire and speaking peculiar languages. It aroused images of my grandmother being scolded and humiliated by a cop, as if she were a child. It brought images of the leering immigrant, who both steals jobs and drains the welfare system.

There were many days I went hungry because I could not bear to be seen eating the ethnic foods my mother made me for lunch. I often avoided having friends over for fear that they might hear my mother speaking Polish. Those were the marks of the lowly immigrant that I desperately wanted no part of. I wanted blonde hair, blue eyes and a cool "Canadian" name, like Brett Smith or Jay Johnson. Those were the marks of the Canadian.

Throughout high school I never dated girls who weren't Anglo. I joined in with my exclusively "Canadian" friends in ridiculing the "Wops" and "Ginos" and other immigrant kids at school. After twenty years of this, I systematically self-destroyed a very important part of who I was, a part I can never get back.

Maria: *"Then and only then was I able to say that I was Polish."*

Having been born in a different country has enabled me to develop a greater awareness of my own ethnicity. When I first came to Canada, I realized that I was different from the people around me. Mainly because the language I spoke was Polish, not English. At that time I felt inferior because of the language barrier, but as my English improved, I was readily accepted by those around me. Since I spoke English, I was seen as a Canadian and no longer as an immigrant. Then and only then was I able to say that I was Polish. At the present time, I feel very strongly about my ethnic background. Even though I now live in Canada, I still want my children to speak the Polish language and practise the Polish traditions and customs.

I feel that being a member of the white race enables me to blend much easier into the Canadian society. My major barrier was being unable to communicate with the language of the dominant culture. Given the fact that I was white, I was no longer considered as an outsider once the language barrier was removed.

Ria: *"As an English-speaking white Canadian ... I fit into our society quite easily."*

I am a Canadian citizen. That might not tell you a lot about who I am because being *Canadian* is an ambiguous term in describing the identity of an individual. Every citizen in Canada has their own unique background because Canada is a country of many races, ethnicities and cultures. Their lives are affected by these backgrounds and more, including their social class and family life. In this essay I am going to explore how being a white Dutch Canadian has affected my behaviour, attitudes and values.

I am a first-generation Canadian with Dutch parents. My parents immigrated to Canada from Holland, their ancestral home. My parents belong to the Christian Reformed Church, which first began in Holland. This church and Holland cannot be separated because they are so closely related. In the 1950s, my parents came here to build a life and raise a family. They followed the "work ethic" that most immigrants do, saving money and working long and hard. I was expected to do the same. A good person was one who was honest in his business and a hard worker.

My family grew up, like most other Dutch families, in the church. They all had a strong sense of family and community, which I still feel with my friends and family. I have been raised to respect the value of life, to do good for your neighbour and to live an honest life. I was also taught stewardship (the proper, responsible care of possessions), the "sacrificing" of pleasure for responsibilities and not to waste. I uphold these values highly and respect those who also do so.

Another part of my Dutch heritage is the Dutch language. I am fairly fluent and find great advantage in that since I am interested in older people, such as my grandparents, who speak Dutch. The older generation is rich in experience and wisdom from which we can learn. The Dutch's cosy homes show the value they place on family and home life, which I feel is important.

Being white in Canada means being in the majority and, as an English-speaking white Canadian, I have been fortunate to fit into our society quite easily. I feel accepted in society and its groups and have had good opportunities for jobs while other racially different people have not. I can say that I feel a steadiness in my overall place in society. Being white has freed me of some prejudices and other racial challenges that others might experience here in Canada. One curious thing I admit to is that I tend to look on other races with a mixture of sympathy for the joking they get, and I mistrust them because I don't know them or associate closely enough with them to fully understand their thinking and lifestyle. My ignorance is a hurdle.

Finally, having been brought up in Canada, I have known the privileges of being able to drive at an early age and of receiving a good education. I have had ample opportunities for jobs, plus the freedom to reside any place I choose. Canada is an affluent Western country full of freedom and choice, which I experience daily. After visiting Honduras, a country of poverty, I especially appreciate this country's affluence and freedom.

Rolie: *"I did my best to acquire the 'Canadian' accent ..."*

Race and ethnicity are terms one rarely uses or prefers as a topic of discussion among friends, acquaintances or fellow workers. They seem to be taboo in Canadian society. And yet, when people see each other, their first thought is, "This person is yellow or brown or mulatto or black or white." It is known that visual data have a far greater impact than those produced by any of the other senses, and hence the impact of skin colour or general features cannot be underestimated. As an individual, and being a first-generation immigrant, I have been rather fortunate in not having had the nasty experience of "culture shock" after having moved to Canada. My knowledge of English and previous experiences in dealing with people from different countries around the world during work and travel made my adaptation and integration into Canadian society easier than it might otherwise have been. Growing up in a large cosmopolitan city, awash in Western influence, was also a major contributing factor in my familiarity with Western culture.

Before arriving in Toronto I had never really given much thought to the importance of race, ethnicity and culture. In fact, I rarely thought about my own culture, probably because I lived it daily. However, after being here for a few days, I realized that knowing the language and wearing Canadian-style clothing was not enough to make the transition to being a Canadian. Also, initially I wasn't sure if I wanted to be one. When asked what I was, my immediate reply was "Indian." I began to wonder if I was the target of discrimination and was going to be judged on the basis of my skin colour. I did my best to acquire the "Canadian" accent so as not to sound like a foreigner, and even became rather good at blowing my own trumpet during job interviews (which is very much against my nature), but I could do nothing to change the way I looked. It was also very frustrating to know that my long years of education in India meant almost nothing here. I began to perceive discrimination in every rejection. Yet I did manage to get a job and thought I'd won a great victory. One hurdle had been overcome, and I felt nothing could stop me from becoming a successful Canadian. However, when at work, white Canadian fellow workers would ask me, "How come you speak such good English?" I could not take it as a compliment. In fact, I always felt insulted and angered that they thought only whites could master the English language. Unfortunately, I felt I was in no position to counter their perceptions except by making an exception of myself.

After being in Toronto for three years, watching people on the transit system, in malls and other public places, after experiencing first hand what it's like to be a first-generation immigrant and becoming partly "Canadianized," I ask myself: "Is Canada a racist country?" The answer, of course, is "yes." Not only do I see and hear and read about racist and discriminatory acts being perpetuated in this country, but I also experience them first hand with neighbours, fellow workers, in the malls, on the transit system and so on. However, this does not drive me away from the country, because, in spite of this, I have been able to achieve a certain amount of success and I'm sure I'll do even better in the future.

Andrew: *"I am bi-racial ..."*

> If I were asked for a definition of myself, I would say that I am one who waits; I investigate my surroundings, I interpret everything in terms of what I discover, I become sensitive (Frantz Fanon, *Black Skin, White Masks*).

I am given multiple names, told I am tragic and made to feel that I must choose to be either Black or white or exist somewhere in the centre, in the benign "happy medium." I am bi-racial and frustrated, because the pundits of mixed-race children, who are usually not mixed themselves, believe in such a thing as "having the best of both worlds." On the same tip, I would not be stupid and naïve enough to say that I live with the "worst" of both worlds, although in many ways I find this reasoning to be the easiest to rationalize when both my "worlds"—Black and white—look at me as some sort of abrogation in a society governed by what W.E.B. Du Bois called the "colour line."

My father is white, my mother is Black, and I am Black. For some this logic doesn't make much sense—"You could pass for white, you know"—and it seriously troubles their minds—"Hey nigger, I'm talking to you"—so much so that they want to probe my mind to find out how I cope with my fissure. Being seen as a "tragic mulatto" seems to be a perennial problem and a source of endless fascination for some white and Black folk, who want to ask, "Is it possible for mixed-race people to be Black?" It seems that there must be a designated camp that I must call home, to be Black or white, or is "bi" the answer? In a world of television talk show mentalities, I know that people want to ask, "Aren't you confused?" Of course I'd answer "yes," but who isn't in this world?

I've heard some people say that it is the coming together of people of different races, ethnicities, and cultures that will help eradicate some of the social dissension in the world, namely racism. Strangely, this philosophy, the miscegenists' dream, sounds like an inspirational jingo from singer

Bobby McFerrin: "Don't worry, think half-breed." I am not an optimist, because some peoples' dreams are others' nightmares, including my own. Because of such thinking, I've grown increasingly suspicious and critical of my parents' marriage, wondering if they really believed that "love sees no colour" shit. It's not the love that I question as, after all, love is one of the last of the humanitarian principles still in existence, but their inability to see that baffles me. Did my father question his white skin and male privilege at the same door that my mother possibly hung her sentiments of self-hatred? And at the same time are there any coincidences of these related facts shaping the dynamics of their relationship? These are serious questions, as they should be, and I feel like I have every right to be suspicious of some, but not all, of the circumstances surrounding my introduction to this world.

As a child it is easy to take what you see for granted, so it didn't seem like such a big deal to have parents who were not the same colour. But there was something that I didn't understand until I started to seriously think about my father's world, the Euro-centric male one, presenting itself as the centre of all of that is correct and normal and my mother's, as a sort of bastardization of the norm. Being a product of the centre and the periphery has a funny way of playing with your head, and there's definitely not enough love in the world to save you from that sort of trauma.

When growing up, I negotiated the world on the politically conservative white side and the liberal Black side. My mother, whom I once cussed in public and called "Nigger," reminded me at one and the same time that I was not white but always to remember that my father was white. In the past couple of years my mother's reminders have seemed to come more frequently as I speak more openly about the social and political lives of Black people. To me her reminders are supposed to serve as some sort of inhibitor to expressing part of me which I believe she has chosen to ignore.

My father, for the most part, chooses to remain silent on the issue of colour. Sometimes I'll receive a book or an article from him where the subject or author is a Black person, which is some sort of acknowledgment that I am, to some degree, Black. We have never had any open discussion about the politics of race or identity; it is not an area that I feel comfortable dealing with, so we just continue talking about jazz, Black athletes and jerk chicken.

Some people who are bi-racial are caught in a sort of world cut in two, an either/or scenario about who they are, how they should be and what they should do. I would be a hypocrite if I said that I have eclipsed this sort of difficulty in my navigation through the mazes of the white and Black worlds. However, it is necessary to understand that hybridity creates a new space, and I am a part of this space for which there is no set archetype. If I say I am Black it does not mean that I am everything that is not white. It is, at the same time, so simple and so complex: I love that.

Elaine: *"I was never proud of my colour, and envied other mixed children who looked Black."*

My biological parents represent two distinct races. My father was born in Germany, and migrated to Canada with his family as a boy. My mother is a Black Jamaican, who came to Canada with her family in the 1960s. My mother and father never married. This was in response to the bigotry and ignorance within my father's family, as they did not want any Black blood "tainting" their Aryan line. This early disownment caused me to feel uncomfortable with the fact that I was born white, and not Black like my mother's family. I was not proud of my colour, and envied other mixed children who looked Black.

Although I was a white child and, in Jamaica, a noticeable minority, I do not remember having any problems because of my colour. On the contrary, when I think back, I realize that being seen with such a fair child was a status symbol for certain members of my family. They frequently paraded me at their functions and with their friends. While in Jamaica, I played with children of many cultural roots, commonly mixed as well.

I came back to Scarborough to live with my immediate family before I started school. Here, my family continues to practise Jamaican culture. I remember a diverse cultural and racial representation among my friends and peers in Scarborough. I don't recall any children (including myself) being isolated and/or teased because of their race or religion. I am very thankful that, from a young age, I interacted with people of other cultures and learned that we are all just people inside.

As I grew older, I discovered just how racially oriented and religiously sensitive our society can be. Although I rarely had to deal with prejudice directly, as I appear racially to be part of the majority, I witnessed many others being treated with varying degrees of cruelty. Paul (Chapter 9) suggests that, within his neighbourhood, if an individual (usually white) was from another culture, they were accepted without discrimination only when they had proven themselves. I have experienced this phenomenon personally (with white people), when it is revealed that my family is Black. Depending upon the degree to which they have "accepted" me, this information is greeted with fascination, awe or discomfort. This is by no means limited to the white population. Many times I have been instantly recognized as a "sister" within Black groups when this same information is revealed.

My experiences with discrimination differ from those of others who have had to deal with it directly on a larger and different scale. They are visibly part of a minority group or community, while I am a member of a small, non-visible minority.

There are many who try to believe that all people are the same. I do not think that. Instead, I believe that every individual is unique and that differences should not be hidden but exposed with pride. The key is not using these differences to degrade others but to appreciate variety, learn from diversity and enjoy change.

SUMMARY

The preceding essays demonstrate the role that race and ethnicity played in these individuals' attempts to fit into the Canadian society, their neighbourhoods, families and peer groups. In her essay, Moran provides details of her experiences as a racial and ethnic minority Canadian, whose ideas, values and aspirations, as she asserts, are very much a product of Canadian and her Chinese culture. She notes that she has "assimilated" some of the dominant cultural norms and values of the society and is, at the same time, very committed to her Chinese culture. She "willingly" accepts the "obligation" to support her parents, and would not wish to "upset" them. However, while she is comfortable with what is expected of her from her family and the Chinese community, she also demonstrates that there are boundaries to these.

The responsibility of supporting her "parents in old age" is acceptable, but she does not consider her inability to speak Chinese to be a liability or an indication of cultural loss. Although Moran has "assimilated much more than first-generation immigrants," and even though she does "not readily mesh" with her Chinese cultural group, she is not protected from the stereotyping and racism that she has experienced throughout her life. She attributes this to the fact that she does "not possess the white privilege that many Canadians of European descent possess," since her "skin colour and her physical characteristics" will always set her apart.

These experiences contribute to Moran's conscious definition of herself as a minority, and ultimately to her cultural identity. As Smith (1991) points out, the development of identity in minority group individuals entails dealing with the sense of initial rejection of one's ethnic group, with moving "from an early stage of unawareness and lack of differentiation to one of ethnic awareness, ethnic self-identification, and increasingly ethnic differentiation on the basis of contact situations" (p.183).

Moran expresses the alienation, ambiguity and doubt that she feels as she questions, "But where do I fit? And where do I belong?" and "Am I in denial of my ethnic roots?" These feelings mirror those of many ethnic minority individuals who are trapped between the dominant culture of the society in which they live and the culture of their ethnic group. This dilemma is created as these individuals begin to come to terms with their "otherness" in a society that has rejected them, but whose culture they have internalized. Moran's experience is not unlike that of Sun-Kyung Yi, a "Korean-Canadian." In her essay "Split Personality" (1992), she writes that she went through the process of acculturation into the host culture aware that only by so doing could she enjoy the benefits that Canada has to offer.

"Whites see whiteness as an 'empty cultural space' and this identity as white people only [takes] shape in relation to others" (Rosenberg, 1997: 80).

Still, she declares that it is "difficult to feel a sense of belonging and acceptance" when you are regarded as an "other."[1]

Like Moran, James is an immigrant, but he has not experienced the same dilemma. He tells us that he "did not have to suffer the potentially painful effects of acculturation." He could also, on occasion, "not acknowledge" his ethnicity. Echoing Peggy McIntosh (1995), James tells us that his identity is never questioned for "people automatically assume that I am Canadian, born and raised." He also alludes to the possibility that he has benefited from white-skin privilege. Although he is uncertain of this, he assumes that this is the case because he "understands how society works." James goes on to say that whites "honestly don't believe that we have ever had any special privileges purely because we are white." This is a very important point. James' seemingly commonsensical understanding of race indicates his unwillingness to concede that he and other whites benefit from their whiteness; rather, he seems to justify their privileges (Phoenix, 1997; Sleeter, 1993)

The same white privilege that James is hesitant to acknowledge enabled him to negotiate and construct his school life in the way he did. It is a

[1] This essay also appears in E.C. Karpinski and I. Lea, *Pens of Colours* (1993): 406-409.

privilege to be able to have "two circles of friends" and to "fit in" as he did, dressing "mainstream" and being "complimented" on his ability to play basketball. In James' case, fitting in was not a dilemma. He had choices.

This was certainly not the case for Joe, who is an Italian who grew up understanding the world as constructed of English, Italian and Others. Like Anthony, Joe suffered "silent embarrassment" because of his "Italian-ness." While Joe and his peers attempted to distinguish themselves "as the more advanced, sophisticated, Anglocized Italians," Anthony seemed trapped by his Italian and Polish heritage, not only because they indicated that he was non-English, but also because they represented the fact that he was an "immigrant." Joe attempted to "fit in" by "Anglocizing" himself, and Anthony distanced himself as much as he could from his family and all that represented the "marks of the lonely immigrant."

Unlike Moran, Joe, Anthony and Maria had other attributes that enabled them to fit in. Joe writes that he could "do a pretty good job of disguising myself as part of the dominant group." Anthony was able to join with his "exclusively 'Canadian' friends in ridiculing the 'Wops' and 'Ginos' and other immigrant kids." Language was not a hurdle, and their white skin allowed them to take advantage of opportunities. While the language barrier initially separated Maria from the people around her, her eventual mastery of the English language and her "being a member of the white race" enabled her to fit in. It was not until she was no longer easily identifiable as an immigrant that she began divulging the fact that she was Polish. Ria too talks about being able to "fit into our society easily" because she is "an English-speaking white Canadian."

Rolie, despite doing her "best to acquire the 'Canadian' accent so as not to sound like a foreigner," and taking on what she believed to be a Canadian cultural attribute–i.e., "blowing my own trumpet during job interviews"–concedes, like Moran, Nadine and Vanessa, that skin colour was something she "could do nothing to change." Skin colour continued to be used by others to justify speculation when Rolie spoke "good English," or to justify asking, in the case of Vanessa, "What are you?"

Ironically, these participants, when compared to Anthony, appeared much more likely to experience the consequences of being identified as immigrants and regarded as "stupid, strange," as an "outsider" (Anthony). However, they seemed much less preoccupied with these consequences and more determined to get on with life. Could it be that they had come to terms with their identities and existence as racialized Others in Canadian society and knew that, unlike Anthony, they did not have the privilege of avoiding their marginalization? Kallen (1995) writes that it is possible for ethnic, compared to racial, minority group members to break out of their identification as minorities by aspiring to and mimicking the racist attitudes and behaviours of the dominant group (p.19). Might this explain Anthony's behaviour in taking advantage of his race-related privilege and power in order to escape the temporary consequences of ethnic identification?

Racial ambiguity contributed to the struggles to fit in of both Andrew and Elaine. Not only did they have to negotiate their racial identity within the larger society, which, as Andrew says (quoting W.E.B. Dubois), is governed by the "colour line," but they also had to confront issues related to race and colour within their respective families. Despite his angry, frustrating and baffling confrontations with his parents, and in spite of his parents, Andrew suggests that he has come to terms with his "bi-racial" identity, something with which neither his parents nor society has allowed him to live comfortably. Similarly, Elaine also relates her frustrations and mentions the significant role of colour in familial and societal interactions. She effectively demonstrates that, in racialized societies, whether Jamaican or Canadian, the colonized mind sees fair skin as a "status symbol." She includes the painful parts, where as a Black person who is able to pass as white (see Harris, 1993), she finds herself in situations where she must endure racist comments directed at people who look like her.

The writers of these essays attempted to "fit in" in a wide variety of ways. For some, fitting in meant dissociating themselves from their ethnic group. For others, it meant symbolically identifying with selected aspects of their ethno-cultural traditions while adopting those cultural attributes that enabled them to attain that to which they aspired. Still others, particularly racial minority group members, attempted to fit in by maintaining some degree of commitment to the preservation of aspects of their ethno-racial cultural heritage while participating, to varying degrees, in the culture of the society (see Kallen, 1995).

SUGGESTIONS FOR DISCUSSION

1. Identify some of the many factors that might constitute "otherness."
2. Discuss some of the ways in which societal institutions force individuals to fit in.
3. Discuss the role of educational institutions in individuals' attempts to fit into society.

Photo: Dick Hemingway

CHAPTER 4

Making Comparisons

A number of scholars point out that the white, European self-construction is fundamentally tied to the construction of Others (Weis and Fine, 1996; Roman, 1997). As Rosenberg (1997: 80) argues, many whites see whiteness as an "empty cultural space," and therefore their identity as white people only takes shape in relation to others. That is, they see themselves *not* as Chinese, South Asians or Blacks, but as the norm. It is for this reason that, in discussions of race, specifically in discussions of whiteness, white participants, as we have seen in earlier chapters, tend to talk of others in relation to themselves (see John and James in Chapter 3). This talk of others, and with others (particularly as they encountered them in the classroom), is, as Roman (1997) asserts, a desire to know the racial Other, which is sometimes linked to their denial of white privilege. This knowledge of Others helps to construct "white as the norm against which all other communities [particularly racial minority] are judged usually to be deviant" (Weis and Fine, 1996).

So how do we go about facilitating a process whereby students engage in talk about Others as well as themselves? How do we ensure that talk about Others is not based on stereotypes and uninformed inferences? How do we ensure that students do not hear only the experiences of minority people through class participants (who often willingly talk about their experiences in classes)? And how do we ensure that, in the absence of other information, dominant group members do not come to think that those who speak represent the experiences of "their" groups?

With these questions in mind, one of the exercises I have used in my classes is to have students visit communities that are predominantly populated by one ethnic or racial group with which they do not identity. Further, they were asked to interview someone from an ethnic or racial group with which they do not identity. I would suggest that the politics of such pedagogical practices enables students to, as Roman (1993: 82) writes, "enjoy the rewards of engaging in the socially transformative practice of critical realism in order to evaluate in a relational way the objective and subjective bases for conflicting claims *to belong to, know and represent the reality* of differentially oppressed and privileged groups."

One student commented on the method and process that were used in the exercise in which he compared his cultural identity, values and experiences with those of a German Canadian.

> **Thomas**: *"The subject has to describe how he or she feels ..."*
>
> To understand how our values and behaviour are affected by our background, it sometimes helps to examine someone with different racial, ethnic and cultural roots. By comparing the two, we will be able to gain a better understanding of ourselves and those around us.
>
> How can one tell if certain values and behaviours should be attributed to someone's ethnic background or simply to their personal experiences? For example, if a person is materialistic, is it because this is a cultural trait or is it simply the person's personality? For the purposes of this paper, any distinct trait of the subject that is shared by other people of the same origin will be considered to be related to the person's cultural background and not to his or her individual experience.
>
> A problem arises involving the interview itself. The interviewer can not simply ask someone to explain how their background affects their values and behaviour. The subject has to describe how he or she feels about something. From these statements, the interviewer can draw conclusions. Although I have tried to be as objective as possible, these conclusions are as I perceive them, and my perception is coloured by my own racial, ethnic and cultural roots...
>
> Human beings are very complex creatures, and it would take a lifetime of study to fully understand only one individual. Not all of us will become sociologists, but if we are open-minded when it comes to dealing with people of different backgrounds, we will be better able to understand, not only them, but ourselves.

This concept of learning about self and others is the basis for the following essays, in which participants make comparisons between themselves and the persons they interviewed. In their analyses, the writers attempt to show how their similarities and differences are related to their racial, ethnic, cultural and immigrant experiences.

The writers are aware that one can not generalize regarding an entire cultural group from an interview with one person. In noting that generalizations can not be made about her, and therefore neither about her subject, one class participant, Carrie, wrote:

> I feel that I am not considered to be a typical member of my culture. Then again, does anyone fit the "norm"? Even though I am a WASP, I behave in a manner which many people refer to as weird.... I also must consider the fact that whomever I compare myself to probably does not entirely represent her cultural group either. Therefore, in interviewing someone from a different culture, I cannot compare my group to her group—it must remain person to person ...

Many of the writers concluded that there are "far more similarities than differences among cultures." This is significant, for in many cases the writers expected to find that, because of differences in race and ethnicity, there

Table 3: Canadian Population by Religion, 1981 and 1991 Censuses

	1981		1991	
	Number	**%**	**Number**	**%**
Total population[1]	**24,083,495**	**100.0**	**26,994,045**	**100.0**
Catholic	**11,402,605**	**47.3**	**12,335,255**	**45.7**
Roman Catholic	11,210,385	46.5	12,203,620	45.2
Ukrainian Catholic	190,585	0.8	128,390	0.5
Other Catholic	1,630	—	3,235	—
Protestant	**9,914,575**	**41.2**	**9,780,715**	**36.2**
United Church	3,758,015	15.6	3,093,120	11.5
Anglican	2,436,375	10.1	2,188,110	8.1
Presbyterian	812,105	3.4	636,295	2.4
Lutheran	702,900	2.9	636,205	2.4
Baptist	696,845	2.9	663,360	2.5
Pentecostal	338,790	1.4	436,435	1.6
Other Protestant	1,169,545	4.9	2,127,190	7.9
Islam	**98,165**	**0.4**	**253,260**	**0.9**
Buddhist	**51,955**	**0.2**	**163,415**	**0.6**
Hindu	**69,505**	**0.3**	**157,010**	**0.6**
Sikh	**67,715**	**0.3**	**147,440**	**0.5**
Eastern Orthodox	**361,565**	**1.5**	**387,395**	**1.4**
Jewish	**296,425**	**1.2**	**318,065**	**1.2**
Para-religious groups	**13,450**	**0.1**	**28,155**	**0.1**
No religious affiliation	**1,783,530**	**7.4**	**3,386,365**	**12.5**
Other religions	**24,015**	**0.1**	**36,970**	**0.1**

— amount too small to be expressed.
[1] Based on sample data, which exclude institutional residents.

Source: Statistics Canada, Catalogue No. 93-319-XPB.

would be very few similarities. This finding indicates that, while we may practise different religions, play different games and dress in different attire, the philosophies behind these various practices and the roles they play in our lives seem to bear some similarity. Furthermore, insofar as every Canadian experiences the Canadian culture and its corresponding values and aspirations, it is understandable that this would be reflected in most Canadians' lives, irrespective of race, ethnicity, religion and group culture.

ENGLISH CANADIANS AND FIRST NATIONS INDIVIDUALS

The following essay excerpts deal with participants' interviews with First Nations individuals. What is instructive here is the little knowledge that participants had of First Nations persons before the interviews, even though both interviewers, Tina and John, went through the Canadian education system.

Tina: *"I became aware of the extent to which some cultures are misunderstood."*

While studying Native Canadians, I interviewed a young lady named Sam. During our talk, I realized that there were some similarities and some differences in our values, ideas and behaviours. In my attempt to point out some of these, I became aware of the extent to which some cultures are misunderstood. We should all stop thinking that our way is "best," and try to relinquish our ethnocentric attitudes.

The Native Canadians are a very religious group. As Sam shared some of their religious practices with me, it occurred to me that, although the methods were different, the purpose and the meaning behind them were similar to my own practices. When Indians go on a vision quest, there are certain steps they must follow. First of all, Indians go on a vision quest to seek direction or to solve a problem. Before they can go out on the quest, they must first enter the sweat lodge to clear their mind and soul of evil or angry thoughts. They enter the lodge without clothing, and they must stay until they feel that they have cleansed their mind. Often prayers of forgiveness are said. After leaving the sweat lodge, they must not tell anyone what went on inside. They then go in search of a spot in the wilderness where they feel a sense of tranquillity, and there they stay, meditating, for about four or five days. Once the vision quest is over and they have returned, they must not tell anyone of their vision, with the exception of the medicine man.

Sam's description of the vision quest made me think of our Roman Catholic "core weekend." Core weekends originated with the Catholic Church, but members of any denomination may attend one. Although the method is different in ways, the meanings are similar. A core weekend is supposed to free you of all your sins and make you more aware of yourself and your relationship with God. At the beginning of the weekend, you must promise that you will not tell anyone outside of the others present during the weekend what took place, with the exception of your priest or minister.

During this time there are healing services, meditation, prayers and confessions. The weekend usually takes place at a school or hall where the clocks and windows are covered so that no one is aware of the outside world—just themselves. You are given simple meals, and there is little time to sleep. When you leave, you are under an oath of silence and you feel cleansed and spiritually fulfilled.

The vision quest and the core weekend are parallel in many ways. In each of these practices, those participating are seeking guidance; whether from Sam's god or mine, everyone needs guidance in his or her life. Both methods produce a cleansing of the mind and soul. In Sam's practice, this cleansing comes before the actual vision takes place, whereas in my practice, the cleansing is the result of the weekend.

Cleansing of the mind and soul are very important for spiritual growth and awareness in both groups. Neither Sam nor I are allowed to share our experiences with anyone except a knowledgeable person like the medicine man or the priest. Only those people will truly understand and advise us properly. Both rituals involve prayer and meditation and a great awareness of one's self.

Of similar value to our two groups are the medicine pouch and the hope chest, respectively. The medicine pouch is a very personal item to an Indian. The items carried inside represent a part of their life. Over the years, Sam will collect items that create positive feelings for her and place them in her pouch. For example, while on a vision quest, she saw a smooth stone and it gave her a powerful positive feeling, so she put it in her pouch. The medicine pouch is usually a gift from someone very special. For Sam, it might be a gift from her mother, grandmother or medicine man. Then, when she wishes, she will pass it on to her daughter or son. The contents of the pouch are unknown to all except the owner. The items are kept secret, not only because their meaning or significance would not be understood by others, but also because, if seen, the items will lose their "power." The medicine pouch is very personal and sentimental only to the owner and to those to whom it is passed on.

As Sam has her medicine pouch, I have my hope chest. My hope chest has great personal value for me. Inside it are stored items from my past that I want to retain, like my first stuffed animal, my baby booties, and the start of my chinaware for when I marry. All of these items are very personal to me and no one would get the same satisfaction from looking at them as I do.

My hope chest was given to me by my grandfather whom I love and admire, and when the time comes, I will pass it on to my first daughter or granddaughter. Unlike the medicine pouch, the contents of my hope chest can be seen by others, although it's hardly worthwhile for them if they don't understand and know me. My hope chest holds great sentimental value for me, and for those yet to own it.

The personality of an individual is expressed in the contents of both the medicine pouch and the hope chest. They reveal a part of each person's culture. By viewing the items in the pouch or the chest, the owner's values can be determined. For instance, the contents of the pouch reveal that its Indian owner values nature, whereas the items in my English-Canadian hope chest reveal my more materialistic values.

Unfortunately, the racial reactions Sam and I each received from other people differed. During my interview, she told me of an incident in which she was blamed because of her race. She was in school with the rest of the students, who happened to be English Canadians. The teacher stepped out of the classroom, and when she returned, something was missing from her desk. Immediately, without questioning anyone, she turned to Sam and accused her of stealing the object. When Sam protested that she hadn't taken it, the teacher accused her of lying. Sam told me that this was not an isolated incident. She has taken the blame unfairly many times because of her race and ethnicity. She is accused and charged without a fair trial.

Being a white English Canadian, I have never experienced problems like this. I've never received the blame without first being fairly tried. I've seen this happen, however, to Blacks, Mexicans and others. Until people are educated in different cultural histories, they will always use these stereotypes and prejudices against other cultures.

During my interview with Sam, I recognized both similarities and differences in the values, ideas and behaviours of our separate ethnic and racial groups. Religiously, in my own way, my spiritual wants are similar to Sam's. We practise our religions differently but the personal fulfilment is similar. Both of us will go through our lives collecting items that are meaningful and special to us, and then pass them on to a loved one.

The difference that I saw was not a pleasant one. Both of us have to deal with racism but in different ways. Sam has to put up with stereotypes from white people, and she hopes that someday things will improve. There is still a lot of education needed. In my case, I have to deal with being a racist at times. I too had my stereotypes about the Native Canadians, but after my interview with Sam and my research on the Natives, I have better insight into the attitudes and beliefs of the Canadian Indians. I think all people should follow this rule: "Do not judge lest ye be judged."

John: *"I was better able to see my own prejudices ..."*

Upon meeting a person from a different culture, a daily occurrence in today's multicultural, melting-pot environment, both individuals are superficially aware of the other's uniqueness. Skin colour, accent and dress all serve to create an initial impression of the "outer self" of that person, but very rarely do we get to delve into their thoughts, beliefs and value system. This, of course, is where the true heart of the person beats. Education, traditions, family rearing and societal influences are all elements that help to shape and mould the human into the special being that he or she is, and it is through the examination of these elements that we can gain valuable insights into our "ethnic" neighbours.

Quite recently I had the opportunity to meet and interview Bill, who is racially and ethnically a native Canadian Indian. Before our meeting, I, of course, held predetermined facts and beliefs concerning him, and I am sure he probably held the same about me. We both, however, were in for an educational experience. Although we did have our inevitable differences, it was the similarities we shared that I found fascinating. Both of us, having been raised in Canada, had some similar experiences; however, even culturally we had some distinct parallels. It is these similarities and differences that I shall examine in this paper, and I will try to give some insight into how these racial and ethnic differences and similarities allowed us to appreciate each other's individuality.

Bill spent his early formative years on an Indian reserve in Northern Ontario, and although he moved to Toronto before his tenth birthday, he considers the North to be his true home and the major influence on his thoughts and feelings. Conditions on the reserve were not very hygienic, and living quarters, he remembers, were generally more like upgraded cabins than houses. He recalls the reserve with a sense of fondness, however, because of the remembered warmth of family memories. He shared his belief that family is very important to the Indians, and "family" included very close friends who were related by values and beliefs. He indicated that the exile experienced by many reserve Indians was due to their isolation from the rest of the populace. This encouraged the close-knit supportiveness that was, in fact, necessary for him to function emotionally. He had found separation from family to be very detrimental to the individual and was in awe when I related my family upbringing.

Although I had been brought up with the belief that the family unit is an extremely precious notion from which support, love and encouragement flow, my experience was somewhat different. I was raised with love and sensitivity but had never felt the bond of which Bill spoke. To him, his family was his mainline; to me, it was quite often a group of people that I sometimes loved more out of duty than desire. Upon examining two other ethnically English families with whom I have had repeated contact, it seems that although the family is respected, relations are somewhat distant and not terribly demonstrative. Perhaps that can be attributed to the British upper-class aloofness and the well-established boundaries of class and respect. Nevertheless, it seems to be prevalent in the three English families I know intimately. Conversely, Bill related that his family, and the Indian families he knew, were very close and expressed as much love physically as they did verbally. Even though we both had a strong belief in the family, I came to recognize that his was a physical reality while mine was more of a concept, and I envied him these ties.

Religion, or lack thereof, usually plays a major role in a person's development and values. Both Bill and I had been raised with a belief in an Almighty Creator and taught to revere and worship this Creator. In my religion, Christianity, the Creator is known as God. In Bill's, the Almighty is referred to in Sioux tongue as *Wakan*. Wakan differs very little from God; both created the Heavens and the Earth and all creatures great and small, and both are fervently worshipped by followers of the faith. It is other aspects of the two religions that reveal their difference.

Bill devoutly believes that every object found on Earth has an essence, whether it be a tiny stone or a mighty waterfall. He believes that all creations are whole, and that any disharmony that ensues after an object is removed or destroyed should be righted by the return or replacement of a similar article. In his opinion, man should always be as one with the environment and sensitive to the natural aura of the Almighty's creations.

He doesn't feel that a place of worship, like the Christian church or the Jewish synagogue, is necessary, because faith is an ongoing process and an individual should show this faith in daily settings and actions and not just in obeisance on a given or acknowledged day.

My new friend further went on to say that it was his conviction that most Indians adhered to the ancient beliefs. Through rituals, such as the "vision quest," a solitary, cathartic journey into one's inner space, they helped to ensure that new generations would be cognizant of the old ways and thereby ensured their continued existence.

I similarly believe that a place of ritual worship is not a prerequisite for perpetuating one's beliefs, but I am at odds with the dogma of my religious leaders. The High Anglican Church states that church attendance is an essential part of faith, and it considers non-attendance and lack of involvement in the religious community unacceptable. This is one aspect of the church with which I do not agree, and I am therefore considered somewhat unworthy in the eyes of the ministry.

Bill and I discussed this notion, and Bill chuckled, stating that the solution was obvious. As I agreed with most of the Indian beliefs on which he had elaborated, he jokingly argued that I should convert to "Wakanism." Although I can well imagine a devout Anglican blanching at the thought, after careful examination I discovered that, even after taking into account the varied differences, the two religions are more alike than I would ever have thought.

Even though Bill, in reality, is the "true" Canadian, my white, Anglo-Saxon, Protestant culture has made me, in the eyes of the majority of Canadians, the recipient of the "true Canadian" title. Because I am a white, English-speaking male from an upper-middle-class family, I have never had to be concerned with how my ethnicity will affect my job prospects, housing enquiries—in short, how others will view me. Because of my social and cultural identity, I am almost guaranteed success in any field I choose. This option is not always available to all members of today's "modern" society, and Bill very ably illustrated this point to me.

Bill is considered a "half-breed"—he has an Indian mother and a white father—and consequently he has physical attributes from both races. His skin is a little paler than that of his mother, a true Sioux Indian, but nevertheless his colouring is certainly far removed from that of a Caucasian. His hair, which tends to be straight, is jet black, and certain facial features, although somewhat softened by his father's genetic influence, are evocative of the Indian stereotype.

I refer here to Bill's physical features because he feels that they have a significant impact on the treatment he sometimes receives. He told me that occasionally people will take a second look at him in their attempt to determine his racial background. He said he encountered very little prejudice when alone, but when seen with a group of Indian friends, the reactions he received were not always so subtle. Ladies clutching their purses tighter when the group came near, obvious sneers directed towards the group, blatant slurs voiced just loud enough to carry, all are experiences Bill and his friends have endured. "I don't know what they think we are going to do," he related to me, "but there often seems to be this tension in the air between *us* and *them*."

As he recounted certain incidents, I realized that, although I had never outwardly behaved in such a manner, I was guilty of harbouring certain similar misconceptions. I almost felt like apologizing. I let him know this and he laughed. He said he expected people to have certain preconceived notions of Indians, due to books, stories and films, and he had learned how to adapt to it. He suspected any minority would agree with his view that adaptation and enlightenment would help to curb such petty ignorances and that, hopefully, in a time not too distant, the aforementioned situations would lessen and then cease to occur altogether.

Upon conclusion of the interview, I began to reflect on some of our discussions. We are two human beings from extremely different backgrounds, yet there was always a common thread of agreement to be found in most of the topics on which we touched. Although I could never expect to fully comprehend his cultural identity, nor he, mine, the opinions of one so far removed from my own upbringing were extremely enlightening. I am better able to see my own prejudices. Although I still tend to see things ethno-centrically from time to time, understanding my own and then another's culture is, I believe, the first step to breaking down some of the racial and ethnic barriers erected so long ago.

Respect must be engendered for the differences of our many cultural heritages, for it is only in this manner that we can learn from and grow with each other. An acknowledgment of our similarities should be recognized, because norms, values and beliefs, although varied, are all based upon love, friendship and understanding. Only after careful examination of a different culture can we begin to see that, although we appear dissimilar outwardly, there seems to be a sameness that is evident only if we make a conscious effort to discover each other's individuality within.

ENGLISH CANADIANS AND FRENCH CANADIANS

Lyn: *"As a member of the dominant group, I don't feel the conscious necessity of reaffirming my cultural heritage..."*

In this discussion of similarities and differences between my own ethnic culture, English Canadian, and the group which I studied, French Canadian, I would like to concentrate on how each group views its heritage, and the importance each group places on its culture. I would also like to discuss how each group views the preservation of that culture and how this is reflected in behaviours and attitudes. In doing so, I will make comparisons between the individual I interviewed and myself.

The individual I interviewed is a Franco-Ontarian and holds many of the values of French Canadian culture, with one of the most important being the commitment to family. This commitment extends to include involvement in the close-knit Franco-Ontarian community. Historically, these values have been strengthened by the position of Franco-Ontarians as a minority within the larger English culture.

Jacques has a strong sense of his own heritage and a sense of loss and isolation from his culture. As he is living in Southern Ontario, it has only been relatively recently that he has had access to French television or radio, and the French community here is very scattered. His language is crucial to him and, as it is to most French Canadians, inseparable from his culture. He cannot practise this culture unless he returns to his home town or visits other French Canadian centres. Therefore, the preservation of his language involves a day-to-day struggle. Because of this, he places a high value on that language and is very conscious of his own ethnic and cultural identity as distinct from English Canadians'.

Although I am an immigrant, I am of English birth, and this places me firmly within the English Canadian ethnic culture. I have been socialized to accept the high value placed on success in the public sphere, on material success and economic status, values that are emphasized more strongly than commitment to family and community. However, it is through such things as economic status or power that English Canadian cultural identity is reinforced.

As a member of the majority (or dominant) group, I don't feel the conscious necessity of reaffirming my cultural heritage as I can practise that culture daily. It is mirrored for me in my day-to-day experience of society—in the institutions that surround me, for example. Although the preservation of ethnic cultural identity may not appear to be an issue, it is shown to be an important one by the ways in which the majority culture perpetuates itself through institutions such as political parties, schools

Photo: Dick Hemingway

The Sikh contingent of a federalist rally during the 1995 Quebec referendum campaign.

and various media and by the strong reluctance to relinquish control over those institutions. The historical denial of official-language status to the French language is a good example of this.

It can be seen then that both groups place a strong emphasis on the preservation of their cultural heritage, which each group values highly. The important difference lies in the assumptions and attitudes that surround that value.

Jacques assumes that his ethnic and cultural identity is continually under threat of assimilation by the majority English culture. He has no occasion to use his language, and his ties are to the Franco-Ontarian communities of Northern Ontario, but he has to work in the south. As a result he is both conscious of and desires to emphasize his identity, his "difference."

I, on the other hand, surrounded by my own ethnic culture, have tended to lose all sight of myself as having an ethnic identity. I and other members of my group preserve our culture by living it without being aware that we are doing so. I don't feel the necessity of emphasizing my "difference" and yet tend to be unaware of the "sameness" which surrounds me as actually having an ethnic cultural basis. This attitude in English Canadian culture has resulted in a strong tendency to deny or ignore those differences. The belief that we are really all the same is based on the assumption of what the same is—namely, like us. When the majority group denies or ignores the assertion of difference, it is also denying the need for accommodation of those differences that could threaten their own cultural "sameness."

This highlights another important issue in the discussion of these two groups and of how they view the preservation of their respective cultures. Both groups consider themselves to be charter members of the Canadian society. If we take this to mean that a charter group's institutions provide the basic structural framework for society, then it can be seen that only English culture has retained this status in Ontario. As a result, English Canadians assume this status to be valid almost without thought. The desire of the French in Ontario for official status appears as either irrelevant or as a vague historical issue, because nowhere do English Canadians see evidence of this status. For the Franco-Ontarians, official status involves the very right to their existence as a distinct cultural and linguistic group. It becomes a crucial issue of survival and far from irrelevant to daily life when their culture is not reflected in the language used or in the priorities of government. Our tendency to deny our understanding of this desire on the part of the French shows how easily threatened we can be. Sharing charter group status is acceptable theoretically, but in terms of "granting" legal status, it somehow becomes questionable.

Both cultures, then, have the same intense belief in the necessity of preserving their cultural heritage and maintaining language and values while living day to day. The key difference here is in what is assumed; on one hand, the conscious effort made towards preservation of identity and, on the other, the largely unconscious perpetuation of culture through which identity is preserved.

In comparing these values and ideas, the differences and similarities of the two ethnic-cultural groups, I have drawn on knowledge of my own group and on my conversations with Jacques. I could see that our differing backgrounds, relative to the culture within which we live, has had an effect on the relative strengths of those values and ideas and on how clearly we perceive their existence. This was very evident in our discussions of Franco-Ontarians, and perhaps it could be generally applied to any other ethnic group living within a different majority ethnic culture. Acceptance and the definition of differences can become crucial in the preservation of a distinct ethnic identity. Awareness of similar needs by the majority culture is also crucially important in preserving both cultures.

Maureen: *"I did not regard having two languages as a tool for survival ..."*

For my paper, I chose to investigate the French Canadians. Part of my investigation involved speaking with Charlotte, a French Canadian born just outside of Quebec City. She is approximately fifty years of age and is married to a non-French gentleman. They reside with their children in Brampton, Ontario.

What follows in this paper is based on the similarities and differences between Charlotte and me. Certainly there are others than those mentioned here, but I have chosen to examine four specific areas—religion, language, education and politics. Please keep in mind that I have developed these views from my own interpretations resulting from conversations with Charlotte, and while I believe I have relayed her beliefs, attitudes and behaviours accurately through comparing them to mine, they do not necessarily reflect her interpretations.

My awareness of and interest in the French people has grown immensely since my study of the French Canadians through library research and after spending time with Charlotte. During our conversations, the subject of religion surfaced more than once. Baptized and raised a Roman Catholic, she has, over the past three or four years, found herself drifting from the church. She explained that this has been a physical separation—not a spiritual one. She has been experiencing some doubt as to the necessity of weekly attendance at Sunday Mass, and feels secure with her decision not to attend regularly. For her, the continual love for God and her fellow man takes precedence over the obligatory Sunday attendance. She usually attends at Christmas and Easter with her husband, a non-practising Catholic. Charlotte displays no hostility towards the demands imposed by the church, but simply feels she is fulfilling her obligation to God by other means.

Religion continues to play such a major role in the French culture that I was taken aback when I heard her personal view. She acknowledged the importance of religion in her culture for the majority of Francophones, but at the same time defended her stand. She sees it as a personal conflict with which she feels she is dealing appropriately.

I, too, am a Roman Catholic and am currently practising. Being of Irish origin, it seems to follow that I am Catholic, but I do not feel I practise because it is a cultural trait. I don't feel I practise it because I am Irish, but because the faith is fulfilling for me, and I enjoy partaking on a regular basis. So while we both acknowledge and appreciate our faith, we follow different methods of practise.

Religion and language are two major aspects of the French Canadian culture. Charlotte is bilingual; I am not. There are certainly more Francophones who have learned English than there are Anglophones who can converse in French. It would appear that we both fit our cultural moulds in this regard. However, the French are accused of forcing their language on the non-French. It appears to be quite the opposite to me.

To date I have made several attempts to learn French, with little success. Perhaps it is just too difficult for my simple mind or, more likely, I do not regard having two languages as a tool for survival. Charlotte does. Not only does she see the French language as an important tool in conjunction with English, but also as a preservation of her cultural heritage. She is proud of her ability to communicate in both languages and recognizes the advantages of these two languages, not only here in Canada, but also for worldwide travel.

While Charlotte's views reflect the practical, the majority of her group regard the situation from a political standpoint—French is one of the two founding languages in this country and both should be spoken and understood by all, for a bilingual Canada.

We both appear to hold education in high regard as we are both currently pursuing new careers through community college. It appears I am following a cultural behaviour shared by my society—that of furthering my education. The fact that the government's financial assistance encourages people like Charlotte and me to further our skills indicates the cultural similarity.

One other area worthy of discussion is that of politics. While we are both opposed to separatism, our knowledge and awareness of the Quebec struggle and Canadian politics in general differ greatly, with me being the more ignorant. Charlotte was able to cite Bill numbers and significant political dates, and could make quick references to names of importance as a result of her culture. Their struggle for distinct recognition across Canada plays a major role in their culture, and Charlotte's political know-how is not uncharacteristic. I also fit my culture's mould to a tee. Because I am a member of the majority, English and white, I feel no need to strive for recognition and pay little heed to the political world around me. This is nothing to be proud of, but is certainly noteworthy and definitely a cultural norm.

Certainly Charlotte and I share more similarities than differences, partly because we are both white and we both speak English. Despite our different methods of practising our faith, the fact that we are both Catholics plays an important role in shaping our values. As for our differences, they appear to stem from religion and language, two of the major cultural aspects of the French Canadian.

JUDAISM AND CATHOLICISM

Mark: *"Is there only one normal way of life ...?"*

As I sat waiting to interview my friend Dave, I attempted to foretell his replies. Dave and I are very good friends, yet we have totally different backgrounds. I am a Canadian Conservative Jew, and he is a Roman Catholic Italian Canadian. Although our ethnic differences are tremendous, we tend to share many similar views on a wide variety of topics, such as marriage and prejudice found in the work force and in daily life. However, because of our dissimilar backgrounds, we hold opposing views on issues such as family relations, having children and religion.

Is there only one normal way of life, one pattern, one single direction that is set for everyone to follow, or is each individual required to discover his or her own personal lifestyle? When discussing our ideas, the issue of marriage emerged. Dave has just recently become engaged. For me, marriage has never been an option—I have never considered *not* getting married. In the Jewish religion, one of the most highly regarded and holy events is the joining of two individuals in the bond of marriage. I feel as if it were a prerequisite for a fulfilling life. This tenet is also held by the Roman Catholic Church.

Dave does not deviate from this aspect of his ethnic group, although he does not see himself as a religious individual. We have both been socialized to marry one day in order to proceed with a normal way of life. In both our family life and our religious upbringing, marriage is considered to be a security to provide us with the strength to achieve future goals. I can remember sitting in synagogue as a child, hearing the rabbi relate tales of the ceremonious marriages recorded in the Bible, which, in turn, created the Jewish religion as well as many other religions.

While Dave was growing up, he learned the beliefs proper to a Roman Catholic Italian, and I learned those that relate to me as a Jew. At the age of twenty-three, Dave now views religion as being "very misleading, hypocritical and no longer spiritual." He also feels it is too judgmental. Dave's parents were strict about following the laws and customs of his ancestors and passed them on to him. When Dave reached an age when he wanted to know why his parents did the things they did, the reasons were not explained to him. For Dave, the laws and customs remained his parents' ways and never truly became his own. Because of this, Dave does not feel any bond with Roman Catholic ways. Therefore, he does not practise the customs at all, other than attending church twice a year to please his parents.

I must admit that I feel differently. While I was growing up, I attended a school on Sundays for two hours where I learned about the laws and customs my parents practised at home. At this school, many of my questions were answered. This established a strong value for my religion. I have acquired values and ideas from my religion and have not disregarded the beliefs of my ancestors. I feel that it is important to learn about one's background from a viewpoint that only a religious outlook can provide. Although I would not say that I follow the laws and customs of the Jewish religion strictly, I intend to pass on my knowledge to my children and provide them with the option to choose how religious they would like to be—as my parents have done for their children.

When we broached the subject of having a family, I felt there were going to be discrepancies. I have always looked forward to having at least two kids. Although having children is an individual decision, my strong family ties and my religion have played a large part in influencing my choice.

I believe I follow the preferential norm for both Judaism and Catholicism. However, Dave has veered from the norm by intending not to have children. He feels it is a personal preference. He states that if he did choose to have a family of his own, among the prerequisites would be a wife who is willing to remain at home with the children, financial stability and a strong relationship with his spouse.

Comparing our lives made me aware of the apparent differences that influence such a decision. Dave drifted away from his parents when he rebelled to establish his own identity. It was difficult for him to follow his parents' strict ways and abide by the laws of the Roman Catholic religion, which his parents follow closely. By understanding Dave's reasons, I am able to empathize with his feelings on this topic. Since his decision has been influenced by an unhappy upbringing and mine by one of happiness, it is evident as to why we hold different views.

As we are both Caucasian, neither of us has ever experienced prejudice based on colour. However, we have both experienced one form of prejudice or another because of being members of a minority group, Italian and Jewish respectively. Dave feels that his surname is a cause of prejudice. His surname is very "Italian." Upon hearing such a name or reading it on an application, people may immediately apply stereotypical views to him. Such a factor may not seem so relevant; however, when an employer is reviewing dozens of applications, every detail on that application is critical information that helps to form an overall impression. At times, a name might destroy a chance at acquiring a particular job if the employer is prejudiced.

The Jews have been discriminated against for as long as I can remember and are often victims of stereotypical views. The fact that Dave and I both come from a minority group has possibly contributed to our deep annoyance regarding this issue. Both of us refuse to judge people for what they are rather than who they are. Personally, I feel that there is not one person I have met in my twenty-two years who is without a single fault. If everyone dwells on each other's bad points, everyday life would be miserable for everyone. We live in an imperfect world.

It is very hard to relate Dave's behaviour and beliefs to his being Italian Roman Catholic. His ancestors came to Canada four generations ago and therefore he feels absolutely no ties to Italy. He views himself as a Canadian. Dave feels that since his parents are Roman Catholic then he must be as well, although, as stated previously, Dave does not believe in his religion.

I too feel that I am more a Canadian than anything else. My final question to Dave was, "If someone were to stop you on the street and ask you what your ethnic background and religion are, what would you answer?" He replied, "I would say I am a Canadian, but if you were to go back and look at my ancestors, you would find that I am of Italian Roman Catholic descent."

Through much examination of Judaism and Roman Catholicism, I have attempted to understand the reasons behind the similarities, along with the differences, among different ethnic groups. In conclusion, one's ethnic group sets standards and provides direction for each member of that group. Our behaviour, derived from the values and ideas that we learn, reflects the amount we have diversified from the pattern set out for ourselves and forms each person's lifestyle.

RELIGIOUS AND FAMILY LIFE

Barbara: *"We both come from cultures where the family is very important."*

For this essay I interviewed Maya, who has been my friend and neighbour for eighteen years. Maya is a Hindu who was born in Delhi and has lived in Canada since 1960. I am a Canadian Jew who was born in Toronto and I have lived in Canada all my life.

Hinduism is not a rigid religion. Hindus worship many deities, and there are many variations among people and within villages and families. There are several sacred texts, and many Hindus use idols or pictures in their worship. Maya has a prayer room in her home, where she goes to pray and meditate.

Maya worships her guru (teacher) as the highest deity. He leads a very simple life and spends his time in prayer and meditation. Her husband also worships the same guru, and they visit him in India once or twice a year for lengthy periods of time. She hopes that one day she will be able to emulate his lifestyle. Maya does not attend a temple, because she feels that she does not need a temple to practise her religion.

Maya believes in reincarnation. A person who leads a holy life is reborn as a better person and so on until the soul reaches the ultimate, a state that her guru has reached. Maya also believes in an omnipresent God, with which the perfected soul lives in intimate and perpetual contact. Since her guru has reached the ultimate, his soul will be released to God when he dies.

I have always received the impression that Maya's religion is very important to her and that it is a very private and very personal part of her life. Her religion also has a quality that is quite foreign to my thoughts and feelings. In contrast to the idols and polytheism of Hinduism, Judaism is a monotheistic religion that does not permit the use of idols in worship. The sacred text for all Jews is the Torah, which, like the texts Maya worships (the Ramayana and the Bhagavidgita), was written by many scholars.

I am not a practising Jew; I have not believed in God since I was a teenager. Even though I was raised in a traditional home, I became an atheist. I think that this happened because I do not need a god to live a satisfying life. Being an atheist also means that, unlike Maya, I have no deity to turn to for advice or solace, and I must depend mainly on my own inner resources.

Just as there are many different ways of being a Hindu, there are also many different ways of being a Jew. Even among the three main subgroups of Judaism, there are many individual variations. Also, like Hindus, Jews are usually born into their religion, although both religions accept converts.

The central tenet of Judaism is to be a good person. However, there is no institutionalized system of rewards and punishment; these come essentially from within the person. Judaism teaches that goodness is reward enough and that, while a wicked person may appear to go unpunished, being bad is sufficient punishment in itself. Because of the emphasis on being a good person, people who make a contribution to society have always been highly regarded among Jews. I have always been attracted to work I consider to be socially useful.

Unlike Maya, I do not believe in an afterlife. There is no well-developed concept of Heaven or Hell in Judaism; Jews seem to be occupied mainly with this life. Since there is no afterlife, Jews believe that it is important to do one's best in this life.

I do not know how widespread the practice of asceticism, to the degree that it is practised by my friend's guru, is among Hindus. As far as I know, it does not exist among Jews, and certainly it was never a part of my life and thought. There are a few Jewish rabbis and scholars who spend a great deal of time studying the Torah. However, this type of learning does not seem to be of high priority among Jewish people. While they value a good education, it is a secular education that is highly prized, because an educated person can lead a richer life and can contribute more to society.

In spite of her high regard for her guru's lifestyle, Maya takes great pride in her home and her possessions. She readily admits this, but considers it a weakness that she must try to overcome. For me, as for most Jews, the acquisition of worldly possessions and comforts is highly desirable and a legitimate reward for hard work.

Both Maya and her husband speak Hindi as their first language and that is the language they use within the family. Both their children speak Hindi well and the family has made many trips to India, where most of their relatives live. During these visits, both children were taught to read and write Hindi, and both can do so fairly well. However, outside their home both children speak only English and also have a fairly good command of French.

Maya thinks that it is unlikely that her children will speak Hindi to their children. While her children enjoy visiting India and feel comfortable there, they both regard Canada as their home. For Maya, however, there is a strong possibility that she will eventually return to India. She says that, while her mind has accepted Canada, her heart is still in India.

In contrast, both my husband and I were born in Canada and English is the only language we speak. Unlike other non-English-speaking minority groups, the Jews in Canada have never had a language to preserve. Most of them came from Eastern Europe and had no wish to speak the languages of the countries that most of them despised. However, I do envy people who are fluent in more than one language, because I feel that it adds richness and colour to one's life.

Unlike many members of other minority groups in Canada, the Jews had no wish to return to their countries of origin, and would not have been welcome if they had returned. With no language or country to call their own, Canadian Jews have been only too eager to learn English and to adopt Canadian customs and habits. Unlike Maya's family, we have spent most of our holidays travelling across Canada and the United States. Like most Jews, I feel, not only a strong loyalty to Canada, but also an enormous sense of gratitude that my parents and grandparents immigrated to Canada. While I have never wanted to live in Israel, I do support a Jewish homeland as a haven for Jews.

Maya and I both come from cultures where the family is very important. While Maya has raised her children to be aware of and to appreciate Indian culture, she understands that in an open society doing this may create difficult choices for her children, since they wish to remain in Canada. In contrast, I have had to make the kind of choices that Maya's children are making. My children, in turn, accept without question that they may choose freely from the many lifestyles that Canada has to offer.

Since neither Maya nor I need the support system of an organized religion, we have never found it necessary or even desirable to live in an area where there are large concentrations of people from our own ethnic group. Her children and mine have had the opportunity to grow up with children from many different ethnic groups.

Like myself, the only expression of prejudice that Maya has encountered has been the occasional remark. Because I do not have a Jewish name and I do not "look Jewish," people occasionally make anti-Semitic remarks in my presence. In spite of these minor expressions of prejudice, we both feel comfortable in Canada and have friends from many backgrounds. Overall, we have great respect for the British cultural base on which English-speaking Canada is built.

Maya and I were surprised at the similarity of our attitudes on abortion, divorce, heritage language classes, affirmative action programs, refugees, inter-marriage and capital punishment. I think that there are several reasons why Maya and I share so many of the same views despite our different backgrounds. We both belong to ethnic groups that have become integrated into Canadian society and have assumed positions of leadership in many areas. Our religions allow for many differences; and we have been influenced by the many social changes that have occurred here.

In my long and close association with Maya, we have both found our similarities to be far deeper and far more important than our differences.

Jackie: *"Because I have not experienced such hate I cannot understand how he felt."*

The religion that has always interested me the most is the Jewish religion, but I wondered if it is solely a religion, or both a religion and a culture. I interviewed David, who is thirty-eight years of age. When I met him I distinctly remember remarking to myself that he looked like the stereotypical Jew: he had dark hair and a big nose. It was my first experience of meeting a Jewish person, and I was terribly ignorant about his religion and his ethnicity. Thank goodness he has a sense of humour.

David is Canadian-born, but his grandparents emigrated from Russia during the Russian Revolution. He considers himself to be a second-generation Jewish Canadian of Russian descent. David believes that his religion and ethnicity are one and the same. During the interview, I explained to him that I was Scottish Canadian but that my ethnicity was Scottish. He insisted that his religion and cultural background are one, as his family never had strong ties with Russia. I argued his point and reminded him that, although I grew up primarily in Canada, I still was a product of a Scottish upbringing. Likewise, he must have some Russian influences in his life. He disagreed. David also believes that the Jewish people consider themselves to be an ethnic group. He explained to me that, because the Jewish people never had a true homeland until 1948 and were from different countries, they joined together as one. I still have difficulty understanding this, but David truly believes it.

I was born in Scotland in 1962, and we immigrated to Canada as a family in 1966. Although the Canadian culture has had a great influence on my behaviour, I still consider myself to be Scottish. I take great pride in my ethnic background as well as great pride in being Canadian.

David was raised in a small community in Northern Ontario where his family were the only Jews. The rest of the community was made up of French Canadians and Anglo-Saxons. This has influenced his behaviour as an adult, and is a factor in how he feels about himself today. He vividly remembers the neighbours commenting to his parents on how they had known a Jew once, or how they had never met a Jew before. As a child he was disconcerted by this as he was made to feel different from the other kids.

I never had that problem growing up in an Anglo-Saxon, middle-class neighbourhood. I was never made to feel that I was different or that I had to prove myself to fit in. But David seems to have experienced this kind of judgment most of his life. Once, when he was six years old, a young boy came up to him in the park and called him a "dirty Jew." Without showing any anger, he turned around and called the boy a "stupid peacock." I did not understand his response at first, but David went on to explain that the other children laughed more at the other boy because, although they did not understand what a "dirty Jew" was, they knew that a peacock was a bird. He walked away from that situation having learned a great lesson—that he should not listen to silly names but that he should feel comfortable with himself and his religion. I found the story sad, but David laughs about it. I guess because I have not experienced such hate I cannot understand how he felt.

David feels that his strong family upbringing has helped him feel secure with himself and his life. His family taught their children that they had the freedom to choose what they wished to do with their life. His interpretation of success is a result of his family's philosophy. He sets his own goals, which in turn are measured only by himself. He has no desire to "keep up with the Jones's" and I can only wish that I had that kind of outlook on success.

I feel that I am always under pressure to succeed. When my parents moved to Canada, they dreamed of giving their children a better life, including education, cultural experiences and so on. That is a hard thing to live up to. I am envious of David's philosophy but am not sure why there is this difference. It

Photo: Dick Hemingway

Schools have an especially important role to play in educating students about difference and in promoting an understanding of ethnic and racial diversity.

could be because my family, when living in Scotland, was lower class, while David's family has been in the middle class for several generations.

David's Jewish culture influenced him greatly until he left home at the age of twenty-five. When he moved into the Toronto work force, he felt that it was no longer necessary to practise his religious beliefs or traditions until he had his own children. He believes strongly in his faith but does not feel it is necessary to go to the synagogue weekly to prove his faith to others.

I have no substantial religious background. My grandparents were once Catholic but no longer believe. My parents felt it was up to me to decide whether I would be baptized or not. I sometimes envy the religion that David grew up in because it seems to strengthen a person. I guess I will always feel that I missed out on something. David feels it is very important to educate his children about their religious roots as it gives them pride in their culture, which he feels is an important part of a healthy upbringing.

There are many Scottish traditions that my family still follows, such as Robbie Burns Day, eating haggis and the wearing of the Kilt on special occasions. We have retained many superstitions that have been passed on for generations. We feel this bonds us to our ethnic background, but David thinks differently. He describes two kinds of traditions: timeless traditions, such as the family unit, and traditions that no longer apply, such as marrying only Jewish women to preserve the "race." It is ironic, but he admits that this tradition is a perfect example of discrimination. David feels that the Jewish religion and traditions go hand in hand. He feels that times are changing and so must traditions—but religion must stay intact.

I have always had a strong work ethic, which I believe is the outcome of my strict upbringing to succeed. I sometimes push myself too hard, however, and end up not enjoying what I do for a living. This can also be a motivating factor, as it pushes me towards more education, which in turn can give me a brighter future. David believes that doing a job well and enjoying it is all that matters. He is an engineer for a large manufacturing company and admits that, although money is important to him, he would not do a job just for the money. My family has always put great importance on how much money someone makes. I tend to go along with David's philosophy rather than my parents'.

David feels that his family and religion gave him his first moral footing but that his peers have been of greater influence on him. My strong moral beliefs were definitely an outcome of my family's teachings. I find it odd that, despite my having no religious background, my morals and values are just as strong as those of a person who came from a strict religious background. For some reason I always felt that a religious person would have stronger morals than I, but now I can see that this is not the case. I must say I feel good about learning this.

David celebrates Christmas in the same spirit as I celebrate Thanksgiving—not in the religious sense, but as a tradition and an opportunity to get together with family and friends.

"Through education at an early age, children should be taught about the different cultures in Canada. They should be taught the differences and the similarities of these cultures and then we will probably see that there are so many more similarities than differences." This was a most profound statement David made while we were discussing discrimination.

I cannot say that I have been discriminated against because of my Scottish ethnicity, but I may have been because of my sex (female). My ethnic background has never been held against me, nor has it hindered me in doing what I have set out to do. David cannot say the same. Before admitting to being discriminated against, he admits quite freely that he discriminates against others. I was quite shocked by his statement, as most people would feel uncomfortable confessing this. David feels that he can sense if a person is discriminatory by nature, and he in turn discriminates against that person—not in action, but in judgement. He admits that if a person doesn't live up to his standards he has no time for them. He hates this aspect of his personality and has tried to change it, but he has come to terms with why he thinks this way.

He still feels that he sometimes has to prove himself twice over to be accepted by the majority. At university, he hung around solely with Italians, because he felt that he did not have to prove himself and that he could relate to their faith and strong upbringing. He felt he did not have to waste his time on people who judged others on their religious or ethnic background. He is fortunate that his parents gave him the confidence and strength to walk away from the ignorance of others, but he admits that perhaps these experiences of discrimination have made him discriminate against others. David's family believes in "an eye for an eye."

I have never been discriminated against. Neither I nor my family have ever felt this direct hatred from others, so how can I possibly begin to understand what people who are discriminated against feel? Anger? Hatred? Or an eye for an eye? I mentioned to David that seeking revenge on others who hurt you can only cause war, but if you turn the other cheek, things may pass. He is quite stubborn in this belief, although he admits it is not always the right way.

I believe David's strength and security are a result of his needing to fight for what he wanted and of keeping his head high when someone made a racist comment. I respect the way he has handled his situation. I believe that, because I have had a lot of things handed to me throughout my life and have never been ridiculed, it has made me a weaker person emotionally than David—not that I want the anger he has experienced, but if I could experience some, it may make me appreciate myself more and allow me to conquer my fears.

It is difficult to think of other significant differences. Religion is an obvious difference, but I am not sure if it is a significant one—I had a strong, close family unit. There is a difference in our of interpretation of success, but I would think that this has more to do with economic status and social class than our culture. Obviously there are dietary differences and traditional differences, but I do not think these differences are significant in shaping our behaviour.

There are many similarities. I did not expect this, as I was naïve about the Jewish culture. Beliefs about education are the same. Our work ethics are similar. The family is the most important entity in both our lives. Both our homes are always open to friends and to those in need. We are both honest and open-minded people.

If everyone in this country could do a report on a culture and recognize that there are far more similarities than differences among cultures, our country would be a lot better off. So would the children of tomorrow, who may yet be ridiculed and teased, who may grow up unsure about themselves in a country they call home.

FAMILY LIFE, ROLES AND VALUES

Sharon: *"Discrimination is something that I … have never faced …"*

My subject's name is Mary. She was born in Hong Kong and immigrated to Canada with her parents and her brother and sister in the late 1960s when she was still a young child. Her family eventually settled in the Brampton-Bramalea area. They were one of the first Chinese families in town. Today, Mary is studying engineering at an Ontario university. Now that Mary's basic background has been established, how does the fact that Mary is Chinese affect her values, attitudes and beliefs?

I asked Mary what she thought she valued most in her life. Her response was her family. In my opinion (and Mary agreed with me) this great respect for family, and for parents specifically, is a trait common to most Chinese. Children are taught from their youngest days that they must respect their elders, for they have an obligation to them. Anything the children may do or achieve at any time in their lives reflects first upon the parents and then on the child. Mary feels that, while there is great reverence for the parents, the parent-child bond is usually an emotionally distant one. Again, this distance can be attributed to the children's upbringing. They are taught to mask their emotions, to be stoic and to hold all feelings in, for emotions can make one vulnerable to others.

In commenting on the fact that most Chinese people work in such fields as business, engineering, math and sciences, Mary stated that she believes it is because these are all fields in which emotions, for the most part, play no part. These positions are ruled by the head, as the saying goes, and not the heart. Therefore, because the Chinese believe that emotional expression should be restricted, it makes sense that they would prefer these jobs rather than positions in such fields as the arts.

Closely related to the issue of respect for parents and elders is the view of marriage. Mary's view of marriage is in accordance with my understanding of the "typical Chinese" attitude towards this institution. Marriage is not to be entered into lightly—it is a serious matter. In the past, most marriages were arranged; however, Mary doesn't hold to this view. She believes in marrying for love.

In Mary's view, there are different roles for men and women within the union of marriage. The man is the master, the breadwinner and the decision maker. The woman's prime duty is to serve the husband and to provide for and take care of the children. Although Mary is spending a great deal of time, money and energy on her education, as soon as she marries she will commit herself to this role of a dutiful wife.

Inter-racial marriage is definitely frowned upon. The reasoning behind this is that, if one were to marry a non-Chinese, that person would be an outsider and would cause problems and strife within the family. This could lead to a break-up of the most important institution, the family. On the night I first called her about the interview, Mary was involved in a family problem. Her parents had discovered that she was dating a non-Chinese. Mary was forbidden to see him. When I last spoke with Mary, this matter had still not been resolved. Although this incident caused a great strain in Mary's relationship with her parents, she doesn't feel that she should have to date only those who are Chinese. However, when I questioned Mary further, she said that in all likelihood the man she marries will be Chinese.

Upon examining my own values and beliefs on family and marriage, I found that basically my beliefs are similar to Mary's, but there is a degree of variance. For instance, in my family, there isn't such a rigid set of rules or a demand for respect. There is respect among the members of my family, but it has not been ingrained in me through the repetition of proverbs and lectures day after day; rather, it has occurred naturally. Also, in my family, the role of various members are not so pronounced. Both of my parents work, so both are breadwinners and both are caretakers. Neither my mother nor my father has one set role. Unlike Mary's parents, they cross over to share the typical "husband" and "wife" duties.

My beliefs also differ from Mary's in my view of marriage. I do not believe that the role of the wife is merely to serve the husband. I believe that, if the wife wants to work, she most certainly should do so. Mary does not feel it is right for the wife to work outside the home. Inter-racial marriage is something that Mary feels is not for her, even though dating outside of her race is okay in her opinion. I feel that both dating and marrying outside of one's race or ethnicity is acceptable. Normally, being a member of the dominant group, the idea of inter-racial marriage might never occur to me. However, I dated someone of a different race for several years. Just as Mary's parents frown on the idea of dating and/or marrying outside of their race, so did my parents. Neither set of parents wanted to risk the potential weakening of the family structure that could result if it were to be infiltrated by someone with different values and ideas.

Discrimination is something that I, as a member of the dominant group, have never faced, but I imagined this might not be the case for Mary. Had she faced any discrimination? When this question was posed, Mary's response was a very quick and almost defiant, "No!" When pressed further, however, she grudgingly admitted that perhaps there had been instances of discrimination in the past. She not only feels that discrimination shouldn't occur but maintains that it doesn't. Several statements like this one led me to believe that perhaps Mary was trying to deny the existence of discrimination by the use of blanket thoughts and ideals, such as "Everyone should be treated equally," rather than dealing with reality. Mary states that discrimination doesn't exist, and yet I have seen her exhibit her own prejudicial tendencies. For example, she often makes derogatory comments about other Chinese, she avoids contact with other members of her race and ethnicity and she actively tries to associate exclusively with members of the white majority.

Mary thinks of herself as Canadian and not as Chinese. However, it is undeniable that Mary's values and beliefs stem from her Chinese background, just as mine have stemmed from my WASP background and upbringing. Whether one chooses to accept it or not, the fact remains that values, ideas and beliefs exist in a causal relationship to one's race, ethnicity and cultural history.

Debbie: *"Initially, physical contrasts cannot be overlooked."*

The Mexican people constitute a small but important part of the Canadian population. Based upon my interaction with Gerardo, a recent immigrant from Mexico, I am now able to draw comparisons between us that are essential to a better understanding of our similarities and differences.

During our first meeting, our racial differences were quite obvious to both of us. His olive skin and dark hair are noticeably different from my fair complexion. Initially, these physical contrasts cannot be overlooked. Being part of the white, Canadian racial majority, I admit that I tend to be somewhat judgmental of people who are racially different. All my life, I have been taught to believe that racial contrasts are indicative of cultures that oppose my own. However, my affiliation with Gerardo has fortunately developed my awareness of this critical and unwarranted perception. I now realize that this ethnocentric viewpoint is overflowing with unnecessary prejudice and discrimination. Although we are different racially, Gerardo and I have much in common.

First of all, our values appear to be the same when analyzing the importance of the family. Gerardo's Mexican background has taught him to value his family members highly, and to treat them with reverence and respect. Similarly, my British ethnicity has been influential in the same way. Like Gerardo, the relationships I have with my parents and siblings are important to me for similar reasons. Consequently, this shared value is reflected in our behaviour. When interacting with family members, we both agree that we are intentionally more patient and compassionate because of their importance to us.

However, this value is not identical in all aspects. When comparing the structure of our families, it became evident to us that the amount of importance we grant to each person within the family unit differs. This disparity appears to have been influenced by our different cultures. Within the Mexican culture, the mother is the dominant family figure. Mexican people believe that the "woman's" place is at home so that she can raise the children and maintain the household. The mother is the parent who holds authority and provides support for the children. For all these reasons, Gerardo respects his mother enormously and values his relationship with her.

In contrast, the relationship I have with my father is most important to me. Within the (British) Canadian culture, the father is still the dominant figure in the household. He holds authority and gives support to the other family members. My own family continues to recognize and honour this traditional role. Consequently, my culture has influenced my feelings of tremendous admiration and respect for my father.

Some differences between Gerardo and me can definitely be attributed to our different cultural backgrounds. However, the importance we grant to our relationship with one parent or another in no way affects the corresponding amount of importance we place upon the "family unit" as a whole.

Gerardo and I also share a belief in the work ethic. Success is highly valued by both of us. However, cultural and ethnic differences have again developed certain variances in our individual perceptions of work and success. Gerardo does not value work for its financial rewards. His ethnic background has taught him to appreciate his job for the stimulation and enjoyment it provides, rather than for the money. It appears that the Mexican culture does not consider financial prosperity to be indicative of individual success. For this reason, he is not overly concerned with his salary. Personal satisfaction and secure relationships with his family and friends are far more important to him.

Unlike Gerardo, my British ethnicity has taught me to believe that one's job is irrelevant if one's pay cheque is substantial, because success can be achieved with financial gain. Additionally, the Canadian culture has also been influential in fostering this particular belief.

Consequently, these different attitudes have affected certain aspects of our behaviour. I tend to be far more aggressive and competitive than Gerardo, because I want to succeed financially. In contrast, Gerardo is more relaxed and less assertive, because financial gain is not a priority for him. Gerardo and I positively agree that these opposing ideas can be attributed to our different ethnic and cultural backgrounds. However, even though our interpretations of success are vastly different, it still remains a value that we both consider to be tremendously important.

In summation, it is fairly obvious how influential our backgrounds have been regarding the development of our individual values, ideas and behaviours. I realize that I have only skimmed the surface of the various similarities and differences that exist between Gerardo and myself. However, in making the comparisons, we have both acquired a better understanding and acceptance of each other, as well as feelings of kinship and mutual respect. Just as important, we have each gained tremendously valuable insights into ourselves as individuals.

Doug: *"I had been able to tap information from this person who had been through so much ..."*

Tsung, who is twenty-five years of age, is a Vietnamese refugee who fled Vietnam with most of his family in 1979. Now his family runs a small corner grocery store. They have assimilated into the community quite well and are liked by their neighbours.

Tsung's parents are Catholics from the southern part of Vietnam. He, in turn, was raised as a Catholic and plans to bring up any children he might have in the Catholic faith. Tsung's immediate family is of extreme importance to him. Having seen what war is like and what it can do to otherwise well-disciplined and civilized people, Tsung is very sincere in this matter. The family is a tightly knit unit that shares just about everything.

I mentioned to him that, in my family, individuals keep many of their problems, especially emotional ones, to themselves. Tsung summed up his situation neatly by saying that, because his family had faced death so many times in Vietnam, the family became closer; and once they were free of Vietnam, they felt a moral obligation to help each other overcome any obstacle. Although I know that my parents love me, saying things of that nature is considered unnecessary in my family. I feel intimacy is lacking in my family. There is a degree of shame or embarrassment in saying that you love or care for someone. Tsung claims these tensions or apprehensions just do not exist in his family. He explained that a family like his, which has been through hell and back, just cannot have those problems.

Tsung and his family celebrate all the holidays that Canadians do and also many of the traditional Vietnamese holidays. Although Christmas is associated with happiness and sharing, it also holds an element of grief for them. One of Tsung's older brothers defected to the North Vietnamese army one Christmas Eve, and Tsung has heard from him only twice since then. Christmas gift giving, according to Tsung, is very personal and done with the utmost sincerity. In my family, gift giving is just something that is done. My brother buys me something so as not to feel guilty; I, in turn, buy him something.

Tsung was not very surprised to hear that I do not attend church. He informed me that he felt guilty if he did not go to church every Sunday and pray. I asked him why he felt he needed to be in church, specifically on Sunday, to pray. The question seemed to catch him off guard. He finally answered that, because his parents do, he does as well. He had never really questioned going to church. It was just something that people did. I suggested that the Good Lord was there, twenty-four hours a day, and all one had to do was talk and He would listen. I also insisted that one did not have to be dressed to the nines to talk to God; that if I wanted, I could talk to Him in the shower, while I was changing the oil in my car, or just about any time or place. As long as I was sincere in my thoughts, they would be heard. Tsung seemed perplexed at the simplicity of my statement as if he expected me to become more technical at any moment. He confessed that my thoughts were worth examining, but maintained that he would still attend church every Sunday.

I asked what he thought about communism and I was quite surprised to hear that he accepts it. He personally does not care for it but accepts it nonetheless. This acceptance of communism became more understandable to me as he explained his version of why North Vietnam would wage war for thirty years to rid itself and the rest of the country of capitalism. Why, he asked, should anybody want to live in poverty all their lives, be worked to the bone in their own country, only to see the fruits of their labour line the pockets of the French land and factory owners? He believes that the North Vietnamese had the right idea when they wanted the French out of the country, but it saddens him to see that they turned to the Soviet Union for help. After hearing Tsung's version, I have to confess

> that I agree with him 100 percent. If I had grown up in the conditions that Tsung described to me, I think that I would be compelled to do something about it as well.
>
> Tsung mentioned that he and his family have not experienced any racism, but he does admit that he thinks others feel sorry for him. He explained that this bothers him to no end, because, if you feel sorry for someone, that fuels the notion that nothing can be done to help the individual, that the situation is hopeless and the person is eternally bound in his predicament. Tsung says he does not want anybody feeling sorry for him; rather, he wants him and his family to be accepted as they are.
>
> My final question to Tsung was whether he had any personal prejudices or if there were a particular type of person he disliked. He answered that he did not have any personal prejudices. When I told him that I thought he might be hiding something, he simply repeated his initial statement, and I left it at that.
>
> I came away from the interview feeling satisfied that I had been able to tap information from this person who had been through so much and was quite willing to share his thoughts with me. Tsung is religious, smart and carries his own thoughts and his family means more to him than anything on the face of the earth. I only wish that the members of my family were as sincere and devoted towards each other.

SUMMARY

With few exceptions, all the participants stated that, while there were differences between themselves and the interviewees, the similarities were "far deeper and far more important than [the] differences." As a result, John suggested that

> respect must be engendered for the differences of our many cultural heritages, for it is only in this manner that we can learn from and grow with each other.... Only after careful examination of a different culture can we begin to see that, although we appear dissimilar outwardly, there seems to be a sameness that is evident only if we make a conscious effort to discover each others' individuality within.

Many of the writers were "fascinated" with the discoveries they made. They talked about being able to "now understand some of the feelings," ideas, values and aspirations of the people they interviewed. These participants talked of having gained insight into the disadvantages that minorities experience and their struggles to retain their cultural identities and gain acceptance, particularly from dominant group members. As Lyn said,

> [For] Franco-Ontarians, and perhaps this could be generalized to any other ethnic group living within a different majority ethnic culture ... acceptance and definition of differences can become crucial in the preservation of a distinct ethnic identity. Awareness of similar needs by the majority culture is also crucially important in preserving both cultures.

Racism was seen as one of the unpleasant differences between minority and dominant group members, as articulated by Tina:

> The difference that I saw was not a pleasant one. Both of us have to deal with racism but in different ways. Sam has to put up with stereotypes from white people, and she hopes that someday things will improve. There is still a lot of education needed. In my case, I have to deal with being a racist at times. I too had my stereotypes about the Native Canadians, but after my interview with Sam and my research on the Natives, I have a better insight into the attitudes and beliefs of the Canadian Indians. I think all people should follow this rule: "Do not judge lest ye be judged."

Is this sufficient? Does a conversation with an individual from a particular racial or ethnic community really provide "insight" into that individual's experiences? What "insight?" Insight that confirms existing knowledge of that community? What if the interviewees' comments had conflicted with the knowledge that the interviewers brought to the conversations? Would they have continued the conversation? Do these interview situations provide individuals, particularly majority group individuals, with the opportunity to engage in the process of Othering and the production of a discourse about their white English selves?

That almost all of the writers featured here are of English Canadian background is largely due to the composition of the classes. It is therefore understandable that many of those interviewed are members of minority groups. Evidently the politics of difference is played out in these interview situations. The interviewer is likely to set the agenda and exercise control by deciding whom to interview, what questions to ask, how far to proceed with a particular point and what information is relevant. The interviewers also decide whether or not to share information about themselves, and if they do so, what and how much they will share. Hence, it is quite possible for these interview situations to re-inscribe the structurally unequal relationships between individuals based on race, ethnicity, language, and immigrant and/or citizenship status, as well as social class and gender.

These structurally unequal relationships are particularly evident in some of the essays. Take for example, John, who interviewed Bill of the Sioux Nation. We first met him in Chapter 3, where he talked about himself only in relation to his "African friend" and the all-African party he attended, and gave us very little information about himself. Here again, even while telling us about Bill's family, religious beliefs and experience with "prejudice," John shares almost no information about himself, so a comparison is really never made. So is it true, as John says, that he has come to understand himself and Bill? Are his "commonsense understandings" (Sleeter, 1993) structured in such a way so as to preserve his privilege and power that has been gained from and perpetuated through structural forms of racism against First Nations people? (Another participant who did little to expose or interrogate her location or identity is Sharon.)

It seems, therefore, that while this exercise helped to expose students to the Other, what is gained depends on the consciousness or frames that inform the approaches of the interviewers, and their willingness and readiness to interrogate themselves–to look deeply and critically at their location. Understandably, participants seek to avoid doing so. What we are likely to see, as is revealed in many of the essays, is evidence of ethnocentricism, ethnicism, racism and religious prejudices, as well as attempts to re-inscribe whiteness as the cultural norm. John's comment contained a telling point: when referring to Bill's mixed heritage, John wrote that "certain facial features, although somewhat *softened* by his father's [white] genetic influence, are evocative of the Indian stereotype"(emphasis added).

In sum, I would suggest that exercises such as visiting communities and having conversations with individuals from particular ethnic and racial backgrounds are useful only if participants are encouraged to critically examine the politics of the situation and their role in it. It seems that those individuals who have acknowledged their cultural selves (in many cases, minorities) are more willing to engage in conversation and share of themselves, rather than merely asking questions to gain information.

SUGGESTIONS FOR DISCUSSION

1. To what extent would you say that exposure to another cultural group is able to provide insights into our own cultural identity?
2. Is exposure or interaction with other racial or ethnic groups sufficient to provide insight into the culture of that group?
3. What is your view of those students who believe that they have gained a heightened awareness of another person's struggles in our society simply by having interviewed them?

Photo: Dick Hemingway

CHAPTER 5

Stereotyping, Racism and Discrimination

Ramish: *"All I wanted was the opportunity to play and to be treated like everyone else."*

Racism has affected me personally ever since I can remember. I lost opportunities, I felt, because of my skin colour and nationality. I love hockey and have been playing since I was young. I remember the name calling and repeatedly being told that I couldn't play hockey because I was not white. I was made fun of and laughed at, and I was usually the last one picked for teams. I grew up in a white neighbourhood, and as all the kids played hockey, I began practising the game in hope that one day I could play with everyone else. After a couple of months of practise I became a better player, as I was faster and much smarter than the rest of the guys. I was asked to play for higher calibre teams because I excelled in the sport. I was always working hard but was still being made fun of by the opposing teams. My team mates learned to accept me. However, when another minority played on another team, they taunted him with the same names used against me by the other teams. All I wanted was the opportunity to play and to be treated like everybody else. I finally learned to work harder and shield myself from the comments. Unfortunately I would go home and feel the effect of the cruelty and meanness of some people. One comment I will always remember is, "You can never skate because your ankles are too weak."

In the above comments, Ramish contends that racism is responsible for his lack of equal opportunity to play hockey, a game he loved and enjoyed. He declares that, despite his hard work and the learned acceptance of his team mates, his "skin colour and nationality" were factors that limited the extent to which he excelled in the game. Is Ramish correct or merely showing that he has "a chip on his shoulder"? (See Camille's comments in the section "Stereotyping" in this chapter.) Is it racism when his team mates accept Ramish but taunt another minority player with the same names? Is it possible that these names are simply "friendly jokes" that Ramish should have learned to appreciate if he really regarded himself as part of the team? Were his team mates really cruel and mean? After all, they played with him. Is Ramish correct in his seeming doubts about being accepted by his peers? And is it really true that certain groups of people do not become good skaters, and hence good hockey players, because their "ankles are too weak"?

If there is any doubt concerning Ramish's conclusion that what he experienced in hockey was racism, then the above questions are worth exploring. Surely Ramish's experiences cannot be explained away as simply coincidences, or on his being in the wrong place at the wrong time. Neither can his lack of success in hockey be attributed to his efforts and skills alone. Indeed, Herb Carnegie (1997) has provided good historical evidence of the extent to which, and the ways in which, skin colour has operated to limit the presence of racial minorities in the game of hockey, Canada's "national sport" (Gruneau and Whitson, 1993). What Ramish is alerting us to is more than peer group taunts and coaches' oversights and preferences, but systemic practices and values that exist, not only in hockey or in sports generally, but in our society as a whole. After all, why would Ramish's team mates understand that the name they had used against Ramish in their taunts would obtain the same results if applied to another minority player? The fact is that racism exists in our society, and it is demonstrated and felt, not only in individual attitudes, speech and behaviour, but also in institutional policies and practices. Racism is structural, or, in another word, systemic. Whichever the word, it means that it is inherent in our society.

We will explore issues of racism in this chapter. While individuals' essays, telling of their values, attitudes, ideas and experiences, will form the basis of our discussion, what is emphasized is the basis of these values, attitudes and experiences. In other words, what structural or systemic factors inform the values, attitudes, ideas and experiences of individuals? In our exploration, it is necessary to define terms in order to establish the understanding we bring to this discussion. These definitions were shared with participants. However, in many cases their essays reflect their confusion with the terms or, more likely, their disagreement with the definitions. One example is the term *racism.* Bearing in mind that many of the participants are young white people, the reader will observe that the word *prejudice* and, less frequently, *ethnocentrism* or *bias*, is used in instances where racism might have been more appropriate. This is, as some participants argued, because they have difficulty seeing and accepting the racism by which they have been informed, live their live, construct others and understand their community, society and the world. As one participant pointed out, attitudes are hard to change.

Donna: Racist attitudes cannot be changed overnight when they have been a part of me for twenty-one years, but I am more aware of the feelings that others have. Although I maintain the belief that whites are biologically superior to Blacks, I appreciate now that Blacks, like all racial groups, are people who, like me, have feelings and bleed red blood.

It is more than the length of time that Donna has held this attitude that makes it difficult to change, for the attitude is sustained by the ideology of racism, like classism, sexism and others, that socializes people in their belief structure. Why would Donna say that, even though she knows better, she "maintains that whites are biologically superior to Blacks"? Evidently, the education she is receiving from school, university, media, courts and religious[1] and other institutions does not help her to challenge her belief. One post-secondary education course, therefore, might be seen by her as providing anomalous information.

In addition to *racism*, sociologists and anthropologists use other terms, such as *ethnocentrism*, *prejudice*, *stereotyping* and *discrimination*, to represent the various ideologies, attitudes and behaviours of individuals. Beginning with ethnocentrism, we will explore the meanings of these terms and use examples to illustrate how individuals understand them and relate their experiences to them. We then explore minority group members' experiences of racism and their reactions to it. Participants critically examine and theorize about the sources of stereotypes in their essays in the section entitled "Seeing beyond the Stereotypes." In the section that follows, their ideas about how stereotyping, racism and discrimination could be eliminated are presented. The chapter concludes with an essay by Adrienne Shadd, who again invites us to think of racism and discrimination not only as pertaining to individuals attitudes and behaviours, but as something that has long been a part of the Canadian society.

According to Shadd, racism is "not simply a phenomenon which afflicts the minds of individuals and causes these individuals to perform discriminatory acts." Rather, "racism is something that afflicts an entire society; it is ingrained and reinforced in all the major and minor institutions of the society." She recounts personal experiences in which individuals expressed negative attitudes towards her and talks about the "derogatory" images of Blacks found in the media. She talks about being discriminated against by the man in the local ice cream parlour who would serve them last, after all the whites had been served; and about "certain eateries, hotels and recreational clubs" that were closed to Blacks. In terms of structure, she writes that, "even in the most seemingly 'objective' of undertakings, such as the writing of our national history, racism has operated to exclude minority groups from the historical landscape, thus rendering their accomplishments invisible, and therefore insignificant."

---

[1] In discussing the education she received from religious institutions on race and racism, one student, Jody, wrote: "'Jesus loves the little children / All the little children of the world / Red and Yellow; Black and White / they are precious in his sight / Jesus loves the little children of the world.' This song, which I sang in Sunday school as a child, never gave me the message that was intended! As Southern Baptists, we sang about people being equal but never believed it. People were only equal if they were white. When reflecting back over our discussions, I realize that I received two very different teachings as a child. My Christian faith taught me to love all of mankind, but my society taught me to love only the white sector of mankind."

ETHNOCENTRISM

It is very common for a person to use his or her knowledge and experience to evaluate another and thus put forth a set of expectations. This practice, however, often leads to *ethnocentrism*, in which we operate on the notion that everyone in our society, irrespective of racial and ethnic background, should speak like us, live like us and participate in all the same activities.

Ethnocentrism refers to the tendency to see things from the perspective of your own ethnic group culture, and to see your cultural symbols as being somehow preferable. It can also mean the assumption that what is true of your ethnic group culture is also true of other cultures (Carroll, 1993: 26). Ethnocentrism, then, can be seen as an uncompromising allegiance and loyalty to one's own cultural values and practices, which are viewed as natural, normal and necessary.

The belief that the culture of one's own group is preferable might appear harmless. Problems arise, however, when individuals establish expectations based on this assumption and begin to use their cultural "standards" as a frame of reference for interpreting and evaluating the behaviour of other groups. Elliott and Fleras (1992) point out that, "not surprisingly, these groups are rated inferior, backward, or irrational. It can be seen that although favouritism towards one's own group can promote cohesion and morale, it can also contribute to intergroup tension and hostility ... [and] to a proliferation of stereotypes about outgroup members" (p.55).

PREJUDICE

Over time, the word *prejudice* has come to mean an unfavourable attitude based on an uninformed judgement (Haas and Shaffir, 1978: 24), or having preconceived opinions that are assumed to be true before having been tested (Driedger, 1989: 350). Elliot and Fleras (1992) define prejudice as a set of biased and generalized beliefs (stereotypes) about outgroups derived largely from inaccurate and incomplete information. It "involves that attitudinal component of identity formation, boundary maintenance, and intergroup relations." These faulty and inflexible generalizations contribute to a frame of mind that makes it difficult to evaluate minority groups "in an impartial, objective, and accurate manner" (p.335).

The word *bias* is often substituted for prejudice. While biases can be both positive and negative, ethnic prejudice is usually negative. It is an unfounded, irrational, rigid judgment involving emotions, attitudes and subjective evaluation. Typically, such attitudes, predispositions or pre-judgments are not reversed or changed even when new information is revealed.

The tendency to categorize and make pre-judgements may be seen as necessary, as the human mind needs to organize the stimuli with which it is bombarded. We need to select and store only some of the many experiences and "facts" available to us in order to effectively react or respond to them. As we acquire new experiences and information, we tend to assimilate them as much as possible into the categories that already exist. This enables us to identify related objects and retrieve information quickly (Driedger, 1989).

Depending on the experiences of a particular individual, this clustering or categorization process will involve some emotion. A person may have more negative feelings about some experiences and related persons than others. Some categories are more rational than others, but the process permits us to slip easily into ethnic prejudice. Erroneous generalizations are sometimes made and, indeed, some categories may reflect, not merely feelings of dislike, but feelings of actual hostility. And, while social distance from others may be the result of a desire to maintain a separate ethnic identity, it can also stem from negative attitudes (Driedger, 1986).

RACISM

Simply stated, *racism* is the uncritical acceptance of a negative social definition of a colonized or subordinate group typically identified by physical features (i.e., race–black, brown, yellow, red). These "racialized groups"[2] are believed to lack certain abilities or characteristics, which in turn characterizes them as culturally and biologically inferior. Discriminatory or unequal treatment towards these groups is often legitimized or justified in this way. Elliott and Fleras (1992) define racism as "a doctrine that unjustifiably asserts the superiority of one group over another on the basis of arbitrarily selected characteristics pertaining to appearance, intelligence, or temperament" (p.52). In his definition, van den Burghe (1967) identifies the link between race and racism. He refers to racism as "an ideology which considers a group's unchangeable physical characteristics to be linked in a direct causal way to physical or intellectual characteristics, and which on this basis distinguishes between superior and inferior racial groups."

Ng (1993) refers to racism as "common sense" or a "taken-for-granted" way of thinking that can be incoherent and at times contradictory. She contends that conceptualizing racism, like sexism, in terms of common sense

[2] Racialization refers to fact that social significance is attached to the physical differences, i.e., skin colour, of these groups (Satzewich, 1998; 1991). In the Americas generally, and Canada in particular, the first group of people to be "racialized" were the Aboriginals. This was part of the process of colonialization.

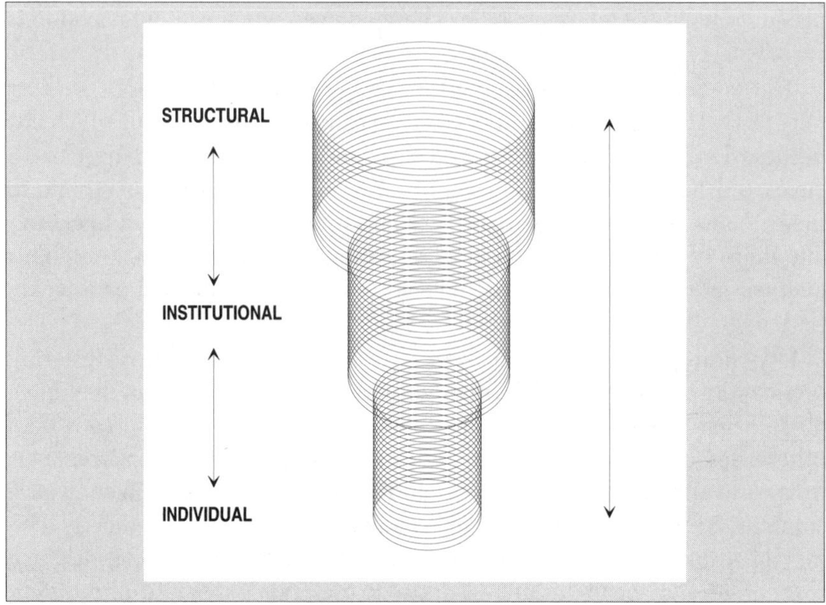

Figure 3: Dimensions of racism.

draws "attention to the norms and forms of actions that have become ordinary ways of doing things, of which we have little consciousness, so that certain things 'disappear from the social surface.'" Quoting Himani Bannerji, Ng states that "racism becomes an everyday and 'normal' way of seeing. Its banality and invisibility is such that it is quite likely that there may be entirely 'politically correct' white individuals who have a deeply racist perception of the world" (p.52).

What is most salient in the way in which racism is conceptualized is not the biological or physical differences between the groups but "the public recognition of these differences as being significant for assessment, explanation, and interaction" (Elliot and Fleras, 1992: 55). A key component of racism is power, not in terms of the "everyday" influence one individual might have over another, but in terms of influence that is supported by ideological, economical, political, social and cultural conditions of the society. In this case, power is seen as a regular and continuous part of everyday human existence, sustained by established laws, regulations and/or policies or by accepted conventions and customs. As sociologist C. Wright Mills (1956) argues, only those with access to the command of the major institutions in society can truly have power.

Racism operates in different forms, and at different levels. Expressions can be wilful, deliberate, conscious, or they can be indirect, unintentional, reflexive and unconscious. These expressions are reflected in individual attitudes and belief systems and in institutional and societal policies and regulations (see Figure 3). To elaborate, *individual racism* is the negative attitudes that individuals hold regarding others. It is an ideology–a set of ideas and related beliefs held by a person who may or may not act on them.

Dobbins and Skillings (1991) explain that racism operates only in cases where individuals, because of their membership in a particular racial group, have access to power and are able to enforce their racial prejudices.

> In this sense, although people of colour can be on the receiving end of racist acts in this society and frequently hold prejudices about members of the dominant group, as a group they lack power to enforce or act on these prejudices. For this reason, it is said that people of colour do not act in racist ways unless they are acting as agents for the dominant power structure (Dobbins and Skillings, 1991: 41).

"White Europeans" (Philip, 1992), and more particularly, "white European men, especially those of British and French descent" (Ng, 1993), are the ones who, because of their ascribed or inherited status in our society, possess power.

Institutional racism, sometimes referred to as systemic racism (James, 1993; Elliot and Fleras, 1992; Arnold et al., 1991), exists where the established policies, rules and regulations of an organization or institution systematically reflect and produce differential treatment of various groups within that organization or institution and in society generally. These regulations "are used to maintain social control and the status quo in favour of the dominant group" (Dobbins and Skillings 1991: 42). There is a reciprocal relationship between institutional and individual racism. The racist policies and practices of institutions are developed and implemented by individuals who, because of their training and allegiance to the organization, understand that they must adhere to the norms (including the role relationships) and sanctions to maintain the "order of things."

The third form of racism is referred to as *structural racism*. Other writers refer to it as cultural racism (Henry, 1994; Anderson and Frideres, 1981), institutional racism (Philip, 1992; Elliott and Fleras, 1992; Satzewich, 1998; Lee, 1985) or systemic racism (Arnold et al., 1991). Like Hughes and Kallen (1974), we will call it structural racism. It refers to the way in which the rooted inequalities of society operate to justify the allocation of racial groups to particular categories and class sites. It explains how the ideas of inferiority and superiority, based on socially selected physical characteristics, and which are found in society's norms and values, operate to exclude racial minority group members from accessing and participating in major social and cultural institutions. Hughes and Kallen (1974) suggest that it is structural racism that is particularly relevant when examining racism and discrimination in Canada. They contend that, because of structural racism, minority group members are denied access to the qualifications, education and skills necessary for full participation in society (p.106).

Other types of racism are mentioned in the literature. One is "red-neck racism"–what some refer to as the "old-fashioned racism." It is characterized by its overt, conscious, deliberate and highly personal attacks (including derogatory slurs and name calling) on those who are perceived to be culturally and biologically inferior (Elliott and Fleras, 1992: 58). "Polite racism," the way in which Canadian racism is often depicted (Philip, 1992; Henry, 1978), refers to "the deliberate attempt to disguise racist attitudes through behaviour that outwardly is non-prejudicial or discriminatory in appearance" (Elliott and Fleras, 1992: 59). Finally, the "new racism," described by Elliott and Fleras (1992) as "disguised and sophisticated," reflects the conflict of opposing values within individuals. More precisely, it is "a contemporary expression of racial hostility towards racial minorities that goes undetected by conventional measures." Within Canadian society, this form of racism is seen to be "an ambiguous and disguised response to the growing presence of increasingly assertive racial minorities" whose activities and demands are criticized as a threat to national identity and social harmony (Elliott and Fleras, 1992: 62).

Ethnocentrism, prejudice and racism are attitudes and ideologies, found among individuals, that affirm the superiority of dominant group members and the inferiority of racial minority group members. The systems of ideas and practices that have developed over time to justify and support the notion of superiority "become the premise upon which societal norms and values are based, and the practices become the "normal way of doing things" (Ng, 1993: 52). Power is the critical component within which the exercise of ethnocentrism, prejudice and racism operate. Specifically, institutionalized power, embodied in the values, norms, regulations, laws and practices of society and institutions, operates to benefit dominant groups over minority groups.

In the following excerpts, participants reflect on their ideas, opinions and attitudes and attempt to assess whether or not their ideas and attitudes are racist. In the first piece, Angella, suggesting that her ideas are "informed" through her experience of "growing up with Indians," and although admitting that the government has something to do with their historical conditions in Canada, still concludes that she does "not think that I could ever change the way I view Indians by trying to look at the situation from their point of view." She seems resigned to living with her racism. This is important, for what we see is that, even thought the information she receives suggests otherwise, Angella thinks that her experience of growing up with Aboriginal people is reason enough for her to maintain her racist ideas. This is evidence of the point made in the previous chapter, that interaction does not necessarily guarantee critical awareness and attitudinal change. Structures will also have to change. This will require that the

Canadian governments put structures in place that address the ideological approach to, and the unequal situation of, Aboriginal peoples.

Angella: *"I have a hard time feeling sorry for people who are not willing to help themselves."*

One thing I have found out about myself, of which I am not particularly proud, is that I am racially prejudiced. I had always understood prejudice to mean an uninformed judgment or negative attitude towards a person or group of people. I have always had a very bad attitude towards Native Canadians, but it was not an uninformed or misleading opinion. I grew up with Indians, and my attitude towards them developed over a number of years. I feel that the Canadian government is creating an inferior race of people by giving them everything. I have a hard time feeling sorry for people who are not willing to help themselves.

I am fully aware of the fact that the white man took their land, and they do deserve some kind of compensation, but there has got to be a better way for the government to deal with the problem. I realize that their culture is one of hunting, fishing and living off the land, but there is not enough land and resources to support all the Indians for the generations to come. It is unrealistic to think that they can live the way their ancestors did.

I know that I am being ethnocentric and that I expect them to change their values and beliefs, but it is hard to look at their situation clearly. I mean, when a community can tell it is pay day on the reserves by the number of Indians passed out on the streets downtown, you become a little sceptical of the way the government is handling the situation. I honestly do not think that I could ever change the way I view Indians by trying to look at the situation from their point of view. My opinion is set from many years of having to deal with these people, and I guess now when people ask me if I am racist, I have to say "yes."

The following reflections of Christine and Brenda are in response to a question that was often raised in class. Often participants would say that one's choice of a marriage partner is based on preference and hence cannot be seen as "prejudiced" or "racist." What do you think? (see also Nadine's comments in the section "Responses of Minorities" in this chapter).

Christine: *"A great friend, but I would never marry him ..."*

Two main topics of particular interest to me are prejudice and stereotyping. Dave, whom I consider to be a close friend of mine, is half Black and half white. His skin colour is very noticeable, but because we are friends, I thought that there was no possible way that I could ever be prejudiced or racist. After learning the definition of prejudice, I realize I was and still am, to a degree, racist.

Certainly Dave is a great friend but I would never marry or even get romantically involved with him because of his skin colour. I am definitely displaying racism. I still don't understand why the colour of one's skin is so important to people when it is their personality that should matter. However, my background is from a strong, white, Roman Catholic family. We hold very closely to the traditional views of white women marrying white men and Black women marrying Black men.

Brenda: *"Would you marry someone of another race?"*

Recently, a friend and I were discussing whether we would marry someone of another race and/or ethnicity. Of course, there is no quick and clear-cut answer to this question as many matters must be taken into consideration. At first, we both agreed that people are people, and just that, whether black or white or yellow or red. When we thought about the fact that we might have been raised to be culturally different, a few doubts surfaced.

My friend told me about a former boyfriend of hers. In his culture, women are placed on this earth only to satisfy man's every whim. This caused a great many arguments, and even though they were both willing to try to adjust their cultural differences, it was too difficult a problem for them to deal with.

After her admission, I became more critical of my self-righteous attitudes. I began to question whether or not I really could marry a person of a different race and/or ethnicity. Even if I could accept this man for who he is, would I be able to cope with the stares and criticism of others? There is much more involved than a simple, "Of course I'm not prejudiced!" Parental acceptance is very important in our society. I know for a fact that my parents would not have wanted me to marry someone of a different race or ethnicity. I concluded that marrying someone of a different race with a different cultural background is not for me.

I was told that this thinking was racist and prejudiced. I felt very wronged. I thought that I saw people only for who they are inside. I thought I would be friends with someone who was of a different race or ethnicity without even considering that fact, but marrying someone is a different matter. It is not the same as being friends. I now realize that this thinking is just as prejudiced as any other.

Rita, a participant who at one time was a partner in an inter-racial marriage, offered the following comment. It demonstrates the structural, and not simply the individual, nature of racism.

Rita: *"Inter-racial marriage cannot be based on love alone, for too many lives are at stake."*

I get the impression that people are very naive about inter-racial marriages. Their first reaction to the question of inter-racial marriage is a quick, "Yes, it's okay." They defend that quick answer by professing that love will take care of all of the troubles such marriages might bring. They never even take time to consider any factors realistically, such as having to deal with parents, churches, social groups, children and unknown prejudices.

I have experienced such a marriage, but before I got married I went through dozens of scenarios making sure that I could back my thoughts with real convictions. I had to know the answers before the questions were asked. I have a five-year-old daughter, and when she came home from school upset, wanting to know if she was white like her mommy or Native Indian like her daddy, I had the right answer for her. I would not walk into an inter-racial marriage with only love to use as an answer, for too many lives are at stake.

STEREOTYPING

The concept of the *stereotype* was first used by Lippmann in 1922 to refer to the manner in which ideas, images and habits are accumulated, shaped and hardened. The term originated in the printing industry of the time, in which a "stereotype" was a metal plate with a uniform matrix of type that was moulded so that printing was standard and unchanging. For the social scientist, the concept of the social stereotype refers to "a highly exaggerated picture, the intervention of supposed traits, and the formation of incomplete images leaving little room for change or individual variation" (Driedger, 1989: 343).

Taylor (1981) delineates stereotypes as people's perceptions or beliefs about others rather than ideas based on factual information. It is characterized by shared beliefs–a set of characteristics believed by large numbers of one group to be true of another. They are flawed judgments of others, since applying characteristics to entire groups involves overcategorization and overgeneralization. This tendency to categorize and generalize about racial and ethnic minority groups is often accompanied by a strong belief in the "correctness" or "truth" of the stereotype and a disregard for fact. Stereotypes sometimes emerge from a person's encounters and experiences (good or bad) with members of other ethnic or racial groups.

Stereotypes serve first to categorize, organize or simplify the amount of extremely complex information that we receive in order to reduce it into manageable units. And when little or nothing is known about a group, stereotypes "fill in" the missing information, thus providing an organized perception of the group. Second, stereotypes satisfy the need for individuals to view themselves in a positive light. Individuals tend to have perceptions and cognitions of their environment that reinforce their positive self-image. If individuals' attitudes towards their own group are extremely favourable and attitudes towards an outside group are less so, this indirectly reinforces their view that they are good people.

To the extent that stereotypes refer "to people's perceptions and beliefs" and contain a "kernel of truth," they can serve a useful purpose when used to understand cultural differences and similarities. They can be guides to behaviour and can play a role in inter-group relations. Indirectly, they can help in defining one's self and social status (Taylor, 1981: 155). When stereotypes refer to a group's attributes in a positive way, the consequences are socially desirable insofar as "the particular intergroup stereotypes satisfy the desires of both groups involved, and where intergroup interaction is not characterized by destructive forms of conflict" (Taylor, 1981: 163). But as Driedger reminds us,

> the assumption that when we know the facts about another person or group, we will act on those facts is not necessarily true. Reason does not always prevail: emotions often impose positive and negative evaluations. When images of others become rigid, like the printer's stereotype, and when they produce the same reaction automatically without further examination, then we have a social stereotype (1989: 344).

The following essay excerpt by Camille, in which she shares her views of Black people, is an example of stereotyping. Where might she be getting all this information? Are her experiences sufficient basis for the conclusions she draws?

Camille: *"They suggest we are being prejudiced ..."*

It is my opinion and that of many others that Blacks carry too much of a chip on their shoulder, and they are too quick to scream prejudice. In working at a track and field centre, I have had much contact with Blacks and have had a chance to observe Black behaviour. What I have noticed is that many Blacks have a very hostile attitude. They are constantly trying to manipulate everything. Since most of the athletes at the centre are Black, the roles are reversed and the white staff is in the minority. If something does not please them particularly, they suggest that we are being prejudiced. There have been a number of occasions when I have asked both Black and white athletes to comply with rules. In response, I have been called prejudiced and a few other choice names by the Black person, while the White person does as I ask without incident. The Black athletes are intolerably rude and unfavourable. I must say here that this is not always the case. I have met many rude white people and many pleasant Black people. Generally, though, aggressiveness in Blacks tends to be greater than aggressiveness in whites.

Geographic location can determine what type of work is available and general working habits. In the case of Black immigrants, they have traditionally worked in tropical plantations and as unskilled labour because that is what is available to them. Their educational system is much different than ours. This lends itself to lower-skilled labour for Blacks according to Canadian standards, leading to increased difficulty in job placement and advancement, low-paying jobs and manipulation into scab labour. The hot climate of Black native lands, such as Jamaica and Africa, requires the Black race to

> be somewhat "laid back" and more relaxed. Lighter work and longer breaks are requirements in a regular work day.
>
> Black social habits also differ greatly from Canadian customs. "Hanging out" as it is called, is a form of leisure, and sexual promiscuity is much more accepted. Unfortunately, when one "hangs out" in Canada, he is the target of criticism and often regarded as a troublemaker. When it comes to drugs and alcohol use, it is a fact that Blacks are more likely to become addicted. This is not because they use the substances more than whites, but rather because their body systems are different; they have lower levels of tolerance.

DISCRIMINATION

Ethnocentrism, prejudice and racism are attitudes and ideologies; *discrimination* is the action that results from these attitudes and ideologies. It is "the process of putting negative cognitions into practice" (Elliot and Fleras, 1992: 56). Specifically, discrimination can be defined as "applied prejudice in which negative social definitions are translated into action and political policy, the subordination of minorities and deprivation of their political, social and economic rights" (Kinloch, 1974: 54). There are typically four denotations of discriminatory treatment: differential, prejudicial, disadvantageous and the denial of desire (Driedger, 1989; Hagan, 1987).

Differential treatment is the difference in treatment of one group by another. This form of discrimination is said to exist when members of a given group who meet all the necessary requirements to participate in activities within the society or institutions are denied the opportunity to do so. They are "not treated in conformity with the nominally universal institutionalized codes" (Hagan, 1987: 338). Insofar as differential treatment is applied to produce equality of results or outcomes, then the context–the social and historical situation of the groups–must be taken into consideration. As was pointed out in our discussion of racism, inequality in power and access to resources produces unequal outcomes. Hence, differential treatment will be required in some cases to produce equality of outcome.

The behavioural expression of prejudice or bigotry results in differential treatment, or perpetrators' behaviour, premised on malice or malevolent motives. The complexity of this form of discrimination is identified by many researchers. For example, Hagan (1987) notes that it is difficult to infer motives from behaviour and that prejudice can be a consequence, as well as a cause, of discrimination. In addition, "historical processes can presumably create self-fulfilling prophecies that may eventually conceal the conditions that created them. For example, patterns of differential treatment can create attitudes of resignation and acceptance on the part of

Table 4: Distribution of Population by Major Religious Affiliation for Selected Ethnic Origins, Canada, 1991

	Catholic	Protestant	Eastern Non-Christian	Other Religious Affiliation	No Religious Affiliation
British	21.5	63.6	0.2	0.3	14.3
French	94	2.7	0.1	0.1	3.1
German	24	63.6	0.1	0.3	11.9
Ukrainian	43.4	24.8	0.1	19.1	12.6
Italian	93.9	3.5	0.1	0.2	2.3
South Asian	7.5	5.4	84	0.3	2.9
Chinese	13.3	15.5	12.3	0.1	58.7
Aboriginal	50.9	34.3	0.3	2	12.6
Canadian	25.8	48.1	0.6	1.3	24.3
Other	39.8	27.4	7.3	15.8	9.7
Total	31.6	49.1	0.9	1.6	16.8

Source: Statistics Canada, 1991 Census.

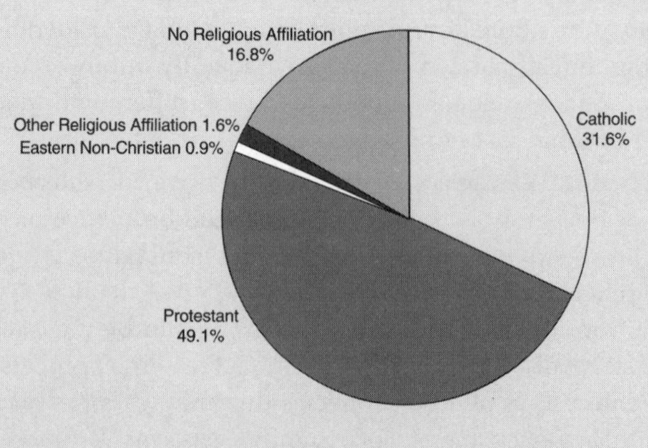

recipients that eventually make moot the possibility of their prejudicial origins" (Hagan, 1987: 342).

Some of the clearest forms of discrimination with which we are familiar are those in which individuals are denied equal opportunity to compete in our democratic society for the rewards to which they are entitled–their "rights." This occurs, for example, when members of ethnic and racial minority groups are abused verbally; when they are the target of ethnic or racial jokes; when they are

> subjected to literature which represents them in a hateful and derogatory manner; and when they are harassed, their property is vandalized, or they are attacked physically. This is referred to as disadvantageous treatment. It is defined as the treatment which occurs when individuals are placed at some disadvantage that is not merited by their own misconduct. It may be characterized as the "effective injurious treatment of persons on grounds rationally irrelevant to the situation" (Driedger, 1989: 351).

Hagan (1987) denotes discrimination that involves "denial of preference" as denial of desire. This is to be differentiated from cases in which particular individuals or groups choose voluntarily not to participate or to take advantage of opportunities in society because they wish to remain in the security of their group (e.g., Hutterites and Aboriginals) (Dreidger, 1989). Individuals who seek full participation and equality are presumed to be discriminated against if they are unfairly denied access to, and opportunities in, education, jobs, housing and so on.

In sum, discrimination is the unequal treatment of individuals or groups through the granting or denying of certain rights. In the case of minority groups, this treatment is often based, not on an individuals' abilities and skills, but on characteristics such as skin colour, language, accent and other physical traits. Discrimination involves differential treatment where restrictions are placed on the aspirations of some members of society, such as their desire to live where they choose, or their desire to work at any job for which they are qualified. Finally, disadvantageous treatment, such as jokes, name calling, physical attacks and ejection from a community, are clearly types of discrimination.

Like racism, discrimination operates at different levels and consists of a complex set of ideas and actions. Researchers indicate that, although there is a causal relationship between ethnocentrism, prejudice, racism and discrimination, they can vary independently under certain conditions. As Elliott and Fleras point out, "fear, threats, sanctions, company policy, or good sense may encourage individuals to compartmentalize their prejudices and divorce them from everyday action" (1992: 56). Like racism, discriminatory practices are known to be inherent in the economic, political and social structure of Canada.

The educational assimilation and genocidal practices against Aboriginal peoples, the enslavement of Africans, the treatment of Black Empire Loyalists, the Chinese "Head Tax," the continuous travel edict that prevented South Asians from entering Canada, the failure to permit the entry of Jews during the 1940s, the incarceration of citizens of Japanese heritage during World War II, the failure to remove restrictions on non-white immigrants until the early 1970s, the segregated schooling, the low educational achievement, the high unemployment and underemployment among racial minorities[3] and the unfair practices in the justice system are all examples of structural and institutional discriminatory practices. These are part of Canadian history and inform our socialization, ideas, attitudes and behaviours. There is no question then, that discrimination is rooted in our society,[4] and we are all affected by it either as objects or as unwitting perpetuators and collaborators. As Henry and Grinzberg (1985) note, discriminatory acts are not performed by an isolated "handful of bigots." They are to be found, not only in the actions of individuals, but also in the societal barriers that deny certain people access to opportunities. Through discrimination, certain groups of people are able to maintain their positions of privilege, largely at the expense of other groups who are deliberately or inadvertently excluded from full and equal participation in society.

Ethnocentrism, prejudice, racism, stereotyping and discrimination are not merely a result of ignorance or misinformation, but are mechanisms that are rooted in the inequalities of society, and promote and sustain existing social relations among racial and ethnic groups. These exist often, not as the result of individual acts, but as "a consequence of rules, procedures and criteria that all together have a discriminatory effect, *regardless* of motive or intent" (Philip, 1992: 158). Therefore, any analysis or discussion of these mechanisms must necessarily take into consideration the structural framework within which they exist. To ameliorate them requires more than

---

3 See Walker, 1980; Philip, 1992; Balski, 1992; Shepard, 1997; Ng, 1993; James, 1996; Anderson and Frideres, 1981; Billingsley and Muszynski, 1985; Abella, Commission on Equality in Employment, 1984; Head, 1975; Henry and Grinzberg, 1985; Haig-Brown, 1993; Henry et al., 1995; Hughes and Kallen, 1974; Ramcharan, 1975; Special Committee on Visible Minorities, 1984; Quamina, 1996; Mannette, 1992 Abella and Troper, 1982; Burnet and Palmer, 1989; Commission on Systematic Racism in the Ontario Criminal Justice System, 1995.

4 In an article entitled "The Canadian Origins of South African Apartheid?", Michèle DuCharme (1986: 2) compares the treatment of Natives in Canada and the then-apartheid situation of Blacks in South Africa. Noting the parallel situation due to colonialism, DuCharme writes that, according to information obtained from government documents in the Public Archives in Ottawa, "South African government official visited Canada at different times ... [between] 1948 to 1963 in order to tour Indian reserves and industrial schools in the West. For example, as late as July 1962, the South African High Commissioner W. Dirkse-van-Schalkwyk visited selected Indian reserves in Western Canada." DuCharme goes on to speculate about the establishment of the apartheid policies of South African in the early 1960s "around the same time that the South African High Commissioner was touring our Canadian reserves."

"exposure" to racial minority group members, such as having them as friends or hearing about them in school or through the media. It requires structural analysis, critical self-reflection and systemic change.

Evidence of racism, prejudice, ethnocentrism and discrimination is not always clear to certain individuals, as is the case for Kim.

Kim: *"After all, they were very much like us."*

I don't remember there being any Black people in the little town where I grew up until I was about ten years old. However, I do remember the first day they arrived at our school. Most of the kids stood around and stared; for most of us, it was the first time we had ever seen Black people. On their first day there, the teacher asked them to tell the class all about themselves. The two boys were twins and had just moved to our community from England. They were both very nice and by the first recess that day they had plenty of friends. After all, they were very much like us. They liked the same sports, they had the same hobbies, and they liked the new country they were living in. It was very hard not to like them, they were so nice.

Kim assumes that, because they eventually came to like the two boys, neither she nor her classmates displayed any prejudiced or racist behaviour. Note, however, that the race of the two boys was considered an obstacle. They had to prove themselves to be "very much like" the other children. Of significance are Kim's comments that "they liked the same sports, they had the same hobbies, and they liked the new country they were living in." What if these two Black English boys had not?

There are also instances in which an individual's "friendly actions" towards racial minorities are in fact based on racism. Actions are used to conceal beliefs and stereotyping. Jane's comments illustrate this.

Jane: *"I feel an astounding sense of intimidation with these people."*

Although one part of me still possesses the steadfast belief that I do not patronize people or treat people of different races with exaggerated kindness, another part of me acknowledges many preconceived stereotypes I have towards people of racial, ethnic and cultural backgrounds that are different from my own. I have also realized that I feel an astounding sense of intimidation with these people. What I mean by this is that sometimes I actually feel that it is necessary to be nice (not in an exaggerated fashion, however) to a person of a minority group even if he or she is not a friendly person. Why? Perhaps because I would prefer to be accepted on a first-impression basis, so that the person would recognize me as an individual who is unlike prejudiced people.

RACIAL JOKES

Individuals verbalize or demonstrate their racist beliefs and attitudes in *racial jokes.* They do so, not only by telling the joke, but also by participating in the process of constructing Others. It is important to ask why the statements or stories about particular groups are seen as humorous. Why do we consider what is said to be funny or worthy of being told as a joke? One class participant said that he "had a racial joke for every ethnic group we discussed," and he found the jokes funny because he "believed that anyone who was not white was inferior." On what information was he basing his beliefs?

The case of Ramish, presented at the beginning of the chapter, illustrates how racial comments can be cruel, mean and hurtful even though they might be directed at others. Ramish felt the effects of comments directed at other minority players. Similarly, Audley, in the following comment, suggests that he cannot "take it easy" for it is never "only a joke"; he is implicated in whatever is said. Disrespecting others who are like him is also disrespecting Audley.

> **Audley**: *"It is only a joke man, take it easy."*
>
> Friendships in life can be both happy and sad. I grew up in a neighbourhood of many white children. I remember times when I would not be invited to attend parties because of my colour. I would usually get picked on. I was called many names because of my colour and nationality. I even remember a time when I was not permitted to enter someone's home because his family was afraid that I might steal something. As time moved on, I simply learned to interact with different types of people.
>
> Most of my friends now are white, and I love them like brothers. Unfortunately they tend to make fun sometimes of racial groups such as the Chinese, Indian and Blacks. I am sad when I hear their ignorance. I bring it up with them and explain that this type of behaviour is not right but wrong. The response I get is that "it is only a joke man, take it easy." I expect more from these guys, but my presence doesn't help. I sometimes feel that they forget my nationality and think that I am white. I feel that the problems with my friends are ethnocentrism and racism. They see racism as a joke, and do it for amusement. Look at it from a minority's point of view, and it is downright stupid.

Consider further the following comments by Ajit Adhopia (1988). In an article in which he explains his process of becoming a "regular Canadian," Adhopia recalls that after making "so many sacrifices to transform my family from strange immigrants to true-blue Canadians," he still experienced racism. In his article "Prejudice and Pride," Adhopia illustrates that skin colour, more than cultural practices, often underlies racist treatment. He writes:

My new Canadian identity was shattered on a Sunday afternoon when I was sitting in my car waiting for a friend.... Three or four boys in their early teens walked toward me. A blond, blue-eyed boy looked straight into my eyes and yelled "You f... Paki." His friends burst into laughter. They did not run, they just walked away leisurely.... Back home I was too angry and embarrassed to share the experience with my family. My anger turned into deep depression and for weeks I pondered upon a question: "Where did I go wrong?"

Finally, it dawned on me. In my effort to become a regular Canadian I had missed one important thing–I forgot to change the colour of my skin. Darn it.... The young blond boy who thought he was insulting me is responsible for giving me the new awakening to my own cultural roots ... (Adhopia, 1988: 6).

RESPONSES OF MINORITIES

How do members of minority groups, who experience racism, stereotyping and discrimination, feel about these issues? Their responses range from frustration and discomfort to hurt and anger, depending on their experiences and struggles for acceptance.

Judy: *"I was really offended ..."*

Whenever a question was asked, a white person would start by saying, "I'm not prejudiced," and continue to answer. I was really offended by this, because it was obvious that they were being prejudiced and just couldn't admit it.

Natasha: *"I was hurt ..."*

After discussing prejudice I started thinking about the majority white race. How easy life is for them, never being stereotyped, but just being taken for who they are—individuals.

Then I wondered what it would be like if I were white. I soon decided I'd rather be what I am. I believe I'm richer, more cultured (for having both Canadian and Guyanese experiences) and more appreciative of life in general because of my colour and where I came from. Although facing prejudice is a horrible experience, I feel minorities have something over the majority group. I feel we are more objective and appreciative because we know what it's like to be discriminated against. White people will never know, and for that reason will always take life for granted.

During class discussions I thought about how prejudiced my classmates were. It was nothing that would be admitted to up front, but underlying prejudice was there. I also thought that if our teacher were white, reactions would probably be more open. I was hurt a few times in class because of racial comments or preconceived notions that my classmates harboured about minorities. I guess it hurt me because these people will never know what it's like to be discriminated against simply because of their skin colour.

I also thought that they were ignorant of what people were really like. But what hurt me more was that they never gave people a chance. They just kept their beliefs and never bothered to find out differently.

Sanj: *"Hearing an ethnic joke makes me self-conscious and uncomfortable ..."*

When interacting with my white friends and white people in general, I am never consciously aware of my colour unless an ethnic joke or remark is made. Then I become very self-conscious and uncomfortable.

Mark: *"Anger flows through me ..."*

Many of my friends are not Jewish and often take part in racial humour. This does not offend me since I know it is done in jest. Such things as "I hear there's a sale on at (such a place)—don't all Jews like bargains?" or "You have a big nose! You must be Jewish!" are often part of their repertoire. If I hear someone speaking in a negative manner about Jews and I sense they mean what they are saying, then anger flows through me. I can vividly remember standing in line one time at a movie theatre with a few friends and having another group of guys throw pennies at us. They screamed at us, "Come on, Jews, pick them up! Come on, you dirty Jews!" I felt so much anger and hate for those people, I just wanted to kill them. I let it pass because I had been taught not to fight unless it was for my own protection. To this day that incident stands out in my mind. Since I have experienced discrimination because of my faith, I have become much more aware of the feelings and the problems that arise when people judge others according to stereotypes.

Donovan: *"I was not truly a Black person ..."*

Stereotypes have been around for countless years, and their damage to the reputation of minority groups is incredible. In my essay I will focus on the stereotypes that have affected Blacks, and me in particular. From experiences in my life I can point out many stereotypes that have affected me personally, but here I'll focus on only two.

One of these stereotypes is the belief that "All Blacks are good athletes." It is easy to see how this stereotype came about, simply because of the Black domination on the playing field of many of today's most popular sports. However, this is indeed a stereotype. Because of this stereotype, a whole group of people are categorized as being better athletes. I personally did not excel at sports, and because of this stereotype, I felt inferior and embarrassed. I felt as if I had to play sports because it was expected of me. When it was discovered that I was not as good as "every other Black person," I felt I was less than them.

This stereotype is compounded by the belief that Blacks are not good at school, but only in sports. This has not affected me personally, but has led to

> many Blacks believing that they are not as smart as the rest of the students, which of course is not true.
>
> Another stereotype with which I have personal experience is that "Blacks are born with natural rhythm and are really good dancers." I was not always that good a dancer and to this day I am still not that great. Because of my lack of dancing ability, I was again made to feel inferior as a Black person. This made it seem to me that I was not truly a Black person because of my inabilities.
>
> The sad thing is that so many Blacks, and not only whites, believe in these stereotypes. This hurts the entire Black community, as they believe that success at sports is their only hope in life. Education seems unimportant to them because sports come easier to them and it is just simply expected of them. This leads to stereotyping Black people as being superior in sports but lacking in academic ability, because Blacks actually believe that they are naturally better at sports because they're Black. Stereotypes, such as the ones I have mentioned, have a terrible effect on the Black population as a whole. Once caught up in a stereotype, it is hard to detach from it and discern that these false truths are not true. If Blacks continue to believe the stereotypes of today's world, the only people who will be hurt are themselves.

Since they have lived with stereotyping, prejudice, racism and discrimination throughout their lives, it is understandable that marginalized racial and ethnic group members would not all steadfastly challenge negative constructions of their own group or others like them. We have already met Anthony (Chapter 3), who engaged in a process of taunting othering Italian individuals like himself. In the following example, Nadine shows how she too engaged in the process of stereotyping and "othering" of racial minority people. She admits that it is "hypocritical" and "shameful" that she, a Guyanese-born Canadian of South Asian descent "who has been on the receiving end of racism," would display such attitudes herself. However, probably most telling is her final comment: "Believe me when I say it's an ongoing personal conflict that I am trying to resolve...." Might this express not only her "ongoing personal conflict" but also the constant bewilderment that she feels as a minority?

> **Nadine**: *"It's okay for me ... because I am a minority ..."*
>
> I guess the most difficult part of the class was dealing with my own prejudices. Being a minority, I never thought of myself as being racist. However, I would never consider going out with a guy of any racial-ethnic background other than white English Canadian. I call it a preference, but in effect it is racism. I say this because I have been approached on numerous occasions by guys from different backgrounds and admittedly I am very snobby. I don't wait to find out what they're like; I snub them because of their colour.
>
> I tell myself it's okay for me to be this way because I have been on the receiving end of racism, but I am just as guilty of racism as the racists I

Photo: Dick Hemingway

Since the coming of the colonialists to Turtle Island, First Nations' peoples have been struggling against racism and discrimination.

have faced. I don't like feeling this way or having this prejudice. As a matter of fact I get extremely upset if one of my white friends makes a comment about a guy of a different race, yet it's probably something I would say.

I am not prejudiced against people in general. I have friends of all different nationalities and races, both male and female. However, when it comes to a boyfriend-girlfriend relationship, then I am racist.

A friend of mine recently asked me what I would do if my daughter (now two years of age) came home with a Black guy (or a guy of any other race). I blatantly responded that I would kill her. I am very ashamed of this prejudice, more so because I am a minority. But it's just the way I feel. I've tried long and hard to find the source of this prejudice but I've yet to come up with the answer.

The most shameful part in all of this is how mad, hurt and upset I get when I find out other people around me are prejudiced. My feelings towards these people are hypocritical, because I am no better. With the prejudices I have I should be able to understand why other people are prejudiced. I guess it all comes down to the fact that I think it's okay for me because I am in a minority. I realize this does not justify my behaviour, but it's what I tell myself to make myself feel better. Believe me when I say it's an ongoing personal conflict that I am trying to resolve, or maybe one day truthfully admit.

SEEING BEYOND STEREOTYPES

Stereotyping and stereotypes are rarely in anyone's best interest, as they result in both the possible misrepresentation of a person or the impossibility of being accepted as an individual. Stereotyping might be convenient for those who practice it, but it can also rob them of the opportunity to know groups and individuals more accurately and more intimately. When individuals participated in exercises that encouraged them to critically explore the stereotypes they held of others, many indicated that "speaking with someone from another culture on a personal level" gave them "an opportunity to see beyond stereotypes."

Annette: *"I realized that my opinions were based on ignorance ..."*

The research project on ethnic and racial groups really opened my eyes. When researching the Old Order German Mennonites, my biased opinions surfaced. I viewed them as "Bible thumpers," peddling their religion whenever given the chance. I also thought they were very serious people, who lived strict, unhappy lives. But what I believed about them proved to be very far from the truth. Upon completion of my research, I concluded that the Mennonites were a very happy people who loved their way of life and kept to themselves. I reflected back on my previous convictions and asked myself why I had thought the Mennonites were that way. After thinking this over for some time, I realized that my opinions, as well as my expectations, were based on ignorance. I was accepting and passing judgement on people I knew nothing about. My preconceived notions, I realized, had come from other equally uninformed people and existing stereotypes.

Jason: *"These are stereotypes and not facts ..."*

Stereotypes exist for every group that organizes itself as a culture, and of course the Chinese are no exception. The stereotypes we held prior to doing this project were ones such as "All Chinese are brains," "All people who work in the 7-11 stores are Chinese," and, "If you want your laundry washed really well, take it to the Chinese." Needless to say, these are stereotypes and not facts. However, by examining various data and history, it is possible to see where these stereotypes originated.

Regarding intelligence: Chinese frequently do well in school, not because of their higher inherent intelligence, but due to their motivation and to the emphasis and value placed on a good education. There is a great deal of pressure from within the family to succeed at anything undertaken since all achievements and failures reflect on the family as a whole.

The belief that Chinese hold only menial jobs may exist because, in the past, there were not very many professional Chinese in Canada. Why? The Chinese were prohibited in the early 1900s from holding certain professional positions. This has changed now—Chinese occupy positions at all levels. We found that these and other such stereotypes could quite easily be dispelled by actively examining them.

Ray: *"Hockey is dominated by the white race ..."*

I, along with many Canadians, enjoy the great game of hockey. When you think of hockey, you automatically think Canada. Hockey is dominated by the white race, and there are several theories that explain why this is so. The theory that I tend to believe in is the fact that every National Hockey League hero has belonged to the white race. They have served as role models for almost every Canadian-born white to look up to and dream of emulating.

The Black race has dominated every other sport except hockey, and they tend to be very agile and quick on their feet. The game of football, soccer, baseball and track and field all deal with running, and the Black race has done exceptionally well in all of these sports. Another important fact is that sports such as soccer, football, basketball, and so on are all played in a warm or room temperature, typical of their home climate. White people of Canada are used to the cold climate and enjoy many winter sports and pastimes.

Black people have also been stereotyped into sports that have been areas of former achievement for Black athletes. The Black race has no role models in hockey, and therefore few young boys show any real interest. Also, prejudice has been a major factor. Due to a common stereotype of Blacks as not being exceptional hockey players, they don't enjoy the same opportunities from their instructors and coaches.

THEORIZING ABOUT SOURCES

Cecilia: *"It is ignorance that fosters prejudice ..."*

Just as many might be frightened of, and avoid contact with, our senior population because they force an awareness of our mortality, we fear and avoid people of other cultures and/or races because they make us painfully aware of our ignorance. It is ignorance that fosters prejudice, and until Canadians can allow themselves to learn to know those considered different, they will continue to be guilty of the cruelty that is so much a part of prejudice. Would it help to think of ourselves as immigrants in a strange land? I think not, for it would be difficult to imagine being a victim of those things that we tend to deny even exist.

Janice: *"Blame the victim ..."*

It was interesting to see the stirring of emotion in our discussions of prejudice and racism. This emotion was strongly indicative of how many of us feel defensive about our prejudices. Speaking of my own ethnic, racial group—white English Canadian—I think that this discomfort often leads us to deny the source of our prejudice. This results in the creation of a kind of "blame the victim" situation. Uncomfortable with our prejudices and our ignorance of other cultures, uncomfortable with the perception that we are in some ways privileged by our whiteness, we shut out not only the issues of prejudice, racism and discrimination, but also the people and cultures who raise the issues in our minds. Rather than face the discomfort or conflict, we avoid that which will bring it out. So, we deny that racism or discrimination continues to exist. We see our culture, not as a product of our racial and ethnic identities, as our heritage in a sense, but just as a normal way of life we needn't question.

Helen: *"We put each minority to the test ..."*

It is interesting to note that my attitude appears to change with that of society. The longer a minority group is here, the more tolerant we become of it. At one time the Blacks were strongly discriminated against; before that it was the Italians. Currently it is the Sikhs who seem to be taking the brunt of discrimination. When looking at the situation from that perspective, it appears we put each minority to the test. "Are they good enough to be part of our country?" Yes, they are. I sincerely say this now, but my realization of categorizing is difficult for me to accept and even harder to write down.

Kevin: *"They had no prejudices ..."*

When some of my classmates made it known that they had no prejudices and then went on to express ideas or opinions that contradicted their original statement, I began to question my own prejudices. I have always felt that I was unbiased, just as my classmates did. However, I have now come to the conclusion that deep inside every one of us is a little bit of fear about a certain race or culture that gives rise to reservations about them. These reservations usually give rise to unjust assumptions or pre-judgments.

Debbie: *"An exception among my perceived stereotype ..."*

All my life, I have been surrounded by certain "significant others" who freely exhibit prejudice and discriminatory attitudes to those people who are racially and culturally different. I feel that my interaction with Gerardo, a member of the Latin American community, was extremely valuable, as it helped me to consciously recognize various characteristics about myself. As he informed me of the discrimination and prejudices he is repeatedly exposed to because he is a member of a minority group, I thought he was exaggerating. I like Gerardo very much, and I could not fathom why he felt so strongly about this belief, and, additionally, I could not believe that other people were not responding positively towards him. He is a very personable, intelligent, compassionate young man.

Looking back on this, I admit that I was regarding Gerardo with an outlook appropriately referred to as "cognitive dissonance." He was an exception among my perceived stereotype of the Latin American people, as he had married one of my closest friends. Therefore, my positive perceptions of him were actually based on their marriage and not on any knowledge I had of him as an individual. We are friends, but I believe this relationship would not exist if it were not for their bonding. I highly doubt I would have taken the initiative to begin a friendship on my own. I am thankful for our interaction now, however, because I feel that I will be far more open-minded in the long run, and my initial stereotype has greatly diminished.

In their comments, these writers have suggested that racism, prejudice, stereotyping and other negative attitudes and actions are sourced in ignorance, avoidance, fear and discomfort with people who are different and whom we might not know. Furthermore, the denial that racism and prejudice exist also perpetuates these attitudes and resultant behaviours. But the knowledge, attitudes and behaviours of these individuals are informed by structural factors represented and disseminated by educational, religious, social and governmental institutions, including the media and the judicial system. These sources too must be named.

ELIMINATING RACISM AND DISCRIMINATION

Awareness and a willingness to look at more than skin colour is crucial to the elimination of prejudice, stereotyping, racism and discrimination. People must admit that prejudice and racism exist if they are going to deal with these issues. We must go beyond the common notion that, because we have friends who are Black, Chinese, Portuguese, Native Indian and so on, we are free of prejudice and racism. Critical and painful self-analysis and self-awareness appear to be prerequisites for working towards confronting and overcoming our racism, prejudice and their accompanying problems. In practical terms, interacting with those who are targets of prejudice, racism and stereotyping might be one more healthy way of becoming better informed.

Annette: *"Try not to be so quick to judge ..."*

I encountered a few difficulties in doing my research. I was uncomfortable with the thought of conducting an interview with a Mennonite. I wasn't sure how I should act around one of these people, or what I should say. I had never seen a Mennonite person, never mind talked to one. I wasn't so sure that I wanted to either. Why, when doing the research, had I thought that all my preconceived notions, attitudes and prejudices were gone, but now that it was actually time to come face to face with a Mennonite person, had they returned? As long as these people existed only on paper, they did not pose a threat to my views and beliefs. I then realized that it is much easier to say that we are not prejudiced than it is actually not to be.

Once the interview was over, though, my fears vanished. They were real people, made of flesh and blood just like myself, but with different views and beliefs. They were nothing like I had perceived them to be. They were happy, loving and warm people. I was somewhat embarrassed by my previous thoughts and was glad that I had had the chance to gain the valuable insight that I did towards the Mennonites' culture.

I feel that my attitudes, biases, emotions and prejudices have changed somewhat. Now I try not to be so quick to judge other people when I know nothing about them. I've learned that the colour of a person's skin, the way they dress and the rituals they practise are not a full indication of what that person is like.

Jason: *"Accept differences ..."*

When I interacted with a person of Chinese background, I found that I always checked what I was about to say before I actually verbalized it. I didn't want to say anything to offend the other person. I was being much more careful in these conversations than I ever would be even with a stranger with the same background as me. I also didn't want to say something that was really stupid, for example, the way some people in the United States ask Canadians if they live in igloos. I wanted to present myself as having a bit of knowledge about their culture.

I think, as the conversation progressed, we both felt more comfortable with each other and were finally able to relax. We then talked as two people, not as a Chinese Canadian and a Canadian. But would we ever be able to "be ourselves" together? After all, isn't our culture a large part of what we are? How can we be completely ourselves in a different culture? It's similar to having a lot of private jokes within a group. When in another group, these jokes are meaningless. Sure, wonderful relationships can be formed, but there's still a part of ourselves that can't be shared and understood.

I tend now to agree with the statement that we are all racist. We do see people in different colours (i.e., yellow, black, red, white). How we behave after this admission determines to what extent we are prejudiced. If we dwell on this fact, and cannot see past the skin and find the real person, then prejudice becomes a problem. If, however, we can accept that difference and continue to form relationships, then I think we are aware of our prejudices and are better able to cope with them.

Simon: *"There are good and bad people ..."*

Looking back to before I initiated my investigation of Sikhs, I must admit that my feelings and attitudes towards them were very negative. There was a time when I didn't even want to look at one, let alone have any kind of interaction with them. I based all the opinions I had of these people on one poor past experience with a Sikh, a taxicab driver. What I realize now is that the cab driver could have been Black, Sikh, white, yellow or purple.

The point is that there are good and bad people in every culture. That driver could have been white and treated me the same way as the Sikh did. Because people don't like a particular minority group, they are quick to judge members of the group when they do something wrong. We do not take time to acknowledge that no one is perfect, regardless of what subculture he belongs to.

Kevin: *"Prejudice needs to be addressed and explored ..."*

I believe that interaction and experience are the best teachers. Whether in a one-on-one interview or a class debate, delicate topics such as cross-culturalism and prejudice need to be addressed and explored personally, for it is only through these methods that true emotions and consequent value examinations occur. Personal growth and development are possible only when such confrontation exists.

It would be very easy for me to say that my prejudices and racism have been vanquished and that I have complete empathy for racial minorities and an understanding of their current situations, but I can't. Many ethnic idiosyncrasies still continue to anger me, and I still find myself generalizing a characteristic of one to a culture of many. The difference in my viewpoint now is that I am aware of my ethnocentrism and this, I believe, is of crucial importance.

Lenore: *"Put yourself in the shoes of a minority person."*

Being an educated white English Canadian has made me readily accepted here in Canada, whereas immigrants and other races who are Canadian-born have the great obstacle of prejudice to overcome. I too had my stereotypes and prejudices towards specific cultures. The easiest way of trying to overcome these mental actions is to put yourself in the shoes of a minority person. Imagine having to conform to a different culture, having to speak the language and still trying to remain an individual. I couldn't do it, so why should I expect any other person to?

There is still so much for me to learn about cultures and people. Customs, values and beliefs are specific to each culture. Within each culture are individuals with individual personalities; there's never a "typical" Black, white, Chinese. No one should have to live with discrimination, stereotyping or racism. Only through educating the "ignorant" will this problem begin to lessen.

Leanne: *"Seeing racism in oneself as something that is learned ..."*

There were times during the discussions on racism that I felt a sense of relief. I had come to recognize that a difficult issue can be talked about, and that it is through discussion and taking risks that learning is made possible. I had come to think that racism itself wasn't the problem. What was reinforced for me, through these discussions, was the belief that it is the refusal to accept the racism that is there in all of us that is the far greater problem. Understanding it, seeing it in oneself as something that is learned and also denied by the larger society, is a way to lessen its strength. When we deny racism because it makes us uncomfortable, we only perpetuate it. I think that acceptance of our own tendency to remain within our own racial group and culture and to deny differences because we are uncomfortable with them is the first step towards changing that tendency. This leads us towards learning respect for and acceptance of other races and cultures.

Angie: *"A little knowledge goes a long way ..."*

I think racism will always be around. Everyone is afraid of the unknown or something different. I don't think you can make a person non-racist, but you can educate them; a little knowledge goes a long way and will eventually bring acceptance. I believe this as I have come a long way from the way I was treated in 1974, when I first came to Canada, to now, when I am treated differently.

Andy: *"An intelligent examination of our beliefs and value systems ..."*

It is my conviction that, although we are not born with racial and prejudicial concerns, through experience, observation, learning and interaction with society as a whole, we soon develop these characteristics. They become ingrained in our personalities whether we realize it or not. I was never told outright that one race was superior to another or that I should not like a certain individual because of their cultural and/or racial heritage. Nevertheless, I have been influenced by media stereotypes, by interactions with specific individuals whose behaviour I have subsequently generalized to their whole culture and by the thoughts and opinions of people I consider important. All these factors have contributed to the manner in which I view different races and cultures, and I believe it would be unrealistic to pretend that even now they don't affect me, be it consciously or unconsciously. It is also my belief, however, that knowledge can lead to understanding and, eventually, to compassion. Through an intelligent examination of our beliefs and value systems, we can perhaps begin to focus on where our biases have come from and help to change where they might be heading.

Advocacy is the one necessary element missing from the efforts the participants articulate to eliminate racism. The individual efforts of these participants must be accompanied by institutional and government efforts. Schools, colleges, universities, courts, media, businesses, social services and religious institutions must also critically examine their policies, legislation and practices, for it is in these that inequities are structured and ideologies, as well as individual attitudes and behaviours, are nurtured. In essence, structural factors that contribute to prejudice, stereotyping, racism and discrimination must simultaneously be dismantled by governments, institutions and members of the society collectively.

Photo: Dick Hemingway

Institutionalized Racism and Canadian History: Notes of a Black Canadian

by Adrienne Shadd

It always amazes me when people express surprise that there might be a "race problem" in Canada, or when they attribute the "problem" to a minority of prejudiced individuals. Racism is, and always has been, one of the bedrock institutions of Canadian society, embedded in the very fabric of our thinking, our personality.

I am a fifth-generation Black Canadian who was born and raised in a small Black farming village called North Buxton, near Chatham, Ontario. North Buxton is a community comprising the descendants of the famous Elgin Settlement of escaped slaves who travelled the Underground Railroad to freedom in Canada in the 1850s. As a young girl growing up in the fifties and sixties, I became aware of the overt hostility of whites in the area when we would visit nearby towns. Children would sometimes sneer at us and spit, or call us names. When we would go into the local ice cream parlour, the man behind the counter would serve us last, after all the whites had been served, even if they came into the shop after us. Southwestern Ontario may as well have been below the Mason-Dixon line in those days. Dresden, home of the historic Uncle Tom's Cabin, made national headlines in 1954 when Blacks tested the local restaurants after the passage of the Fair Accommodation Practices Act and found that two openly refused to serve them. This came as no surprise, given that for years certain eateries, hotels and recreational clubs were restricted to us, and at one time Blacks could only sit in designated sections of movie theatres (usually the balcony), if admitted at all. Yet this particular incident sent shock waves through the nation, embarrassed about such evidence of racial "intolerance" going on in its own backyard.

Somehow, this kind of racism never bothered me. I always felt superior to people who were so blind that they could not see our basic humanity. Such overt prejudice, to my mind, revealed a fundamental weakness or fear. Although, instinctively, I knew that I was not inferior, there was not one positive role model outside our tiny community, and the image of Blacks in the media was universally derogatory. Africans were portrayed as backward heathens in the Tarzan movies we saw, and Black Americans were depicted through the characters of Step 'n Fetchit, Amos 'n Andy, Buckwheat of "Our Gang" fame, or the many maids who graced the television and movie screens in small bit parts. (Black Canadians were virtually non-existent in the Canadian media.) I used to wonder if it could really be true that Black people the world over were as poor, downtrodden, inarticulate and intellectually inferior as the depictions seemed to suggest.

At the age of ten, we moved to Toronto. In the largely white neighbourhood where we lived, I was initially greeted by silent, nervous stares on the part of some children, who appeared afraid of me or at least afraid to confront me openly. Later, as I began to develop an awareness of the Civil Rights and Black Power movements through my readings, certain friends would respond with a frozen silence if I brought up the name of Malcolm X, or, for that matter, the latest soul record on the charts. Looking back, I can see that things ran fairly smoothly as long as the question of race could be ignored, and as long as I did not transgress the bounds of the artificial "colour blindness" under which I was constrained. This, apparently, was the Torontonian approach to race relations.

I share these reminiscences to illustrate the different forms which racism has taken over time, and in varying locales in Canada, whether in the form of overt hostility and social ostracism as in Southwestern Ontario, or in the subtle, polite hypocrisy of race relations in Toronto in the sixties.

But how, you may ask, do these personal experiences represent examples of institutionalized racism? Do they not depend on attitudes which vary from individual to individual? Are not our Canadian laws and policies very clear about the fundamental rights of all people to equal treatment and opportunities?

The problem with this line of thinking is that it fails to recognize how powerfully attitudes and behaviour are shaped by the social climate and practices around us. If the only image you have of Black women is derived from the one on your pancake box, then there is something wrong with the media portrayal of racial minorities. If there are no visible minorities in the boardrooms of the corporate world, and few in positions of influence and authority in the work force, this sends a message far more potent than the Human Rights legislation set up to create a more equitable distribution of rewards and opportunities. When generation after generation of school children continue to be taught primarily about the accomplishments of white Europeans in Canada—mostly men—the myth that this is "traditionally a white country," as I heard a reporter say the other day, will persist, unchallenged.

The selective recording of some historical events and the deliberate omission of others has not been accidental, and they have had far-reaching consequences. Blacks and other people "of Colour" are viewed as recent newcomers, or worse, "foreigners" who have no claim to a Canadian heritage except through the "generosity" of Canadian immigration officials, who "allow" a certain quota of us to enter each year.

But this myth that Canada is a "white" country is insidious because, on the one hand, it is so ingrained in the national consciousness, and on the other hand, so lacking in foundation. There is a tendency to forget that Native peoples were here first; Blacks, first brought as slaves in the 1600s and 1700s, were among the earliest to settle on Canadian soil; the presence of the Chinese is traced to the nineteenth century. In fact, people from a wide variety of races and nationalities helped to build this country. Unfortunately, this reality is not properly reflected in our school curricula.

The long Black presence and contribution to Canada's development continues to go unacknowledged. People are surprised to learn, for example, that ten percent of the Loyalists who migrated to British North America after the American Revolution were Black. Their descendants, particularly in the Maritimes, have been living in quasi-segregated communities for over 200 years. Blacks were one of the principal groups to enter the country during the nineteenth century when 20-25,000 fugitive slaves and free people "of Colour" sought refuge in Canada West (Ontario) between 1815-1860.

Standard textbooks never mention that in 1734, part of the city of Montreal was burned down by Marie-Joseph Angélique, a Black female slave, when she learned of her impending sale by her slave mistress. Most Canadians are not even aware that slavery existed in this country. Women's history courses fail to acknowledge that the first newspaperwoman in Canada was a Black, Mary Ann Shadd, who edited a paper for fugitives between 1853-1859 in Toronto and later Chatham, Ontario. Heart-warming stories such as that of Joe Fortes, a Barbadian-born sailor who came to British Columbia in 1885 and subsequently, as the lifeguard of English Bay, taught three generations of young people to swim—such stories are all but forgotten. Fortes is considered a true Canadian hero to those who are still around to remember him, but it seems that many younger British Columbians believe Fortes was a white man. And did any of you know that the term "the real McCoy" was coined after the inventions of a Black man, Elijah McCoy, born in Harrow, Ontario in 1840?[1]

Today's students, Black and white, look to the United States for information regarding the Civil Rights movement, unaware that a gripping saga occurred right here in Ontario. In the forties and fifties, organizations such as the Windsor Council on Group Relations, the National Unity Association of Chatham-Dresden-North Buxton, the Brotherhood of Sleeping Car Porters, and the Negro Citizens' Association of Toronto fought segregation in housing, accommodations and employment, as well as racist immigration laws. Much of the anti-discrimination and human rights legislation that we now take for granted are a direct result of the struggles which these groups waged.

Certainly, these few bits of information alter our perception of what has traditionally been taught in Canadian history textbooks. At the very least, they lead us to question the prevailing assumption that Canada was settled and built strictly by white Europeans. The educational system could be at the forefront in dispelling many of the myths and stereotypes which fuel racist thinking today. Instead, it aggravates the problem by channelling disproportionate numbers of Black children into low-level academic courses and ultimately, dead-end positions in life.

The point I am making is that racism is not simply a phenomenon which afflicts the minds of individuals and causes these individuals to perform discriminatory acts. Racism is something which afflicts an entire society; it is ingrained and reinforced in all the major and minor institutions of the society. Even in the most seemingly "objective" of undertakings, such as the writing of our national history, racism has operated to exclude minority groups from the historical landscape, thus rendering the accomplishments of these minority groups invisible, and therefore insignificant.

Second, racism is not something which simply affects its victims in various adverse ways. It also benefits all those against whom it is not directed, by affording certain privileges. Just remember that for every visible minority who is denied a position because of his/her colour there is a majority group member who is awarded that same position because of his/her colour. Many well-intentioned white Canadians fail to recognize that their lifestyle and position in society is based on a system of class and race privilege. Of course, men enjoy additional privileges based on their gender.

Rather than focusing energy on helping the victims of racism, some of these people should examine the problem from the standpoint of their own situations of privilege. Perhaps in this way, more creative solutions to inequality can be initiated in the light of this kind of alternative outlook.[2]

On a more personal level, even the most subtle and polite forms of racism can be detrimental, especially as they affect children. In my own case, when we moved to Toronto I was made to feel different, alien, even though no one specifically referred to my racial origin. It is a feeling which has never fully left me and perhaps explains why to this day I do not feel comfortable in the company of a group of white people. And when some whites think they are paying Black people a compliment by saying "We don't think of you as Black," as my sister's friends have told her, this is not just a misplaced nicety—it is an insult. We are not seeking "honourary" white status.

Before we as a society can liberate ourselves from the grip of racism, we have to acknowledge that it exists, and that it is not something which has been blown out of proportion; neither is it the figment of some people's imaginations. If we can do this much, we will at least have moved out from under the thick shroud of self-delusion and deceit. That in itself would be a refreshing step forward.

Adrienne Shadd is a researcher, writer and editor in Toronto.

Notes

1. Canadian feminists have grappled with this issue to one degree or another in recent years. White, middle-class women, who have always dominated the movement in terms of leadership and theory, have begun to realize the necessity of proactive strategies in ensuring that women from all racial, ethnic, religious, class, sexual orientation, and so on, backgrounds are represented in every facet of the women's movement. By proactive, I mean strategies that actively recruit women from all those backgrounds. In some instances, they have "stepped down" from their positions of power so that women of colour could take the lead, as in the case of the two most recent presidents of the National Action Committee on the Status of Women: Tanzanian-born Sunera Thobani and Jamaican-born Joan Grant-Cummings.
2. In his mechanical work on railway engines, McCoy invented a lubrication cup or graphite lubricator used on locomotives. This invention made it unnecessary to stop the machines for oiling, hence saving seven minutes per one hundred miles of travel. Between 1882 and 1940, forty-five patents were awarded to McCoy, with all but eight pertaining to lubrication devices for heavy machinery.

SUMMARY

"Why can't we all just get along?"– the now famous words of Rodney King, the African-American man beaten by police officers in Los Angeles in 1992, echoes in many of the comments by class participants. Specifically, in their exploration of the issues, many seemed to side-step the systemic and structural basis of racism–suggesting that prejudice, not racism, is what accounts for how they understand, think and talk about racial and ethnic minorities. They believe that prejudice is the result of ignorance, misinformation and lack of contact; and so, with time, information, education and cross-cultural interactions, prejudice will disappear.

For many, racism seems to be too negative a word to acknowledge as part of the Canadian social fabric. This approach ignores the fact that racism is an ideology that is embedded in the economic, political, social and cultural structures of our capitalist society, and therefore influences everyone. In this chapter, I have tried to point out that racism is not the same as prejudice and ethnocentrism. Racism is more than individual attitudes and ideas. It is structural; it is part of our social and cultural system that operates to inform our construction and naming of others, our beliefs about them, and ultimately our interactions with them. Stereotyping and racial jokes, in this sense, are mechanisms that operate to perpetuate the system.

Many participants suggested that racism, ethnocentrism, prejudice, stereotyping, and discrimination can be eliminated through personal efforts. Surely, personal efforts–and, more importantly, collective action–are needed and necessary. But they are necessary not only to change attitudes, but to change the systematic and structural factors that foster such attitudes and practices–factors such as the laws, policies and practices that operate within our social institutions, and society generally, to maintain racism and discrimination. It is important to keep in mind that discrimination is the action or practice that results from racism; racism, on the other hand, is the ideology that informs discrimination based on race. Adrienne Shadd makes these points quite eloquently in her essay on institutionalized racism.

SUGGESTIONS FOR DISCUSSION

1. What is the difference between ethnocentrism, bias, prejudice, racism and discrimination?
2. How would you describe the procedure by which ignorance leads to racism? How do the lack of awareness, education and exposure combine to make a person "racist"?
3. What is the relationship between individual, institutional and structural racism? Identify some of the major examples of structural racism that are evident in Canadian history.

Photo: Gary Gellert

CHAPTER 6

Immigrants and Refugees

> National growth in the Canadian population declined substantially … between 1990 and 1995. By 1996, natural growth accounted for only 47% of the total growth, while immigration accounted for 53%.… An aging population reduces natural growth since it is accompanied by an increase in deaths. At the same time, the number of births continues to decline, and will likely [continue] falling for a number of years.… By the year 2020, Canada's natural growth will probably approach zero.… These developments accentuate a situation anticipated for some years, namely that population growth in Canada will depend increasingly on immigration. Immigrants represented 17.4% of the population in 1996–the largest share in more than 50 years (Statistics Canada, 1998; quoted in *Transition,* September, 1998, p.8.).

The issues of immigration, multiculturalism and employment equity produced some of the most heated discussions and debates in class. For most of the students, the significance of these issues had to do with, not only their hopes of eventually realizing their career goals, but their understanding of how competitive the job market had become. For young white males in particular, immigration, multiculturalism and employment equity were seen as impediments to their achievement. Immigrants were perceived as "a drain on our social services" and as "taking jobs away from Canadians," "causing an increase in crime" (particularly Blacks and Asians) and "coming into our country and changing our culture" (with reference to Sikhs). Connections were often made between the increase in immigration and "what is wrong with multiculturalism." The latter was seen as facilitating changes in the "Canadian way of life." Employment equity was also perceived, like multiculturalism, as making it difficult for "Canadians" to eventually obtain the jobs to which they aspired. Participants spoke about these factors as causing "unneeded tension and frustrations among 'Canadians' (read white and British), 'immigrants,' the target groups and the government."

The essays in this and the following two chapters illustrate how participants, particularly young white males and females, related these three issues. The discussion that follows attempts to contextualize and clarify the ideas and some of the misinformation and myths that underlie several of the prevailing attitudes and positions that are so often displayed in the general society. It bears repeating that the ideas expressed by the participants also represent many of the perspectives found in our society generally and in major socializing institutions such as the media, schools, governments and others.

***Bill**: "I resented the fact that a Canadian didn't come first."*

I used to resent immigrants and refugees. I always looked at them as taking from the Canadian social services system. I thought this was unfair. This negative attitude was formed when I was out of work and looked into upgrading my education through the unemployment office. The waiting list was long, and what infuriated me was that the list of names of those waiting to enrol were ones that I couldn't pronounce. All these people were ahead of me, and I resented the fact that a Canadian didn't come first. It has taken a bit of attitude adjusting to come to terms with it—this is what Canada is all about. These people belong to Canada, just as I do.

Dave: *"I would like to see these people protesting about Canadian issues ..."*

I cannot understand why immigrants who come to Canada, after making the choice to leave their place of birth and adopt Canada as their new home, would protest in the streets of Canada about issues back in their home country. Canada is filled with problems, and the country needs people who will come here and contribute to the welfare, progress and development of this country. I would like to see these people protesting about such Canadian issues as the lack of jobs, the GST, taxes and other social issues that affect them, because this is where they are living.

Ryan: *"Individuals who do not wish to assimilate ... can leave."*

I am in some ways prejudiced. I feel that individuals who do not wish to assimilate and abide by our society's rules and regulations can hop back on the boat and leave. We live in a country where individuals need to work as a team, as one mass—we don't need sore thumbs.

I have a problem with the Pakistan Sikhs. They come to Canada to seek a better life, but instead they remain prejudiced against others. They march down our streets saying, "Bring my mother over, save her from persecution." These individuals need to realize that they are part of the Canadian society. If they refuse to conform, they will not last very long. They are in a new country now and are called Canadians. I don't want to hear all about their country's problems, because they ran away from their country's problems.

We need people who will work as Canadians. We need people who will work with Canadians. We need people who will work to be Canadians. We need people who will fight for Canada. Prejudice will weaken the bond between Canadians.

Individuals who wish to come to Canada are welcome if they possess qualifications that are in demand. As part of a growing society, it is up to all these new individuals to assimilate and conform so that we, the people around them, can relate to them and they can relate to us.

Jane: *"Canada cannot be seen as a dumping ground ..."*

On the issue of immigrants (women) being allowed to stay in Canada because of persecution and harassment in their home country, I believe that most of them should be allowed to stay. I say most of them, because Canada cannot be seen as a dumping ground or a place where people can concoct a story and easily get in. Also Canada must respect the culture of laws of another sovereign country, and we cannot be viewed as a judgmental country that decides what is right or wrong for other people or how they should live their lives. But once someone has embraced our shores and expressed a desire to remain here in Canada, because of justified fears and a dissatisfaction with the oppressive, sexist and discriminatory policies of their own government, then I believe they should be allowed to stay.

One issue I find irritating is that immigrants come to Canada, an English-and French-speaking country, and apparently make little or no effort to speak English or even to get involved in English as a Second Language classes (ESL). They continue to wear traditional clothes, and also want to wear their traditional clothes at their place of employment.

Nancy: *"They want nothing to do with people that are not of their ethnic background ..."*

The issue that I wish to discuss involves the immigrants who come to Canada and settle with their own ethnic group. I realize that when someone comes to a new country they feel safe in a community that is similar to the one they left behind. However, I feel that this only forces people of different cultures further apart rather than bringing them closer together. I am not saying that it is wrong for people to be actively involved in their cultural community—I feel that it is important to maintain your heritage and pass it down to future generations—but I think that heritage is something that should be shared with others and not kept to yourself.

I am an active participant in a Ukrainian dance group and have been for eight years. Within this time I have seen how these people interact with non-Ukrainians. It seems as though they want nothing to do with people that are not of their ethnic background. They all belong to Ukrainian churches, schools, sports teams, camps, country clubs. They have relatives in Ukrainian rest homes, and on their vacation they drive up to their Ukrainian community cottages.

When I first joined this group, it seemed as though the coordinators wanted me to forget my Scottish and Irish background and just concentrate on being a Ukrainian. There came a time when I was almost embarrassed to admit that I also had another heritage.

When people of the same ethnicity cling together they become so involved in their own culture that they are not willing to open their eyes and experience what other cultures have to offer. It becomes impossible for them to do so because they have spent so much time in their own community that they cannot communicate with anyone outside of it. For example, I knew someone who had been in this country for sixty years. He could hardly speak a word of English, and therefore how was he supposed to communicate with anyone outside his ethnic community? He had trapped himself inside it.

I don't feel that to be a Canadian you have to change your name or behaviour, but I do feel that a true Canadian can admit to being one. I found that I myself was almost considering myself to be Ukrainian. I hardly ever called myself Canadian, which my family has been for three generations.

Raj: *"It is expected that many traditional habits and practices will be muted ..."*

People coming to Canada should be informed or enlightened about what to expect when they arrive here. It is for this reason that the transition period is so difficult for so many people. I respect peoples' culture, traditions and beliefs, and I expect people to respect mine. Many Westerners complain of the treatment they receive in many Middle Eastern countries if they dress "disrespectfully," i.e., in Western clothing, especially women. They are often not allowed to commute or to live in certain areas, because it is felt they will corrupt the natives with their culture. Yet these very people come to Canada and expect us to accept them in their traditional garments, and to work side by side with them. That is not fair. Canada is a sovereign nation with an identity.

I wonder what foreigners would say if they arrived in Canada to find people in various modes of dress, some with turbans, working as police officers, some with daggers, attending schools, others wearing kimonos or saris. They would obviously be confused. I don't believe that Canadians should wear a national uniform or dress, but I disagree with immigrants coming to Canada and insisting on wearing their traditional dress on the job. The world must be able to recognize Canadians for who they are; Canadians should have an identity. I believe this is one of the many reasons that white people are viewed as Canadians, and most non-whites are seen as immigrants. I am not saying that we non-whites should try to conform to the ideals and mouldings of whites, but the integration process is one of blending in. It is expected that many traditional habits and practices will be muted; for the immigrant, Canada is a new country, a different culture and a new way of life.

CANADA'S NEED FOR IMMIGRANTS AND REFUGEES

A poll conducted in 1989 showed that 49 percent of Canadians believed that immigrants take jobs away from Canadians. The same study also found that Canadians were concerned with the lack of effort of newcomers, particularly racial minorities, to integrate into the society (Angus Reid, 1989). These ideas remain, and are reflected in the above essay excerpts.

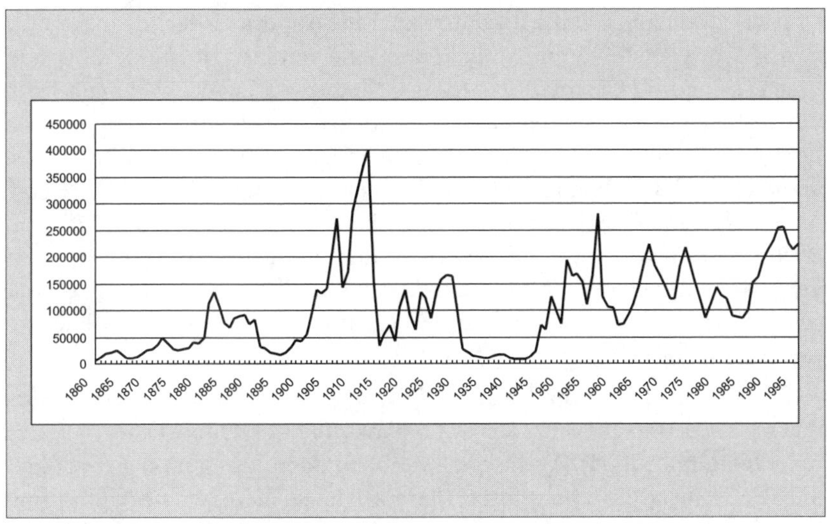

Chart 3: Historical perspectives on Canadian immigration.

More generally, it is felt that the changes in the economy, the double-digit unemployment rate, the need to preserve "our" cultural identity and the rising tensions among the various ethnic and racial groups are enough reason for "the Canadian government to stop immigration altogether or drastically reduce the numbers coming in." Unfortunately this position fails to take into consideration Canada's needs and the significant role of immigrants in the economic well-being of Canada.

At this point it is important to clarify the difference between an immigrant and a refugee, the confusion of which is reflected in the comments made by participants. An immigrant is a person who takes up permanent residence in Canada, while a refugee, or Convention refugee, according to the United Nations' definition and adopted by all member countries like Canada, is:

> Any person who, by reason of a well-founded fear of persecution for reason of race, religion, nationality, membership in a particular social group or political opinion, (a) is outside the country of his (her) nationality and is unable or, by reason of such fear, is unwilling to avail himself (herself) of the protection of that country, or, (b) not having a country of nationality, is outside the country of his (her) former habitual residence and is unable, or by reason of such fear, is unwilling to return to the country (Employment and Immigration Canada, 1978: 11).[1]

[1] It should be noted that people do not simply enter Canada and claim refugee status. Canada must first recognize the country of which claimants are citizens as refugee-producing countries, with reference to the United Nations' definition. Other factors that are taken into account in granting refugee status to claimants are age, level of education, job skills, knowledge of English or French and security and health considerations.

There is evidence that we would experience a serious decline in population if we were to significantly reduce the number of immigrants and refugees entering Canada. According to Statistics Canada, we have a birth rate of 1.7 and an ageing population; there are more Canadians dying than being born; and well over 10,000 people emigrate from Canada (with most going to the United States) each year. Because of this situation, the Canadian government, despite many Canadians' opposition to immigration, continues to allow some 250,000 or so immigrants into the country each year. Many demographers and statisticians claim that we need this number of immigrants to enter Canada each year if we are to have a viable economy and social stability.[2]

The ageing of our population is of particular importance. It is estimated that by 2036, one in every four Canadians will be sixty-five years of age or older (Gauthier, 1994). As the post-war baby boom generation grows older and drops out of the labour force, there will be an increased need for immigrants to meet labour force demands, which in turn will provide a steady tax base to fund the high quality health and social service needs of that generation.

In order to sustain population levels and meet labour force demands, Canada's immigration policies have traditionally sought to attract the youngest, healthiest, best-educated and most resourceful people (see Jakubowski, 1997; Satzewich, 1991). Since the introduction of the immigration point system[3] in 1967, all immigrants except close family relatives of Canadian citizens and permanent residents have been assessed according to age, education, training and experience, demand for their occupation in Canada, presence of pre-arranged employment and/or knowledge of one or more of Canada's official languages. Over three-quarters (77 percent) of all immigrants admitted to Canada during the 1980s were under the age of forty; over half (57 percent) were under thirty (Logan, 1991: 11). Adjusted for age, the 1986 census shows that 28.2 percent of immigrants, compared to 22.3 percent of native-born Canadians, had some university education (Jansen and Richmond, 1990: 6). Although educational attainment data includes pre-school and school age children, a full 33 percent of new

[2] In fact, according to the Law Union of Ontario (1981), Canada's population would begin to decline by the year 2000 with an annual immigration rate of 100,000.

[3] In addition to the refugee class of immigrants, there are also, as set out by the Immigration Act of 1976, family and independent classes. The family class refers to those who may be sponsored by relatives (e.g., parents, siblings, children), or nominated by a husband, wife or fiancée, who are Canadian residents or citizens, eighteen years or older. Sponsors must agree to provide maintenance for up to ten years. Independent immigrants include assisted relatives (not in the above category), entrepreneurs, investors and retirees. Those entering through this class must qualify by scoring a minimum of 70 points out of a possible 100 based on age, level of education, job skills, occupational demand, knowledge of English or French, "personal suitability" (i.e.,capacity to adapt to Canada), and security and health considerations (see Table 4). Entrepreneurs must intend to operate a business and employ one or more Canadians. Investors must have a net worth of $500,000 and invest a minimum of $150,000 in a project that creates jobs and is economically beneficial.

Table 5: Selection Criteria for Independent Immigrants (Business Immigrants, Skilled Workers and Assisted Relatives)

Factor	Units of Assessment	Notes
Education	16 maximum	
Specific vocational preparation	18 maximum	
Experience	8 maximum	0 units is an automatic refusal, except for persons with arranged employment or designated occupation
Occupation	10 maximum	0 units is an automatic refusal, unless arranged employment, designated occupation or self-employed. N/A for entrepreneurs and investors
Arranged employment or designated occupation	10 maximum	N/A for entrepreneurs, investors and self-employed
Demographic factor	8 maximum	Established by the Minister
Age	10 maximum	10 units if 21 to 44; 2 units deducted for each year under 21 or over 44
Knowledge of English or French	15 maximum	
Personal suitability	10 maximum	
Bonus for assisted relatives	5	
Bonus for self-employed immigrants	30	

Minimum Selection Units Required Per Category *

Entrepreneur	25	
Self-employed	25	
Assisted relative	70 (includes 30 bonus points)	

* The Province of Quebec has some variations of these.

Source: Citizenship and Immigration Canada, 1998 (April). *Canada's Immigration Law.* Internet: http://cicnet.ci.gc.ca

Photo: Dick Hemingway

It is in the workplace that we also learn about each other, and learn to live with each other, while we contribute to the economic growth of our country.

immigrants had some post-secondary education; among refugees, 28 percent had some post-secondary education (Employment and Immigration, 1989b: 22).

People are particularly sensitive to factors that might operate as barriers or hurdles to the realization of their aspirations and goals when they are at the point of entering the job market. It is understandable that the student participants believe that immigrants are taking jobs to which Canadians citizens are entitled, given the degree to which this view is supported in the media. Economists argue that, by creating demands for goods and services, immigrants create jobs for Canadians. According to one government study, immigrants and refugees admitted to Canada between 1983 and 1985 created 9,000 jobs over and above those they filled, and single immigrant entrepreneurs were expected to create or maintain an average of six jobs (Employment and Immigration, 1992a). Another study estimated that immigrant investors created an estimated 10,000 jobs between January 1986 and December 1991 (Employment and Immigration, 1992b). While immigrants are to be found in significant numbers, and in some cases are overrepresented, in certain industries and businesses in comparison to native-born workers, this is certainly not the case in the labour force as a whole. Because the majority of immigrants are selected on the basis of education, skills, experience and "national and regional population goals and labour market needs" (Employment and Immigration, 1978: 25), they tend to fill labour market gaps. Immigrants fill jobs for which there are no Canadians or jobs that Canadians do not want.

The notion that immigrants are a drain on our social services is not supported by research data. For instance, according to the Economic Council of Canada, 12.5 percent of the newcomers to Canada between 1981 and 1986 received some government social assistance cheques compared to 13.8 percent of native-born adults; and only 3.5 percent of those who were foreign born received welfare in 1987 compared with 5.5 percent of those born in Canada (Jansen and Richmond, 1990). This indicates, as has so often been said, that newcomers tend to make less use of the social service system than native-born Canadians.[4] They tend to turn to their sponsoring relative or community for social and financial assistance rather than to government. Immigrants generally aspire to be self-sufficient, and this can only be achieved through their own work efforts. Their inexperience with government assistance programs, particularly of those from "developing nations," would likely cause them to feel that accepting such assistance is an admission of failure and contrary to the reason for which they immigrated in the first place. As one minority member of Metropolitan Toronto comments, "You have to understand that back home, we don't have social insurance or anything of that kind.... Everyone's social insurance policy is [their] relatives and friends. If you grow older, or you are somewhat poor, you always rely on the people you know and your relatives. We always depend on each other" (Watson, 1991: A11). Immigration policy requires that immigrants be economically self-sufficient; nominated immigrants are the responsibility of their nominating relative for at least ten years or until they become citizens.

The myth that there is a correlation between crime increase and an increase in immigration is an example of media-fed xenophobia and racism in Canada. It is fuelled by stereotypes of race, ethnicity and the countries of origin of members of minority groups. The Immigration Act stipulates that persons convicted or suspected of criminal offences and persons who would constitute a danger to national security are inadmissible. A study by Samuel (1989) showed that the criminality rate of immigrants from source areas such as Africa, Asia and the Caribbean was less than one-third of that of immigrants from the United States and Europe. Further, Weinfeld (1998) points out available evidence indicating that "criminality, measured by incarceration in federal penitentiaries, is less for the foreign born than for the native born." (See also the *Report of the Commission on Systemic Racism in the Ontario Criminal Justice System.*) Generally, the criminal behaviours of any population must be examined in relations to that group's access to opportunities. We need to examine how, as the host

---

[4] With reference to the 1991 census, Torczyner et al. (1997) showed that, compared to the total population, Black Canadians, the majority of whom were immigrants, tended to obtain less government financial support.

society, our accommodation practices provide immigrants access to the necessary employment and education opportunities.

The excerpts above indicate that a distinction is not made between immigrants and racial and ethnic minorities (see also *The Toronto Star*, 1990). In fact, these minorities, especially racial minorities, are often constructed as immigrants. They are perceived as having "come to our country," settling within "their own ethnic groups" and then protesting "in the streets of Canada about issues back in their home country." Some suggest that Canada's multicultural policy is responsible for what is viewed as immigrants (or racial and ethnic minority group members) "taking advantage of our liberalism" to the extent that they try to change "our identity," "our laws," and "our culture." However, an honest examination of our demography will indicate that "ethnic" neighbourhoods abound throughout the country and have done so for many, many generations.

Neighbourhoods populated by people of similar background, whether by language, social class, ethnicity, race, nationality or sexual orientation, provide members of that community with an available support system. The associations, organizations and businesses located in these neighbourhoods strengthen individual and group identity, nurture community spirit and foster economic self-sufficiency and productivity. Insofar as immigrants must adjust to a new environment and are likely to experience barriers to full participation in the society, particularly as racial and ethnic minorities, it is inevitable that they would seek alternative ways of participating. It is within these communities that they find the space and the voice to experience the life they wish. Further, all members of a democratic society have the right to live where and with whom they choose, as well as participate in the way they wish. Hence, where they live and the ways in which they participate should remain individual choices and privileges, rather than prescribed options.

In his essay, Ryan points out that immigrants should not "protest in the streets of Canada about issues in their home country." Rather, according to Dave, they should "protest about Canadian issues." An interesting question that this raises is: Do not *all* Canadians have the freedom to exercise their rights as citizens, including the right to express their political positions about (and hence influence) local, national and international issues? Similar objections are not often articulated when members of the dominant group protest about international issues. In such cases, they are perceived to be protesting, not out of self-interest, but from a position of concern and empathy. This same behaviour, when exhibited by racial and ethnic minorities, is invariably interpreted as the actions of "others"–outsiders and immigrants.

"SPEAK ENGLISH!"

Noteworthy in the discussion of immigrants is the issue of language. It is quite possible that, in the comment that follows, Lisa's view represents that of many Canadians.

> **Lisa**: *"Immigrants arriving in Canada should learn English ..."*
>
> I always held the firm belief that immigrants arriving in Canada should learn English and should adopt the customs held by the majority; not to do so is a snub to all Canadians and implies the attitude, "Although I am here now, I shall carry on as I did before." Nothing infuriated me more than seeing "immigrants," especially of college or university age, conversing in their mother tongue while ignoring the language that surrounded them—English. I figured that, when in Rome, you should do as the Romans do. This belief included dress, attitude and especially language.
>
> This very point was discussed numerous times in class. Although I was vehement at times in agreeing with the side that upheld what I have just stated, my view now, although not completely changed, has somewhat softened.
>
> I realize that assimilation does take time and that there is security in conversing in one's mother tongue among friends. I also realize that culture is an integral part of one's sense of being. Without it, an essence of the self is lessened. Although I still feel my old sense of ire stir whenever I am riding on public transit and am seated near others who are using a foreign language, I can now at least comprehend some of the troubles they might have functioning in what may be a different society and why they continue to maintain their old behaviour.

When individuals, especially young people who are highly likely to have a facility in English, infuriate people such as Lisa by speaking languages other than English, what can we say about Lisa's and others' appreciation of bilinguality as an asset? Is there a language, other than English, that Lisa would tolerate?

It is true that we often encounter Canadian residents who have been here for many years yet do not speak English or French. In many cases, these individuals circulate within communities where they are able to do business, shop, bank and interact primarily with members of their own ethnic group. In some cases, employees of schools and other government institutions even communicate with them in their "own" language. Many who ask how such a situation could occur do so out of the belief that these people should be speaking English–their inability to do so should not be catered to. By providing information and/or translation services, we are merely allowing them to retain their own language and condoning their

Table 6: Canadian Immigrant Population by Place of Birth, Showing Period of Immigration before 1961 and between 1991 and 1996

Place of Birth	Period of Immigration*			
	Before 1961	%	**1991-1996****	%
United States	45,050	4.3	29,025	2.8
Central and South America	6,370	0.6	76,335	7.3
Caribbean and Bermuda	8,390	0.8	57,315	5.5
Europe	953,360	90.4	197,480	19.0
United Kingdom	265,580	25.2	25,420	2.4
North & West Europe without UK	284,285	26.9	31,705	3.1
Eastern Europe	175,430	16.6	87,900	8.5
Southern Europe	228,145	21.6	52,455	5.0
Africa	4,945	0.5	76,260	7.3
Asia	32,580	3.1	592,710	57.1
West Central Asia & Middle East	4,975	0.5	82,050	7.9
Eastern Asia	20,555	1.9	252,340	24.3
South-east Asia	2,485	0.2	118,265	11.4
Southern Asia	4,565	0.4	140,055	13.5
Oceania & Other	4,250	0.4	9,875	1.0
Total Place of Birth	1,054,930	100.0	1,038,992	100.0

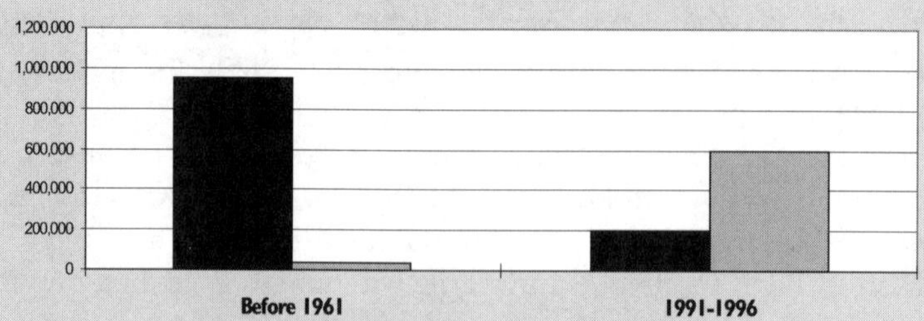

*Non-permanent residents are not included.
**Includes only the first four months of 1996.

Source: Statistics Canada. 1998. *Census 1996*. "Population by Selected Age Groups and Sex for Canada, Provinces and Territories," Internet Catalogue No. 93F0023XDB96005, the *Nation* Series.

failure to become truly "Canadian." After all, "When in Rome, do as the Romans do."

This insensitivity to non-English speakers reflects, in some cases, an ethnocentric attitude. Such is the case with Ria, who in the following comment argues that, if she could learn English, so can all other immigrants.[5]

> **Ria**: Are they really trying or do they want to keep to themselves and not assimilate into the Canadian society? If people come from another country with a different language and are unable to understand people in their new country, they should make an effort to learn the new language so they can be understood, feel more at home and become a part of the majority of the people. I feel very strongly about this as I went through it when I came to Canada thirty-four years ago. I did not understand or speak the English language. I took English lessons and worked among English-speaking people because I wanted to learn our new language. I also kept up my Dutch language.

Also consider the following comment.

> **Sue**: I am able to understand that "a person's language is a symbol of their culture and therefore part of that individual's identity." However, I have to recognize the feelings of frustration and impatience I experience with those who do not speak English fluently. And perhaps most difficult to acknowledge is my insensitivity towards these people, when it is this very attitude I abhor in others who do not understand Sign Language as part of a deaf person's culture.

This ethnocentric, insensitive attitude is based, not only on the feelings of frustration and impatience that English-speakers such as Sue (and in some cases French-speakers) experience, but also on a cultural ideology that indicates that English and French are the languages that every Canadian should speak. Hence, the inability to speak either language becomes a factor in the "othering" of language minority Canadians.

To understand why some people would speak in or try to retain their mother tongue while residing in Canada, we must bear in mind that language not only enables us to send messages and exchange ideas with each other, but it also plays a key role in the development, maintenance and evolution of a culture (Avison and Kunkel, 1987: 51). The symbols that are defined in a language mirror the items, worldviews and values considered important to that culture.

---

[5] While it is understandable that individuals will evaluate others based on their own experience and situation, it is important to recognize the limitations of doing so. What is true of one person's or group's experience cannot be generalized to another.

As such, language is symbolic and an integral part of cultural identity. The first language of minority group members enables them to communicate with and maintain contact with relatives, as well as deal with pragmatic concerns such as economic, social and familial issues (Schecter et al., 1996). Also, for some, depending on age, familial responsibilities, learning experiences and expectations, learning a new language can be a difficult process. So while some language minority members may embrace English, for others, the social, familial and psychological cost of doing so might limit their success at learning the new language. However, those who think like Lisa, Cindy and Sue need not worry, for research tells us that minority languages cannot survive in a context that does not favour their maintenance (Schecter et al., 1996).

THE EFFECT OF IMMIGRATION POLICIES[6]

Elsewhere (James, 1997) I argue that "how and when a group of people is permitted to enter a country, and the ways in which they are accommodated and expected to participate economically, politically, socially and culturally," sets the stage for how they come to be perceived and treated by members of the "host" society. "Mythologies and 'overgeneralized truths' help to construct social images or stereotypes" that justify the treatment they receive and the position they come to occupy in the economic and social structure of the society (James, 1997: 310). That ethnic and racial minority group members (more so racial or "visible" minority group members) are often regarded as immigrants (see also *The Toronto Star*, 1990; Mukherjee, 1993; Shadd, 1994) is, in part, a reflection of racially based immigration policies. In controlling entry into Canada, these policies articulate a notion of who best qualifies to be a "Canadian" and who will remain a "foreigner"–i.e., immigrant (Jakubowski, 1997; Satzewich, 1992; Jansen, 1981). And built into the term *immigrant* is not only the construction of ethnic and racial minority persons as "foreigners" but also the concomitant social images that have been used to justify their exclusion and ultimately the social and occupational positions they occupy in Canada.

Kalbach and Mcvey (1971) report that, since confederation, the bulk of immigrants to Canada have come from the United States and Britain; and "when the proportion of immigrants from 'other' areas of origin began to increase rapidly, so did attempts to control the quality and character of immigration.... The only persons to enter Canada with a minimum of red tape were those who belonged to the preferred groups, i.e., United States

[6] It should be noted that our discussion here refers to federal immigration policies and practices and not to those of Quebec which is the only province with a separate immigration policy. However, this is not to suggest that what is said here does not apply to Quebec; indeed, it is very likely.

citizens and British subjects[7] by reason of birth or nationalization" (Kalbach and Mcvey, 1971: 37). Factors such as race, ethnicity, nationality and social class were used to control the quality and character of immigration and ensure the "assimilability" of those who immigrated (Kubat et al., 1979; Porter, 1965). This meant that white Western Europeans were initially the preferred immigrants.[8] Successive governments and parliamentarians in general debated the necessity of and their commitment to keeping Canada white. For example, in 1908, Robert Boden, the Conservative Minister responsible for immigration, bluntly stated that "the Conservative Party stands for a white Canada." The Liberal government that later came to power, in keeping with that same policy, introduced an Order in Council in 1911 that was designed to stem the "tide" of some thirteen hundred Black American homesteaders who were immigrating from Oklahoma to Alberta (Shepard, 1997). Evidently, while Americans were classified as "preferred immigrants," this referred only to white Americans.

Canadians' prevailing attitudes regarding those who would best qualify as immigrants at that time is probably well represented in the writings of J.S. Woodsworth. Quoting from Woodsworth's 1909 book, *Strangers within Our Gate,* John Porter, in his seminal work, *The Vertical Mosaic* (1965), reminds us of Woodsworth's views at that time.

> For Woodsworth, English orphans and pauper children with their "inherited tendencies to evil," were "a very doubtful acquisition to Canada." He expressed the fear "that any large immigration of this class must lead to degeneration of our Canadian people." The Scandinavians, "accustomed to the rigours of a northern climate, clean-blooded [*sic!*], thrifty, ambitious and hard-working" would be certain of success. The Bohemians "constitute no peculiar 'problems' as they readily adapt themselves to American or Canadian conditions." But the Slovaks of northern Hungary, "closely akin to the Bohemians," were "distinctly a lower grade." The capacity to do certain kinds of work was attributed to centuries or generations of breeding. "Much of the rough work of the nation-building in Western Canada is being done by the despised Galician ... working with a physical endurance bred of centuries of peasant life." Of the southern Italian, who "usually lands here almost destitute," it was thought that "his intelligence is not higher than one could imagine in the descent of peasantry illiterate for centuries." In the discussion of Syrians and Armenians Woodsworth quotes Dr. Allan McLaughlin: "Their wits are sharpened by generations of commercial dealings.... These parasites from the far East ... are ... but detrimental and burdensome." Of orientals there was no question. They could not be assimilated (Porter, 1965: 65).

According to Clifford Sifton, the Minister of Immigration in 1922, the individual judged as making the best immigrant was, "a stalwart peasant in

[7] Apart from those born in Britain, and as spelt out in the policy, people from Ireland, Newfoundland, Australia, New Zealand, and the Union of South Africa were also considered to be British subjects. Of note is that people from other African countries, as well as India, Pakistan, Ceylon, the Caribbean and other so-called Commonwealth countries, were not included in the list.

[8] As we will see, although European by birth and nationality, Jews were not regarded as part of the group of white immigrants.

sheep-skin coat, born on the soil, whose forefathers had been farmers for generations, with a stout wife and a half-a-dozen children" (cited in Porter, 1965: 66). Referring to these views and attitudes, Porter writes: "Reputed biological qualities were thus used for and against the immigration of particular groups, for it was these qualities which suited them for particular tasks" (p.65).

It is clear that until the second half of the twentieth century, Canadian governments sought to ensure that Canada remained largely white. They attempted to restrict the entry of Chinese immigrants into Canada with such policies as the $50 "Head Tax," levied against the Chinese in 1885. This tax was increased to $100 in 1900, and to $500 in 1903 (Bolaria and Li, 1988). And through various bans and other restrictions, such as limiting the number that could enter, governments maintained control of Chinese immigration.[9] Not only did this serve to limit the number of Chinese men who could afford to come to Canada to work on the railroad, but it also impeded family unification, because many were unable to raise enough funds to bring their families over. It was expected that after the men were through with working on the railroad they would return to China. We now know that many of the men eventually grew old and died in Canada without ever re-uniting with their families.

The number of Japanese immigrants allowed into Canada was similarly restricted. For example, by 1920, this number was limited to 150 per year (Kalbach and Mcvey, 1971). The treatment of Japanese Canadians during World War II is well known. However, the way in which the Canadian government handled Japanese immigration after the war may not be so well known. Like the Germans and Italians, the Japanese were considered enemy aliens during the war, so they not allowed to immigrate to Canada. Yet, while the label was lifted for the Germans in 1950, it was not lifted for the Japanese until two years later. Commenting on this point, Jansen (1981) writes:

> Up until the end of the second world war, Canada's immigration policy tended to be based purely on ascribed characteristics of perspective immigrants, in particular race and national origin. But even after the war the racial aspect played an important role–and was considered more 'threatening' to Canadian society than national characteristics. This is clearly seen by the fact that while Germany and Italy were considered to be 'enemy' countries during the war, the ban on immigration of these ethnic origins was lifted immediately after the war ... (p.19).

Prime Minister Mackenzie King's statement to the House of Commons in 1947 is representative of the government's attitude towards Asian immigrants. He stated that "Canada is perfectly within her rights in selecting the persons whom we regard as desirable future citizens. It is not a 'fundamental

[9] The Chinese Exclusion Act that barred Chinese immigration to Canada was made law in 1923 and repealed in 1947.

human right' of any alien to enter Canada. It is a privilege. It is a matter of domestic policy.... The people of Canada do not wish, as a result of mass immigration, to make a fundamental alteration in the character of our population." He added that the "large-scale immigration from the Orient would not be permitted to change the fundamental composition of the Canadian population" (House of Commons, 1947).

Entry by Asians from India was also restricted. Bolaria and Li (1988: 170) point out that Canada was unable to reach a "gentleman's agreement" with India as it did with Japan. Not wanting to take direct action against the Indians because of the British interest in India, Canada introduced "indirect" measures that functioned to limit immigration from India.[10] One such measure was to increase the amount of money that immigrants from India were required to have from $25 to $200. Most telling, however, was the 1908 "Continuous Voyage" legislation. According to this measure, entry into Canada was restricted to those who came "by continuous voyage from the countries of which they were natives or citizens and upon through tickets purchased in that country." Interestingly, at that time the only company able to offer a continuous journey from India to Canada was the Canadian Pacific Railroad, and the government of Canada issued a directive that they were not to sell any through tickets to Canada (cited in Bolaria and Li, 1988: 170). In 1914 this legislation was tested by an Indian businessman. He chartered the ship *Kamagata Maru*, and arrived in Vancouver Harbour on May 23 with 376 passengers aboard. The few passengers who were dependants of earlier immigrants were allowed to enter the country, but most were denied entry and remained on the ship for two months. During this time, the ship was guarded by police, and upon leaving, it was escorted out to sea by a naval ship (cited in Bolaria and Li, 1988: 171).

Like other non-Europeans, Africans were deemed an inadmissible group, despite their having settled in Canada since the 1620s (initially as slaves), the Underground Railroad, and the resettlement of Jamaican Maroons[11] in Nova Scotia. As already mentioned, some who tried to immigrate from Oklahoma were barred from doing so. However, a limited number of people from the Caribbean came to Canada during the late 1800s and early 1900s. Calliste (1994) reports that, by the end of the eighteenth century, a small number of Black Caribbean males, who paid Canadian schooner captains a transportation fee (a business venture), were able to come to Canada on the schooners. Most of these men settled in Nova Scotia and worked in the coal mines and the coke ovens of steel

---

[10] Canada's action here was motivated also by its desire to be perceived as working in solidarity with other members of the Commonwealth, with India being one.

[11] Maroons are Africans who were transported to Jamaica and who escaped slavery. They were considered by the British colonialists to be unlawful and a threat to the social stability of the island. In an attempt to rid the island of them, they were shipped to Nova Scotia in 1796 as a form of punishment (Walker, 1980).

plants, not only because of discriminatory labour practices, but also, as Calliste (1994: 135) writes, "because of the myth that blacks [*sic*] could withstand the heat better than whites." In the early 1900s, Caribbean women were allowed into Canada as domestics based on the Caribbean Domestic Scheme (1910-1911), which was the result of an agreement between the Canadian and Caribbean governments (Calliste, 1994; Satzewich, 1992; Silvera, 1984).

The immigration policies pertaining to Blacks was consistent with Canada's attitude towards non-European immigrants. Simply put, Blacks were restricted because they were "unassimilable." This idea is well represented in the comments of then-Deputy Minister of Immigration, when on January 14, 1955, he stated:

> It is from experience, generally speaking, that coloured people in the present state of the white man's thinking are not a tangible asset, and as a result are more or less ostracized. They do not assimilate readily and pretty much vegetate to a low standard of living …; many cannot adapt themselves to our climatic conditions. To enter into an agreement which would have the effects of increasing coloured immigration to this country would be an act of misguided generosity since it would not have the effect of bringing about a worthwhile solution to the problem of coloured people and would quite likely intensify our own social and economic problems.

Preference was given to refugees from Europe, with the exception of Jews (they too were denied entry when a number of them arrived seeking refugee status during the war). (See Abella and Troper, 1982, for an extensive discussion.) *The Globe and Mail* of January 25, 1939, reported from Ottawa:

> Opposition to immigration in general and to the admission of Jews to Canada, was voiced in the House of Commons tonight by H.E. Brundle (Lib., Champlain). He said he believed Canada's natural resources should be developed by and for Canadians. "I object strongly to the entry of Jews en masse or otherwise into Canada," he said. "I have no brief against the Hebrew race, but since they have, justly or unjustly, created great difficulties in other countries, we should be careful. They nearly always live in the cities, and that means they will be on relief or take jobs from other workers" (reproduced in *The Globe and Mail*, January 25, 1989: 15).

Even when called upon to demonstrate a humanitarian spirit, the immigration policies that served to construct who was best suited to become a citizen of Canada placed entry barriers for those considered "unassimilable."[12] Noting that Jews suffered from the prejudices of Canadian immigration policies, Burnet (1984: 19) writes that "Canada drew the line even at admitting Jewish refugees from Nazism during the 1930s." And commenting on Canada's discriminatory practices towards non-white immigrants, Burnet further (1984) writes:

> The immigration policy bore hardest upon those peoples who were considered unassimilable; they included peoples physically different from the dominant groups.

[12] Kubat et al. (1979: 24-5) report that, in 1956 and 1957, 38,000 Hungarians came to Canada as refugees; in 1968 and 1969, about 12,000 Czechoslovaks; in 1972 and 1973, about 5,600 Ugandan Asians; during 1973 and 1974, about 1,200 Chileans; and in 1980, about 20,000 Vietnamese.

Table 7: Canadian Immigration – Top Ten Source Countries, 1994, 1995 and 1996

	1994			1995			1996		
COUNTRY	**Rk**	**#**	**%**	**Rk**	**#**	**%**	**Rk**	**#**	**%**
Hong Kong	**1**	44,169	19.73	**1**	31,746	14.94	**1**	29,871	13.33
India	**3**	17,225	7.69	**2**	16,215	7.63	**2**	21,166	9.45
China-mainland	**4**	12,486	5.58	**4**	13,290	6.25	**3**	17,479	7.8
Taiwan	**5**	7,411	3.31	**6**	7,691	3.62	**4**	13,165	5.88
Philippines Rep. Of The	**2**	19,097	8.53	**3**	15,149	7.13	**5**	12,923	5.77
Pakistan	**14**	3,746	1.67	**10**	3,996	1.88	**6**	7,724	3.45
Sri Lanka	**6**	6,671	2.98	**5**	8,925	4.2	**7**	6,117	2.73
United States	**7**	6,234	2.78	**9**	5,185	2.44	**8**	5,789	2.58
Iran	**20**	2,694	1.2	**15**	3,683	1.73	**9**	5,770	2.58
United Kingdom	**9**	5,971	2.67	**8**	6,160	2.9	**10**	5,559	2.48
Bosnia-Herzegovina	**10**	4,905	2.19	**7**	6,270	2.95	**11**	5,098	2.28
Vietnam Soc. Rep. Of	**8**	6,230	2.78	**11**	3,953	1.86	**19**	2,476	1.11
Total for Top Ten only	-	130,399	58.25	-	114,627	53.94	-	125,563	56.04
Total Other Countries	-	93,476	41.75	-	97,864	46.06	-	98,487	43.96
Total		**223,875**			**212,491**			**224,050**	

Rk refers to the ranking of that group relative to others during that year.

Source: Statistics Canada, 1996 Census, *Nation* tables.
http://canada.metropolis.net/research-policy/f&f/index_e.html

> It is unnecessary to repeat the history, now widely considered to have been shameful, of overt and covert exclusionary measures directed against Chinese, Japanese, South Asians, and Blacks. As late as the 1950s, one federal minister of immigration after another had to defend regulations on allegedly scientifically grounds that most natural and social scientists regarded as nonsensical. For example, the restrictions on Black immigration were said to have been imposed because it had been "scientifically proven" that Blacks could not endure cold climates (p.19).

In establishing preference in terms of racial, ethnic, class and biology, Canada's immigration policies over the years have determined who would eventually be classified as "Canadian." These policies explain, not only why the majority of the racial minority citizens came within the last half of this century, but also how, the multiculturalism policy notwithstanding, some "immigrant" groups (taking into account that, with the exception of the Aboriginal peoples, we are all immigrants here) have become socially constructed as "Canadian." The fact that most non-European immigrants came at a time of increased urbanization has contributed to their social construction as people who have caused "the problems of urbanization and the concomitant ills of megalopolises" (Kubat, 1979). The requirement that immigrants must be able to assimilate into Anglo-Canada indicates the extent to which the ideology of racism has framed the stereotypes and the racialization of some Canadians as racialized Others, who are perceived as not able to, or never will, assimilate or conform to Canada and hence are least likely to become "good citizens" of Canada.

IMMIGRANTS: RESOURCEFUL RESOURCES

Informed of the history of immigration in Canada, participants such as Cindy reacted by making connections between current and former responses of Canadians to the social, psychological and political dilemmas faced by refugees.

Cindy: *"We are fortunate to live in a good land."*

I was annoyed when I heard comments such as, "Why should those boat people be allowed into Canada?" and "They should have gone through the proper channels." I thought to myself, obviously these people do not know anything about political and religious persecution or about living in fear for their lives as many refugees have. In drastic situations, people do drastic things. We have been so fortunate to live in a good land, true and free, and not to have experienced such realistic nightmares. I grew up aware of the political dissidents in the Soviet Union, who were languishing in labour camps and psychiatric hospitals. I was aware partly because of my Ukrainian Canadian background. I felt that in some small way this set me apart from the other students. They seemed so ignorant,

Table 8: Canadian Immigration by Levels Component, 1994, 1995 and 1996

	1994		1995		1996	
IMMIGRATION	#	%	#	%	#	%
Immediate Family	52,404	23.41	44,094	20.75	43,149	19.26
Parents and Grandparents	41,289	18.44	33,007	15.53	24,417	10.9
Total Family	**93,693**	**41.85**	**77,101**	**36.28**	**67,566**	**30.16**
Skilled Worker - Pr. Appl.	28,619	12.78	34,537	16.25	41,733	18.63
Skilled Worker - sp. or Dep.	40,522	18.1	46,893	22.07	55,486	24.77
Business - Pr. Appl.	7,024	3.14	5,294	2.49	6,151	2.75
Business - Spouse or Dep.	20,341	9.09	14,134	6.65	16,212	7.24
Prov./Terr. Nominees	-	-	-	-	231	0.1
Total Economic	**96,506**	**43.11**	**100,858**	**47.46**	**119,813**	**53.49**
Live-in Caregiver - Pr. Appl.	4,743	2.12	4,654	2.19	3,580	1.6
Live-in Caregiver - Sp. or Dep	208	0.09	792	0.37	917	0.41
Deferred Removal Order Class	-	-	423	0.2	3,313	1.48
Retirees	7,426	3.32	304	0.14	145	0.06
Total Other	**12,377**	**5.53**	**6,173**	**2.9**	**7,955**	**3.55**
Total Immigrants	**202,576**	**90.49**	**184,132**	**86.64**	**195,334**	**87.2**
REFUGEES						
Government Assisted Refugees	7,629	3.41	8,113	3.82	7,836	3.5
Privately Sponsored Refugees	2,828	1.26	3,213	1.51	3,040	1.36
Refugees Landed in Canada	9,249	4.13	16,347	7.69	17,216	7.68
Dependants Abroad*	18	0.01	34	0.02	393	0.18
Total Refugees	**19,724**	**8.81**	**27,707**	**13.04**	**28,485**	**12.72**
Total Immigrants/Refugees	**222,300**	**99.3**	**211,839**	**99.68**	**223,819**	**99.92**
Backlog	1,575	0.7	652	0.31	231	0.1
Total	**223,875**	**100**	**212,491**	**100**	**224,050**	**100**

*Dependants (of a refugee landed in Canada) who live abroad
Source: Statistics Canada, 1996 Census, *Nation* tables.

http://canada.metropolis.net/research-policy/f&f/index_e.html

> although I now realize that I might also have been making assumptions about these students.
>
> After hearing about the various racial and ethnic groups, I was saddened by the reminders of the part played by my country in denying entry to certain groups of refugees—putting their very lives in jeopardy. Knowing that this was none of my doing personally does nothing to reduce the sense of guilt I feel as a Canadian.

Similarly, Jeff, having admitted to his ignorance of and now embarrassment at Canada's history of immigration, is left with the question of how immigrants manage to succeed in Canada, when he has not been able to.

> **Jeff**: *"I always thought of Canada as a warm, caring country."*
>
> How could I have been so ignorant? I have always prided myself on being "a man of the world." I have travelled to many places and thought I had a good understanding of other cultures. I was shocked to learn of the positive effects of immigrants on our society. It is because of immigrants that we are able to live in a buoyant labour market. I was also shocked to learn of how early immigrants were manipulated and suppressed. I had always thought of Canada as a warm, caring country. My investigation of Jews almost made me embarrassed to say I am Canadian. How could such a warm country refuse thousands of Jews who were fleeing for their lives during the Holocaust? As for education, I had to ask myself why many immigrants become successful while I remain financially stagnant. Could it be that I am the uneducated one?

It is not Jeff's education that is responsible for his financial stagnancy in comparison with many immigrants. It is more likely that, as a non-immigrant, he does not have the "immigrant drive" or "immigrant strategies" that seem to be responsible for the successes of immigrant Canadians. Indeed, as we have noted, immigrants are not randomly selected to come to Canada. Our governments have always sought to admit immigrants who would benefit Canada economically (Satzewich, 1992; Jakubowski, 1997). In current immigration criteria, in addition to occupational and professional experience and expertise, educational qualifications, age and demands for the immigrant's skill, there are points given for what is termed "personal qualities" or personal suitability," which are awarded by immigration officers. One is left to guess on what basis the officers assign these points.

The National Film Board's 1989 video *Who Gets In* reveals that country of origin, life circumstances, wealth and responses to the questions of immigration officers determine who gets into Canada. Specifically, the video demonstrates that Vietnamese refugees in Hong Kong and Filipino women working in Hong Kong and wishing to immigrate to Canada as domestic workers were not treated or questioned in the same manner as the Hong Kong entrepreneurs who were expected to bring thousands of dollars and invest it in Canada. For example, an entrepreneur with an untested business idea and $3 million seemed to undergo a very easy interview and, before long, was given permission to immigrate here. In some cases, individuals within this "investor class" of immigrants were represented by immigration lawyers and consultants, some of whom were Canadians working in Hong Kong.

The video also shows that the Africans and South Asians in Kenya did not receive the same respectful treatment that the Chinese entrepreneurs of Hong Kong received.[13] The cases in Kenya were largely of dependants of Canadian citizens and permanent residents and refugees who were seeking asylum. One case is particularly telling. A former prison guard, Mr. Tulumba of Zaire, had assisted political prisoners in escaping incarceration. He had fled to Kenya because he believed his life was in danger. Even though Mr. Tulumba impressed the immigration officer, as the officer himself said, and demonstrated his courage, determination, ambition and tenacity (illustrated, among other things, by the fact that he was able to learn English in six months while in a refugee camp), he was refused entry to Canada. As the officer explained, "He is very, very bright. A remarkable man under any circumstances. But it doesn't necessarily mean that we want him in Canada. I would rather have him spend a couple of years growing tomatoes or something, and kind of get that sharp edge off him before we can think of introducing him into our society." As a refugee applicant, Mr. Tulumba failed the "personal suitability" test because, according to the officer, he did not seem like a person who could "move in next door to my mom," or like any person living in a small community in Canada.

It is certainly not the unmotivated and unambitious who typically get into Canada, but individuals who are willing to work hard to become economically and socially successful; and if they do not succeed, then they seek to ensure that their children do.[14] In a longitudinal study in which my colleagues and I have been engaged for the past three years, we compared the educational and occupational achievements of children of foreign-born parents with those of children of Canadian-born parents. The initial study of the educational and occupational aspirations of Ontario Grade 12 students, first done in 1973 by Professor Paul Anisef of the Department of Sociology at York University, found that students of foreign-born parents,

---

[13] The CBC reporter Ann Medina, who narrates the video, also points out that there were only three officers in Kenya serving about one-third of Africa, while thirteen officers were serving Hong Kong alone. As one immigration officer argued, Hong Kong was worth $2.5 million (1988) in income to Canada.

[14] Morton Weinfeld (1998) suggests that, "to the extent that some immigrants (grandparents or older children) perform unpaid labour such as child care or helping out in a small family-owned business, 'the economic contributions of immigrants would be underestimated in most econometric models'" (*Transition*, 1998: 8).

who in some cases were themselves foreign born, tended to have high educational and occupational aspirations (Anisef, 1975). This finding is similar to many other studies that report that the high aspirations of immigrant children tend to be supported by their parents and their respective communities who place confidence in education as a means to success (Lam, 1994; James, 1990; Larter et al., 1982).

Our follow-up study of the Class of 1973, who are now in their early forties, reveals that many have managed to fulfil their aspirations. Specifically, the findings show that, while the children of foreign-born parents were disproportionately more likely to come from working-class family backgrounds, they sought out and acquired the education (in some cases with the financial support of the parents) necessary to attain the careers and occupations to which they aspired. Noteworthy is the fact that, when compared to their female counterparts of Canadian-born parents, female respondents of foreign-born parents were less likely to be unemployed and twice as likely to be self-employed.

> As newcomers, the foreign-born are challenged to question conventional strategies for achieving success and may lack the social capital available to Canadians. Yet … foreign-born parents are made more reflexive by their migration experiences, and aspire to do well in Canada by actively supporting the ambitions of their children. Canadian-born parents might well learn from the experiences of … the foreign-born in helping broaden the life experiences of their children and preparing them to deal effectively with the 21st century (Anisef et al., forthcoming).

In another study with Professor Celia Haig-Brown, we examined the educational experiences of immigrant and refugee students currently in university who had graduated from an ethnically and racially diverse school in a working-class area of Metropolitan Toronto. Apart from the educational and social ambitions demonstrated by the students in the interviews, we also noted their strong desire to contribute to both their geographic and ethnic communities, which they agreed had contributed much to their educational success. Most striking were the comments of Nguyen, who came to Canada with his parents at a young age as a refugee from Vietnam. Nguyen expressed his indebtedness to his community, school, teachers and, most of all, to Canada for the opportunities he has had. Contrary to his parents' wishes that he go into business, where it might be "easier to get jobs … and [he would] probably make more money," Nguyen was thinking of going into teaching, where he could more directly "pay back" his community and society.

> But also, I'm thankful to be here, so I'm paying, well it's not really paying back, but I want to return my dues, so if I'm going into teaching, I'm probably going to go into some service field.… It's very silly but it's deep rooted in me that I'm thankful to be here … so this is why business is not for me.… I think you're in business for yourself … not the community or the country, whatever (James and Haig-Brown, 1998).

In another study, Professors Jansen, Plaza and I investigated the employment experiences and social mobility patterns of Caribbean immigrants to Canada, specifically those of African and South Asian (or Indian) origin. Of the 328 individuals surveyed, 92 percent were born in the Caribbean, most arrived as children and 82 percent are now citizens of Canada. Also, 82 percent reported having completed some post-secondary education. During interviews, some 50 men and women with post-secondary education reported that institutional and systemic discrimination in their work place operated, not only as a barrier to their gaining employment, but also as a so-called glass ceiling that prevented them from reaching their potential and attaining their occupational and/or professional aspirations. Nevertheless, despite these barriers and limitations and their failed dreams, most, relying on their own initiative (and, to a lesser extent, family and friends) have persevered and found work largely in the service area. And, in keeping with their strong will and determination, slightly more than three-quarters (78 percent) said that they were satisfied or very satisfied with Toronto as a place to live, two-thirds (66 percent) felt that Toronto was a good place to raise their children, and only about one-third (32 percent) said that they would return to the Caribbean if conditions were right (Jansen et al., forthcoming).[15]

By and large, immigrants to Canada have managed to confront the limitations before them and have applied themselves in ways that make it possible for them to take advantage of the opportunities and possibilities for success in Canada. As Keren Braithwaite (1989) said of Caribbean parents, if they do not succeed in the ways they wished to, they hope that their children will. Hence, immigrants will utilize their energy and resources in reaching this goal. It is this immigrant drive, ambition and determination that immigrant-receiving countries have long recognized, and they therefore have supported (though in the case of some immigrants, reluctantly) the idea of immigration.

In the following essay, Zena, while certainly not representative of all immigrants, articulates a perspective that should always be borne in mind: that immigrants and refugees are not poor, uneducated people who enter Canada seeking handouts and who do not wish to actively participate in the social, political, economic and religious life of the county. Zena considers herself an insider–a “Canadian”–and expects the rights, respect, privileges and acceptance that this citizenship entails.

[15] It is also worth noting that well over half (57 percent) of the respondents said that they felt that Black men were the most vulnerable to discrimination in Canada as compared to any other ethnic and racial group. The police were identified by more than half (56 percent) of the respondents as treating African Caribbean men with little respect.

Zena: *"As an 'unhyphenated' Canadian, I see myself as a citizen, sharing the same future with other Canadians ..."*

An immigrant Canadian, I am a part of the much-talked-about Canadian ethnic mosaic. I epitomize the diversity of this mosaic: an East Indian by race, born and raised in East Africa (a second-generation African), a practising Shiite Ismaili Muslim and with a working knowledge of three languages (East Indian, Swahili and English). A Tanzanian national by birth, I left my country in 1971 as a result of political considerations for a four-year stay in the United Kingdom prior to immigrating to Canada in 1975.

It was during the 1960s that Tanzania (then Tanganyika) and the other countries in the region attained independence from Britain. The colonial affiliation meant that, until 1970, the school system, the judiciary and other institutions were modelled along the lines of those in Britain. For example, the medium of instruction in schools and the predominant language of commerce and government was English. I was therefore brought up with an understanding and appreciation of British culture—the predominant culture I subsequently found in the U.K. and in Canada.

A strong part of what I am is formed by the Ismaili community to which I belong. The Ismaili faith, one of the seventy-two sects of Islam, takes the Islamic concept of religion as a way of life (i.e., unlike the strict Augustinian distinction between material and spiritual, Islam considers both to be equally important) even further. The community encourages and has developed major programs in education and social and economic development. Higher education, excellence in commerce and in the professions is put on par with prayer, as is enterprise with a conscience and self-help. My faith has instilled strongly in me the existence of God, and a balance between the pursuit of material things and prayers for the soul.

Culturally, I consider myself a Canadian Ismaili. This would not be different if I were asked this question on a visit to Tanzania or at Jamatkhana (the Ismaili prayer/community house). As minorities in all the countries they reside in, Ismailis' first loyalty is to their country of residence. There is no Ismaili code of conduct; they adopt the language and dress code of the respective countries. As an "unhyphenated" Canadian, I see myself as a citizen, sharing the same future with other Canadians, all equal and without special privileges.

As someone who left her country of origin because of political reasons, I am able to appreciate the stable political environment, democratic values and institutions and the various freedoms (of expression, religion and so on) far more than Canadians who were born and raised here. This is reflected in my active participation in, and support of, civic affairs; for example, the fact that I vote in all elections, my membership in a political party, my open-mindedness in accepting various differing opinions, my interest in reading newspapers and in particular editorials and opinion pieces and my support and respect for law and authority.

Similarly, I am able to appreciate the high standard of living in Canada after having lived in a Third World country where electricity and running water are considered luxuries. I place a high premium on education. It was a luxury back home, both in terms of user fees and availability—Tanzania, with a population of 25 million, has only one university. Although I was born and raised in relative luxury, the poverty of and lack of opportunities for most Tanzanians are permanent reminders that, to most of the people in the Third World, getting three meals a day remains a major preoccupation.

These "backgrounds" have also given me a high regard for the work ethic and self-help. Social security programs (medicare, pensions and so on) do not exist in Tanzania or India (the country of my great-grandparents' birth), and therefore this dependence on government is an alien concept to me. Although as a liberal-minded, social democrat, I support the UIC and welfare systems, I would find it difficult to collect from these programs. The work ethic, pursuit of excellence and self-help are reinforced by all my background influences (nationality, ethnic and religious). As a parent, I expect to pass along these values to my children and related ones of thrift and of carrying as little debt as possible.

My being a member of a visible minority that is frequently negatively stereotyped is another major influence. The ignorance of my fellow Canadians as to the many different peoples generalized as East Indians (a Tanzanian Ismaili like myself has as much in common with a Tamil from South India as a WASP would have with a Ukrainian—they are both white) is disappointing. I am frequently drawn into the role of educator, explaining about different Eastern cultures and religious backgrounds.

Unfortunately, the only thing many Canadians know about the world's second largest religion (Islam has 1 billion followers) is the political violence and terrorism in the Middle East. This is like equating Christianity with violence because of the struggle in Ireland between Catholics and Protestants. People lose sight of the fact that Moslems, like everyone else, can be poor or rich, tolerant or intolerant, honest or dishonest, illiterate or scholarly. In personal terms, this has cultivated a tolerance in me for other cultures, a desire to learn more about them and a sympathy for the negative stereotyping to which they might be subjected.

Another effect of this is that I try very hard to be a model citizen, because, as a member of a visible minority, I feel that my shortcomings will be attributed to my race, ethnicity and so on. A beneficial result of this (sort of a "backward compliment") is that this makes me a winner, since I try harder than I would have otherwise.

SUMMARY

The essays on immigration suggest that participants see immigration as impeding economic growth and positive social relations in Canada. Immigration is perceived as largely unnecessary, particularly at times of high unemployment and social tensions due to crime and ethnic differences. But in answer to the question, "Are immigrants a strain on our society?", Darren rightly mentions the economic benefits produced by immigrants.

> **Darren**: *"Immigrants will enable Canada to become prosperous."*
>
> One of the benefits of having immigrants come into the country is economic. The immigrants will obtain jobs and receive wages in return. They will then spend money on necessities, such as food, shelter and clothing. Companies must then produce more of these products in response to the demands of the new immigrants. When this happens, new jobs are created. This is beneficial to economic growth, and will eventually benefit the whole country. This aspect is one that a number of Canadians do not take into consideration when they oppose new arrivals to the country.
>
> Without immigrants, our population would not increase. The reason for this is that the number of children born is very low and does not equal the number of deaths and emigrations that occur each year. The influx of new immigrants into the country will help to compensate and eventually even out and expand the population. This will enable Canada to become economically stable and prosperous.

As Fleras and Elliot (1992) state, "the immigrants of today are likely to underwrite the costs of the delivery of social services in the future. For this reason alone, we are as dependent on immigrants as they are on us" (p.46).

Many people see a link between immigration and multiculturalism–a link between two unnecessary evils. It is believed that the large numbers of immigrants, with their assertiveness and expectation that their ethnic and religious values and practices will be recognized, contribute to disharmony and a loss of "Canadian identity." But as one participant argues, this perception of multiculturalism, immigration and immigrants is due to the fact that "we are resistant to change and anything foreign. What we don't understand, we destroy. The cold hard fact is that we need immigrants more than they need us."

SUGGESTIONS FOR DISCUSSION

1. Account for the various viewpoints of the impact that immigrants and refugees are perceived to have on Canadian society.
2. Speculate on the effects that stopping immigration would have on the economy of Canada.
3. Which seem to be more significant and why in sustaining Canada's economic growth: independent/entrepreneurial or sponsored/ nominated immigrants?

CHAPTER 7

Culture, Multiculturalism and the Ideology of Integration

> If birds were suddenly endowed with scientific curiosity they might examine many things, but the sky itself would be overlooked as a suitable subject; if fish were to become curious about the world, it would never occur to them to begin by investigating water. For birds and fish would take the sky and water for granted, unaware of their profound influence because they comprise the medium for every act. Human beings in a similar way occupy a symbolic universe governed by codes that are unconsciously acquired and automatically employed. So much so that they rarely notice that the ways they interpret and talk about events are distinctly different from the ways people conduct their affairs in other cultures (Barnlund, 1988: 14).

According to Barnlund, "cultural myopia" characterizes the members of every society. This explains how individuals understand, and are able to identify, culture. Jackson and Meadows point out that "for most people the term [culture] is vague because individuals live the culture and seldom explain it or consciously think about or evaluate it" (1991: 72). No society is without culture–a core set of values and expectations that exert tremendous influence on our lives, structure our worldview, shape our behaviour and pattern our responses. Adler asserts that "all human beings share a similar biology, universally limited by the rhythms of life" (1997: 27). We all move through a similar sequence of phases in life: from birth, to infancy, childhood, adolescence, adulthood, middle age, old age and death. He continues:

> The ultimate interpretation of human biology is a cultural phenomenon; that is, the meaning of human biological patterns are culturally derived. Though all human beings are born, reproduce, and die, it is culture which dictates the meaning of sexuality, the ceremonials of birth, the transitions of life, and the rituals of death (Adler, 1977: 27).

In this chapter we will explore culture as a social construction that frames the life experiences and responses of individuals to social and environmental factors. The objective is to arrive at an understanding of culture–the core set of norms, values and expectations to which Canadian residents adhere–and to explore how people living in Canada and in particular communities are expected to integrate into a set of cultural values and aspirations. These are informed by the ideology of multiculturalism, which promotes a culture that reflects social, ethnic and racial stratification.

TOWARDS AN UNDERSTANDING OF CULTURE

Simply defined, culture is the way in which a given society organizes and conducts itself as distinguished from that of other societies.[1] Culture consists of a dynamic and complex set of values, beliefs, norms, patterns of thinking, styles of communication, linguistic expressions and ways of interpreting and interacting with the world that "a group of people has developed to assure its survival in a particular physical and human environment" (Hoopes and Pusch, 1981: 3). Therefore, members of any given society will not only be influenced by the culture of that society, but can also contribute to shaping it. The location of various groups within the social stratification system will determine the ways in which they are able to influence the overall culture of the society. The term *social stratification* refers to the hierarchical system in which segments of the population are ranked on the basis of their power and access to wealth and prestige. This ranking or social class structure is determined by a complex interplay of property ownership, income, education and occupation, as well as factors such as gender, ethnicity, race, length of residency and citizenship status.

Given this stratification and the resultant hierarchical or social positioning of the various groups in society, the culture that emerges will largely mirror that of the group with the most economic and political power. Specifically, the cultural elements (i.e., the norms, values and expectations) of the ethnic group with the most power will be dominant or considered to be the "norm" in society. Yet it is these very cultural norms, values, moves, practices and so on that are considered "invisible" and are possessed by "people without culture"–those who are "we." The cultural elements that are "visible" are perceived to be possessed by those "with culture"–the marginalized members of society (Rosaldo, 1993: 199).

It is important to stress the dynamic nature of culture. Changes within a culture are due to global influences, the movement of people from one country and/or region to another and the interaction of various racial, ethnic and social groups. Changes also result as structures respond to the tensions and conflicts that occur as groups agitate for space, resources, recognition and survival.

Culture is therefore much more than costume, food, music and dance. As Jackson and Meadows explain, "Culture must not be treated as a loose amalgamation of customs, as a heap of anthropological curiosities" or be seen merely in terms of artifacts such as languages, specific knowledge of customs and rituals (1991: 70). These are the symbols of a culture, and they

---

[1] Carroll defines a "society" as any fairly large group of people who share common cultural values, have inherited a common set of historical traditions, engage in a relatively large amount of mutual interaction and are associated with a particular geographic area (1993: 26).

too change. Observable aspects of culture are merely tangible reflections of a complex, inter-connected set of elements that fulfils specific functions in the lives of the members of that society.

Simple actions such as boarding a bus, making a dental appointment, dropping by to see a friend and attending classes are aspects of culture. These behaviours are governed by the shared assumptions and rules of the culture. The existence of these common values makes it possible to predict and control behaviour. For example, teachers and students with similar social histories know what to expect from each other on the basis of commonly understood rules about schooling. We routinely operate on the assumption that all of us know the rules and will conduct ourselves accordingly. This enables us to depend on each other to behave in predictable ways. Students and teachers from other cultures may not share these assumptions or unspoken rules.

We adhere to particular rules or ways of doing things because we place a value on them. We respond to behaviour with disgust, horror, pleasure or disdain, not only because we consider some rules useful, but because we judge them as right or wrong. And while we continually evaluate these rules, members of society are still punished and rewarded on the basis of their loyalty to them. The result is that people are powerfully motivated to abide by societies' rules and to attempt to force others to do so.

Variations in cultural expressions within a society exist as a result of social and historic factors that preserve and generate differences. For instance, the region, gender, class, race, ethnicity, religion and sexual orientation with which people identify are factors that contribute to the variances. These social characteristics help to determine the variation in cultures or what some social scientists refer to as "subcultures." For instance, although individuals may share the belief that formal education is related to future career success, their understandings of career success may differ depending on the norms, values and expectations of their cultural groups. This would then determine the kind and quantity of education that they pursue.

A "subculture" or what I shall refer to as *group culture* is expressed by "a group of people within a larger socio-political structure who share cultural (and often linguistic or dialectical) characteristics which are distinctive enough to distinguish it from others within the same culture" (Hoopes and Pusch, 1981: 3). The elements of cultures that find expression in the society sometimes conflict with the "culture of the society" as a whole. As such, they are likely to contribute to changes within the culture of the society. As accommodations are made, a new culture emerges, with new dimensions. Individuals can be members of a number of different cultural groups and possess a combination of values, customs and patterns of thinking derived from the culture of the society in which they live, as well as from the many groups to which they belong. Adler (1997) points out that "the cultural identity of a society is defined by its dominant group, and this group is usually quite distinguishable from the minority sub-group with whom they share the physical environment and the territory they inhabit" (p.26).

ETHNIC AND RACIAL DIVERSITY AND CULTURE

In order to establish a reference point for discussion, we will use terms as defined by social scientists. *Ethnic group* refers to a group of people who tend to share a common ancestry and history, who may or may not have identifiable physical or cultural characteristics and who, through the process of interacting with each other and establishing boundaries with each other, may identify themselves as being members of that group (Smith, 1991: 181). Ethnic group members often, but not always, speak a common language. They tend to be identified as a distinct group based on a common set of values, symbols and histories (Smith, 1991: 182). Sometimes religion or religious affiliation is also part of the ethnic identification. The group's identity tends to be maintained over generations, not only because new members enter the society, but also because members develop or maintain interest in their ancestral group and culture and identify with select markers of the ethnic culture (Fleras and Elliot, 1992). Fleras and Elliot (1992) also point out that the culture of ethnic groups is not necessarily based on the original immigrant culture, but on a "reconstructed" ethnic culture in which tradition is "invented" on the basis of ongoing adaptations to the environment and to the social situation in Canada (p.51)

According to Jones (1991), the term *racial group* refers to "a group of people who share biological features that come to signify group membership and the social meaning such membership has in the society at large. Race becomes the basis for expectation regarding social roles, performance levels, values, norms and morals of the group and non-group members alike" (p. 9). Skin colour is often the basis upon which status allocation and group membership take place.

Ethnicity and race are significant when groups are identified and acquire status according to social and physical traits. Cultures based on ethnicity and race are not related to any inherent qualities. Rather, they exist as a reflection of the social meanings that society has attached to these characteristics, and the ways in which individuals and groups operate with these meanings. Particularly significant are the meanings that respective groups give to these characteristics in the context of the society in which they live. The behavioural patterns that individuals develop as a consequence of these social meanings are referred to as *ethnic* or *racial group cultures.*

The terms *dominant* (or *majority*) *group* and *minority group* refer to the relative relationship of groups to the societal power structure. The dominant group in society tends to influence the economic, political and social participation of other members of society. Members of the dominant group usually occupy elite or privileged positions. Power and access to economic and political resources, rather than greater absolute numbers, characterize the dominant group. For example, while women outnumber men in most societies, they lack the power base of men and are therefore considered a minority group in terms of their relationship to power.

As pointed out earlier, other terms are used in place of minority group. For example, *racialized groups* is sometimes used to refer to racial minorities; so also is *marginalized groups* used to convey the status of groups within the society. Minority groups are often constructed on the basis of perceived physical, cultural, economic and/or behavioural characteristics. Members of these groups are seen as subordinates in society and often receive different or negative treatment. According to Smith (1991),

> we use race and ethnicity to define one's power status within the society. Each multiethnic/multiracial society develops a social distance scale which is usually anchored in the mainstream society's cultural value and feeling about the minority group. Those groups against which majority members have strong sanctions are those that they perceive as being the most unlike them, and therefore, the group from which they feel the greatest amount of social distance (p.70).

Inevitably, the status of a group within the social hierarchy (or stratification) will influence its cultural patterns with respect to ethnicity and race. Dominant group members are likely to enjoy the privileges of their status in society and gain access to the social, economic and political institutions without compromising their cultural identity or having to overcome barriers related to race, ethnicity or language (McIntosh, 1995). Minority group members are likely to experience exploitation and oppression (Smith, 1991: 70). In addition to their own group culture, minority groups also possess knowledge of the dominant group's cultural norms and values. This knowledge is often necessary for survival, causing them to be "inescapably bicultural" (Hoopes, 1981: 22).

The relationship of a group's members to power is mediated not only by race, ethnicity, language and immigrant-citizenship status, but also by social class, gender and other characteristics. As noted in Chapter 2, social class might be of more significance to a person's social interactions and successes within society than race and/or ethnicity. However, as race and ethnicity do play a significant role in the social positioning of people within Canadian society (Porter, 1965), it is important to explore how they operate in the lives of individuals and in the production of culture.

Given its power and control over institutions, the dominant cultural group often cajoles or coerces minority group members to conform to the existing culture of the society in which their culture is constructed as the "norm."[2] Driedger (1989) refers to this as "a nationalist attempt" to have the minorities in society inculcate the values, norms and habits of the society; in other words, to acculturate or assimilate.

According to social scientists, *acculturation* is the response of minority groups and immigrants to overt or systemic pressures from the dominant group to adopt, conform or adjust to dominant values, customs, behaviours and psychological characteristics (Sodowsky et al., 1991: 195). *Assimilation* is identified as an aspect of the acculturation process. During acculturation, individuals incorporate cultural elements of the dominant ethnic group. During assimilation, considerable elements of their ethnic or racial subcultures are relinquished in order to "fit in." This theory of assimilation is premised on the idea that the power of the dominant group will be too much for any minority group to resist, and therefore the group will assimilate into the dominant group (Driedger, 1989). We usually consider this to be the American "melting pot" approach to accommodating diversity.

Assimilationist theorists claim that, as racial and ethnic minority group members interact with dominant group members, particularly in major institutions[3] where the dominant group's norms and values predominate, some kind of conformity is inevitable. This is all the more likely as minority group members recognize that success or upward social mobility is dependent on their being able to operate within the larger society. It is suggested that these group members seek to avoid poverty, alienation and harassment, which are the consequences of the sanctions against those whose culture deviates too far from the "norm." Assisting this process of assimilation and/or acculturation are mechanisms such as ethnocentrism, prejudice and racism, which are often sustained by stereotyping and discrimination. The significance of these mechanisms is evident in the role they play in preserving and perpetuating the structure and the cultural ethos of the society that favour the dominant group (see Chapter 5).

---

[2] It should be noted that many theories have been developed to explain what happens in modern, heterogeneous, technological societies. These are (a) assimilation and amalgamation, which "assume that the urban industrial forces of technology and majority power will cause some loss of ethnic identity"; (b) modified assimilation and modified pluralism, which "predict that minorities will retain ethnic characteristics partially or in changed forms"; and (c) ethnic pluralism and ethnic conflict, which "emphasize that ethnic solidarity and identity can be maintained despite industrialization in both rural and urban settings" (Driedger, 1989: 34). My argument is that, while the power of the dominant ethno-racial group is a significant force within the cultural evolution process, the active ways in which groups seek to maintain their respective cultures will not lead merely to their acculturation into the existing dominant cultural frame, but to a cultural frame that enables them to cultivate and display the values and aspirations of their cultural group.

[3] Major institutions refers to government (politics), education, society, culture (ballet, opera), recreation (hockey, baseball).

The premise of acculturation and assimilation suggests that minority groups are not likely to actively resist coercion and hence will not be able to maintain their cultures in any form. Neither does their definition indicate that the culture of the society as a whole will change regardless of the limitations of the dominant ethno-cultural group. If the society is to survive and contain the many challenges, tensions and conflicts that result from the various groups' struggles for recognition and their rightful and equal place in the society, then some sort of "accommodation" will or must be made. It is inevitable then that the cultures of minority groups will help to determine the culture of the society that emerges. That general culture will be influenced by the relative number of the groups; the time and rate of entrance of the respective groups; where they settle; the extent to which they are isolated or segregated; the age and sex composition of the groups; the influence of individuals either in opposing or encouraging assimilation; the crises that are experienced in the society (Berry, 1958: 240) and the political, economic and social actions of the groups.

THE POLICY OF MULTICULTURALISM

There is a common belief in Canada that, in contrast to the assimilation policies and practices of the United States, "we are multicultural."[4] Many of the class participants declared this to be so. Indeed, there is a Multiculturalism Act, which states:

> [T]he Constitution of Canada ... recognizes the importance of preserving and enhancing the multicultural heritage of Canadians...; [and] the government of Canada recognizes the diversity of Canadians as regards race, national or ethnic origin, colour and religion as a fundamental characteristic of Canadian society and is committed to a policy of multiculturalism designed to preserve and enhance the multicultural heritage of Canadians while working to achieve the equality of all Canadians in the economic, social, cultural and political life of Canada (The Multicultural Policy of Canada, the *Canadian Multicultural Act* [July 1988]).

According to the Standing Committee on Multiculturalism (1987), it is the integration of racial and ethnic groups that is encouraged, not the assimilation. The Committee defines integration as "a process, clearly distinct from assimilation, by which groups and/or individuals become able to participate fully in the political, economic, social and cultural life of the country" (Standing Committee, 1987: 87). Prime Minister Pierre Elliott Trudeau, on October 8, 1971, attempted to reassure the Canadian population that assimi-

[4] George Elliott Clarke (1998), in his essay "White Like Canada," writes, "Canadian identity, such as it is, defines itself primarily in opposition to the United States. Canadians are nice; Americans are trigger-happy. Canadians also claim to be uniquely sensitive to multiculturalism. Whereas the American paradigm for assimilation is the "melting pot," Canada celebrates a gorgeous "mosaic" of peoples permitted to maintain their ethnic particularisms. The most significant difference between Canada and the U.S. is, finally, that America has a race problem. In Canada, the party line goes, there are no racists save those who watch too much American television ..." (1998: 100-101).

lation or conformity was not an objective of the official federal policy of multiculturalism. In part, he declared that

> there cannot be one cultural policy for Canadians of British and French origin, another for the original peoples, and yet another for all the others. For although there are two official languages there is no official culture, nor does any ethnic group take precedence over any other.... A policy of multiculturalism within a bilingual framework commends itself to the government as the most suitable means of assuring the cultural freedom of Canadians.... First, resources permitting, the government will seek to assist all Canadian cultural groups that have demonstrated a desire and effort to continue to develop, a capacity to grow and contribute to Canada, and a clear need for assistance, the small and weak groups no less than the strong and highly organized. Second, the government will assist members of all cultural groups to overcome cultural barriers to full participation in Canadian society. Third, the government will promote creative encounters and interchange among all Canadian cultural groups in the interest of national unity. Fourth, the government will continue to assist immigrants to acquire at least one of Canada's official languages in order to become full participants in Canadian society (cf. Palmer, 1975).[5]

Fleras and Elliot (1992) point out that the policy of multiculturalism addresses the experiences and expressions of members of society at the "individual, group, institutional, and societal levels" (p.23). At the individual and group levels, the policy assumes that discriminatory attitudes and cultural jealousies can be overcome if all Canadians share the same amount of cultural freedom. But can this belief in cultural pluralism as the very essence of Canadian identity be practised in a society in which inequality and racial and ethnic stratification are institutionalized? Probably Jaenen (1977) answered this question best when he observed:

> It should not be assumed ... that by defining Canada as bilingual and multicultural the federal government and the various provincial governments are making a definitive sociological analysis of Canadian society. Rather politicians are responding to electoral exigencies, to lobbies, and more optimistically also to the historical context and constitutional dialogue. It was obviously impossible to maintain the initial policy rubric of biculturalism, although bureaucrats as well as social scientists realize that the term multiethnic comes closer to defining Canadian social reality than does the term multicultural (p.81).

Consider also Price's (1978) idea that cultural pluralism is a myth. Price contends that the customs of the minority ethnic groups "that survive are usually these innocuous ones that escape the conforming crush of law, such as religious practices, music and tastes in food. These, then, become the hallmarks of ethnic difference, remnants of once truly different cultures" (p.85).

The notion of cultural pluralism can therefore be seen as a way in which Canada sought to accommodate different groups, as well as to avoid or

---

[5] Today, the multiculturalism policy is law. It is the Canadian Multiculturalism Act (Bill C-93) passed in July of 1988. In addition to reinforcing the sentiments of the earlier policy, the Act emphasizes the promotion of positive race relations and cross-cultural understanding in a society where multiculturalism is a "fundamental characteristic of our evolving Canadian heritage and identity."

resolve tension and conflict between the various groups in the society. It remains true, however, that our society is stratified by gender, ethnicity, race and class upon which acculturation and assimilation have operated as "there are limits beyond which cultural freedom cannot go" (Berry, 1958: 339). Hence, contrary to the notion of cultural democracy, groups, though speaking their own languages and following their own customs with respect to food, dress, rituals, recreation and worship, must carry out their day-to-day living within the boundaries of the established legal, political, economic, cultural and social institutions if they are to be "acceptable" members of the society. Most of these institutions represent the perspective and worldview of the dominant cultural group.

Further, contrary to the claim that conformity is not an aim of multiculturalism, a critical examination will show that, insofar as "the political, economic, social and cultural life of the country" (Standing Committee, 1987: 87) is in fact constituted and controlled by the dominant ethno-cultural group of the society, there are overt and covert pressures towards conformity. How else would immigrants and minority group members "fully participate"? Indeed, critics (James, 1998; Bannerji, 1997; Walcott, 1997) have long argued that Canada's multiculturalism, set as it is "within a bilingual framework," and claiming that "there is no official culture, nor does any ethnic group take precedence over any other," merely reinforces the British and French ethno-cultural identities. It does so while promoting assimilation under the guise of integration of "other ethnic groups" and while alluding to "the undisputable role played by Canadians of French and British origins in 1867, and long before Confederation" (Innis, abridged version of the Bilingualism and Biculturalism Report, 1973: 1).

In a paper entitled "Multiculturalism Diversity and Education," I write that these "Other Canadians" are represented in the multicultural program as "people with a 'heritage' from elsewhere and whose 'foreign' cultural values and practices remain static and based on their past experiences in other countries"(James, 1998: 4). Multiculturalism promotes a discourse of "difference," signalling that culture is primarily carried in and exhibited by people with "foreign bodies" who are "linguistically different" (i.e., non-English or non-French speaking, with "accents") and "do not look and sound Canadian." The popularly held notion of "Canadian-ness" is related to the construction of Canadians as "phenotypically white" (Walcott, 1997) and without accent (in other words, Anglo-Celtics) (James, 1998: 4; see also Bannerji, 1997; James and Shadd, 1994; Roman and Stanley, 1997; Quamina, 1996). This conception of "Canadian" and "culture" is evident in the following comments:

Table 9: Canadian Population by Aboriginal Groups and Sex, Showing Age Groups, for Canada, 1996 Census – 20% Sample Data Canada

Aboriginal groups and sex	**Total Age groups**
Total population	28,528,125
Male	14,046,875
Female	14,481,245
Non-Aboriginal population	**27,729,115**
Male	13,656,005
Female	14,073,105
Aboriginal population	***799,005***
Male	390,870
Female	408,140
North American Indian single response	**529,040**
Male	258,335
Female	270,700
Métis single response	**204,115**
Male	101,430
Female	102,685
Inuit single response	**40,220**
Male	20,180
Female	20,040
Aboriginal multiple responses	**6,420**
Male	3,175
Female	3,240
Other Aboriginal response	**19,220**
Male	7,750
Female	11,465

Notes:
(1) Depending on the area under study, the data for North American Indians may be more affected than most by the incomplete enumeration of certain Indian Reserves and Indian Settlements. In the 1996 Census, a total of 77 Indian Reserves and Indian Settlements were incompletely enumerated. The populations of these 77 communities are not included in the Census counts.
(2) Includes those with registered Indian and/or Band member response without self-reported Aboriginal response.

Source: Statistics Canada, 1996 Census, *Nation* tables.

> **Andrea**: Call me naive, ignorant, or sheltered from the real world, but I thought in order to have a culture a person had to be of a different racial group. Since I was born in Canada, I thought I was just "Canadian." Now I am told I have a culture....

> **Richard**: As far as my culture goes, I am at a loss. I am Canadian. Period. There are no special traditions or attitudes that have been passed on to me by my parents or grandparents. My parents have taught me what they think is important for me to know. I have no traditional food or drink, no cultural costume. I am Canadian.

We have already made reference in Chapter 2 to one student who, in the introductory class exercise, was asked to identify himself in terms of ethnicity and race and refused to say anything other than that he is "Canadian." However, he suggested that he would not accept that single descriptor from a Black or Chinese person because "they do not look Canadian."

The political, social and cultural messages that Canadians receive through multiculturalism contributes to the homogenization of "foreign bodies"; in other words, a construction of "cultural groups" based on "likeness" or "sameness" (James, 1998). This was quite evident in the way students discussed some of the minority groups, specifically Blacks. The seeming overgeneralization or stereotyping of Blacks as being more likely to engage in criminal activities than other racial and ethnic groups led one participant to reflect the following at the conclusion of class.

> **Troy**: We argued and argued over the matter of the Black community and the police. My argument, and I think I can speak for at least one-quarter of the class, was that Black people tend to be more involved in crime. From statistics or police documents I can draw this conclusion. But one cannot make this type of conclusion because statistics mean nothing. All they are saying is that so many crimes are being committed by these types of people. There are bad apples on every tree. I believe that all people are good. Just because there are some bad ones does not mean that the entire race should be discriminated against. I also hold the belief that a criminal has no colour. A criminal is a wrong-doer, and all criminals shall be dealt with by the law.

Multiculturalism, as many critics argue, is a state ideological mechanism used to manage the difference and dissension that are to be expected in any society, and, of course, within a diverse society (Ng, 1993; Bannerji, 1997; Walcott, 1997; James, 1998). Further, scholars argue that the current multiculturalism policy is the re-conceptualization of an old Canadian policy of assimilation of minority groups. Historically, policies have articulated the "assimilation" of First Nations people and "other" Canadians. Now the word used is integration (Leslie and Maguire, 1978; Jaenen, 1977; Driedger, 1989).

EXPECTATIONS OF ANGLO-CONFORMITY

There is no denying that Canadian governments have always sought to bring about Anglo-conformity through the assimilation and integration of ethnic and racial minority groups and Aboriginals. Historical evidence shows that the British settlers expected, through the legal, political, economic, and cultural institutions they established, that the Aboriginal people, the French and subsequent immigrant populations would assimilate to an Anglo-Saxon way of life. Leaders such as Lord Durham hoped that "somehow even the French would finally amalgamate into the dominant culture although not without conflict and competition. [These leaders] assumed the desirability of social institutions and expected all others to learn the English language" (Driedger, 1989: 41). It was felt that the core of nationalism must remain English while French institutions, language and history would take a lesser role.

The cultural debasement and social indoctrination of the Aboriginal peoples serve as a testament to the importance placed on assimilation in the institutionalization of Anglo-Canadian cultural norms. At the beginning of European settlement, First Nations' peoples spoke different languages and lived in complex, self-governed societies. The 1876 Indian Act was a determined effort to eradicate the cultures of the Indian, Inuit and Métis peoples. The Act declared that all Indians who married non-Indians or who received an education in a Christian residential school would be recognized as "civilized" and "fit for white society." All of these "enfranchised" Indians and their families would then be required to leave the reserve. As Frideres points out, the assumption of many was that the longer "our individual native resides in an urban area, the more likely integration into the dominant society becomes" (Frideres, 1993; see also Monture-Angus, 1995; Haig-Brown, 1993). Today, there are few Aboriginals alive who have not been influenced by the enormous impact of European culture on their traditional way of life (see Adams, 1989; Bedassigae-Pheasant, 1996; Pleasant-Jetté, 1996: Monture-Angus, 1995; Wotherspoon and Satzewich, 1993; Mannette, 1992).

What is the place of First Nations or Aboriginal people within the multicultural policy, given the fact that they are certainly not part of the "other ethnic groups" and the Indian Act already regulates their relationship to the State? The 1971 multiculturalism policy did not attempt to bring First Nations under its jurisdiction. Understandably, First Nations people took the position that, since they were not part of the "foreign," constructed Other, they were outside the ambit of the policy. However, the Multiculturalism Act of 1988, in assenting that the policy and practices of multiculturalism apply to "all Canadians," indicates that, as "Canadians," Aboriginals are indeed included. The 1991 pamphlet *Multiculturalism:*

What Is It Really About? points out that "many of the issues to which multiculturalism responds–racism, understanding different cultures, and preserving culture–concern aboriginal peoples" (p.18). The pamphlet goes on: "However, many of their political, social, and economic concerns are beyond these programs. Other federal government departments have policies and programs designed to deal with these issues" (p.19).

The educational system established in Upper Canada by Egerton Ryerson, a former Methodist minister, influenced educational institutions throughout Canada. It was premised on the principle of "fitting children for their place in the social hierarchy" (cf. McNeill, 1974: 134). In the words of Ryerson, the purpose of education was to "impart to the public mind the greatest amount of useful knowledge based upon and interwoven throughout with sound Christian principles [and that they must] render the system in all its various ramifications and applications the indirect but powerful instrument of British Constitutional government" (cf. McNeill, 1974: 133).

Over the years, education, like other institutions, has operated to "Canadianize" immigrants and minorities. Ashworth writes that "the goal of public schools was to assimilate immigrant children into the Canadian way of life. The 'hidden curriculum' was biased towards white Anglo-Saxons.... Concepts contrary to the religious beliefs of some groups were stressed, and Christian beliefs and values were promulgated" (1988: 27-8). Hence, as the English had authority over the government, the courts, religion, the educational system and all the other important structures of the society, this ensured the survival of the British culture.[6]

The fact that some ethnic and racial groups reside in enclaves, whether in large urban centres or on rural reserves, does not mean that they do not undergo this "integration" process. While it may be true that many still practice aspects of their ancestral cultures to varying degrees, they all reside in Canada, and the process of conformity is sure to influence their cultural values and behaviours. Furthermore, members of these groups must attend educational institutions in which they are taught the dominant values, norms and behavioural practices. Like other Canadians, minority group members are socialized to elements of culture through the textbooks used, the languages spoken and the daily routines of educational institutions.

---

[6] It should be noted that education was established under provincial jurisdiction as a consequence of the British North America Act. It meant that the education systems of each province developed differently. In Quebec for instance, while French education was supported, English control over education and the possibility of assimilation was very much a fear (Jaenen, 1977). Provinces such as Ontario, Manitoba, Alberta and Saskatchewan committed what Jaenen (1977) refers to as "linguistic genocide in the name of efficiency." By instructing students in English alone, they would be "Canadianized," thereby producing "Anglo-conformity" (see also Tomkins, 1977).

STUDENTS' VIEWS OF MULTICULTURALISM

Ed: *"The Multiculturalism Act has given everyone the chance to change Canada ..."*

I was never a fan of the Multicultural Act and, if anything, I find myself even more opposed to it now. Although many people would like to say that this makes me a racist, I believe that I am not. A racist is someone who hates or discriminates against a person or people because of a difference (or perceived difference) in colour or religion. While I have never been like that, it sure makes my blood boil to hear that Sikhs can wear their turbans in our police forces or that schools are required to remove all symbols of Christmas from the classroom. Just because I do not like to see these events happen doesn't mean that I dislike the person for succeeding in his or her quest. I am developing a strong discriminatory attitude towards the government.

On the topic of a Canadian identity, I can remember a government official (I cannot remember who) stating that one of Canada's greatest problems is that we haven't been able to create a feeling of being truly Canadian. This same politician stated that many of the problems that we are experiencing with Quebec could be amended if we could just inspire a feeling of Canadian-ness within the people. That statement blew my mind. This same politician supports the very Act which is, with the government's blessing and money, destroying what remaining Canadian identity there is. Not only does Canada open its arms and borders to accept immigrants from all over the world, which is something that doesn't bother me, but it also willingly changes *Canadian* traditions and customs to accommodate them. In essence, what the Canadian government is doing is saying, "Hi! Welcome, culture. Don't worry about learning one of the two official languages of the country. In fact, if there are any traditions that have been around in Canada for a long time that you do not like, let us know. We will either exclude you from them or change them all just for you."

What the Multicultural Act has really done is given everyone a chance to change Canada and make it more like the country they left in the first place. If you want to inspire a feeling of Canadian pride, leave Canada's laws and customs as they are and encourage people to assimilate and contribute to the country in a positive way. As John F. Kennedy so eloquently put it, "Ask not what your country can do for you, but what you can do for your country!" Although this was an American President, I believe this country needs to do some real flag waving to wake it up.

Jeremy: *"Canadians don't know enough about the history of French Canada ..."*

During the last week, the issue of sovereignty for Quebec has been competing with the Gulf War for the news headlines. This issue sparked after the failure of the Meech Lake Accord. The collapse of the Accord created an even stronger feeling of patriotism in Quebec. This event sealed the fate of Canada's future. French Canadians are often thought of as extremist, separatist and selfish. I believe that English Canadians don't know enough about the history of French Canada to be able to be make a fair and unbiased assessment of them or the situation. During the next few paragraphs, I will express my opinion and try to clarify the situation as a "Quebecois."

I don't believe anyone can fully understand the situation unless they've lived it. I was born in Montreal, and I went to a French school until I came to college in Ontario. I believe that this enabled me to see through many of the lies that the media was reporting. The greatest concern for the French is the preservation of their language. They live in a continent dominated by the English language. They are influenced by this through music, television, the media and of course the political system. Many tactics used by the Quebec government to ensure the safety of the French language are questionable. The greatest example is Bill 101; this affected the province on many levels: economic, educational, social.... I believe that it violates human rights, especially in the domain of freedom of speech. But is it justified? I believe it is. If the rest of Canada is almost solely English (road signs, store signs), why not? There is one aspect that I haven't made up my mind about: immigrants or Canadians whose parents did not go to an English school are obliged to go to a French school, although I believe that going to a French school is the first step towards becoming a "true Canadian" (most immigrants already know a bit of English!).

If you have taken a good history course, you will know that Canada did not start out with equality between the English and the French. I remember learning that the English had tried to assimilate the French by forcing them to go to English schools and by not allowing them to have any Catholic establishments. Eventually the French got some of their rights back—not because of the fairness of the English, but because of their strong will and their patriotism. The one thing that will never change is their devoted patriotism towards the Quebec flag and their language. Proof of that can be found in Quebec's music and theatre and is especially in evidence on Saint Jean Baptist day (national holiday). For the first time this summer, I participated in the holiday celebrations, and I was blown away by the number of people in the streets carrying flags and chanting, "Vive le Quebec!" That day I was proud to be a "Quebecois"!

The thing that annoys me most is when other Canadians complain that, when they go to Quebec, nobody speaks to them in English. What do they expect? The French know just as much English as the remainder of Canadians know French. If French people were to travel to anywhere in Canada outside of Quebec, they wouldn't expect everyone to speak French to them. Let's not have double standards!

I believe it's time that Canada realized that Quebec has a completely different culture. The way things are going, Quebec will separate, and it will prove to be a great loss for all Canadians. It's time we opened our eyes and accepted Quebec for what it is and not for what we want it to be. Without "La Belle Province," there will be no Canada. It's about time all Canadians discarded their differences and tried to live together as one!

Ron: *"I don't think that it is right that a Sikh may change that rule."*

The idea that Sikhs are allowed to wear their turbans while on duty for a Canadian police force makes me very, very mad. I know that everyone in Canada has freedom of religion, and there is nothing wrong with that. However, the Charter of Rights and Freedoms is like rules and regulations. The police force has rules and regulations, and under those, there is a uniform rule that states that every police officer must wear a hat. I don't think that it is right that a Sikh may change that rule. It is not fair to the rest of the police force. In fact, I think that it is an insult to this country. If I went to their country, there would be no way in hell that I or any other white man would be able to change any of their rules. I do not have any prejudices against the Sikhs or any other nationality or skin colour, but people from other countries are treating Canada like garbage and they are taking advantage of Canada and its people. I think that in order to change this problem, Canada has to take away some privileges and change the Charter of Rights and Freedoms.

Simon: *"The very essence of the multicultural policy within Canada is being ignored."*

Although the past few decades have seen numerous changes in Canada's constitution regarding racist attitudes, statutes and laws founded on bigotry, the recent confrontation between the minority Sikhs and the majority white Canadians over the issue of the Sikhs wearing their ceremonial daggers proves, in my opinion, that the system of social stratification and inequality among minority groups is far from being eradicated.

Being labelled as a minority within the Canadian culture tends to lead to certain stigmas and attacks that are based on the colour of people's skin, as well as on the rites or rituals that take place within the subculture of minority groupings. Sikhs have recently become the target for attack, such as this one regarding their traditional dagger, which a great many Sikhs see as an essential part of their heritage.

When Sikhs come to Canada and become citizens of this country, they, as well as all other minorities, are granted full freedom of religion, language and all heritage rights. I believe that, by depriving the Sikhs of their right to wear the kirpan, the very essence of the multicultural policy within Canada is being ignored. The Sikhs view their dagger as something to be honoured and deeply treasured—not as a weapon—just as Christians view their cross.

I think it is sad that the prevalent attitude among so many Canadians is, "We let them into this country, so they should do as we tell them to. You don't see us going to their country and making all these demands." I believe that this type of statement reflects the way the Canadian population has been reared with close-minded and bigoted attitudes, handed down from generation to generation.

Many more changes need to be made before Sikhs or any other minority group can appreciate the freedom that they deserve. Although Canada is proclaimed as a multicultural country, it really is not. Until multiculturalism is fully enforced and regulated, minority rights will continue to be undermined and stepped on. Changes need to be made now.

Chuck: *"Multicultural ideals are in fact counter-productive ..."*

The formula is quite simple: if you want access to opportunity, you must be able to assimilate and become part of Canadian culture. If a Canadian moved to any other country in the world, he would have to adapt to its culture if he wanted to succeed. The multicultural ideals are in fact counter-productive to the economic growth of Canada. For Canada to truly arrive at being an integrated society, we have to begin behaving as though we are all Canadians; that we have our own culture and that all of the various cultures that compose our great nation should work towards blending into a harmonious society. Unfortunately, racism continues to exist in every imaginable way among all races. But we are certainly more likely to make inroads against these attitudes and make progress towards actual equality if we learn to view one another as human beings and not as Blacks, African Canadians, Jewish Canadians, Aboriginal Canadians and so on.

These comments by students reflect the commonly held notions that (a) those with culture are primarily "foreigners"–ethnic and racial minorities, non-English or non-French-speaking people and immigrants who identify with their country of origin while in Canada, and (b) that they should "maintain" the languages and traditions of "their" country while living in Canada. Ironically, many of these same students claim that "there is no Canadian culture," yet they voice resentment, as do Ed and Chuck, that Canada's culture is being changed. Their understanding of culture as something made up of observable, distinguishable elements, possessed primarily by immigrants and people who are racially and religiously different, is indicative of what has been communicated to them through the multiculturalism discourse. Further, it illustrates the observation made by Barnlund (1988) that the cultural norms of the society so completely surround them, so permeate their thoughts and actions, that they do not recognize the assumptions and the structures on which their lives and worldview rest (p.14).

It is the Anglo-Celtic structures that individuals such as Ed, Simon, Chuck and many others are seeking to maintain–that core set of values, norms, practices and aspirations to which all of us within the geographic boundary of Canada are expected to adhere. Despite the claim of cultural freedom or multiculturalism, there are evidently strong and not-so-hidden messages that promote conformity to Anglo-Celtic (and in Quebec, French) ideas, knowledge, symbols, customs, languages goals and aspirations, as well as views on how people should or should not behave. These social, linguistic, cultural and political expectations are governed by legislation, policies, rules, practices, values, sanctions and so on. These are reinforced through schools, workplaces, courts, police forces, businesses and media socialization. In promoting cultural conformity, these institutions help "to organize, integrate, and maintain the psychological patterns of the individual, especially in the formative years of childhood ... that are unique, coherent and logical to the premises and predispositions that underlie the culture" (Adler, 1977: 28).

On the notion of cultural sanctions and conformity, one class participant observed that, as a business employee, it is likely that her attitudes towards minorities and immigrants "who hold unfamiliar values and customs" was likely to have contributed to their conforming.

> **Jillianne**: Recently a Chinese lady came to the bank where I am employed, and presented me with documents stating that her Chinese name had been changed to a Canadian name. I asked if changing her name would make her life easier. "No," she replied, "it will make things easier for *you*." How true! This brief incident clarified for me how Canadian immigrants struggle with the attitudes of the dominant group, how they are often forced to adapt and assimilate to our Canadian ways.

One aspect of our cultural diversity with which many Canadians seem to struggle is that of religious freedom–the right of individuals to engage in their particular religious practices. As some of the essays indicate, religious practices, for example, those of Sikhs (often cited), are perceived to contravene "our laws" and will inevitably change "our Canadian identity." Particular references are made to Sikhs being allowed to wear turbans on our police forces. Participants insisted that religious practices such as those of Sikhs are contrary to our laws even when informed that the Canadian constitution and the Multiculturalism Act claims to support these practices. Specifically, the constitution "provides that every individual is equal before and under the law and has the right to equal protection and benefit of the law without discrimination and that everyone has the freedom of conscience, religion, thought, belief, opinion, expression, peaceful assembly and association." Further, the Multiculturalism Act states, in part, that

> whereas Canada is a party to the *International Convention on the Elimination of All Forms of Racial Discrimination*, which Convention recognizes that all human beings are equal before the law and are entitled to equal protection of the law against any discrimination and against any incitement to discrimination, and to the *International Covenant on Civil and Political Rights*, which Covenant provides that persons belonging to ethnic, religious or linguistic minorities shall not be denied the right to enjoy their own culture, to profess and practise their own religion or to use their own language . . ..

Criticisms are very often made by some dominant group Canadians whose religious practices and symbols are well-preserved by the laws and institutions of our society. Generally, Canadians do not know that the Sikh religion has been in Canada for generations; that the first Sikh temple or *gurdwara* was opened in Vancouver, British Columbia, in 1908 (Burnet and Palmer, 1989). On the basis of longevity alone, shouldn't we think of it as a well-established Canadian religion?

The principles of equity and social justice should underlie what is put in place to ensure the rights and privileges of Canadians. The aims and objectives of the multiculturalism policy claim that the rights and freedom of all members of society will be ensured. But as historical and contemporary evidence has shown, Canadian multiculturalism policy and programs as currently constituted do less to promote equity, social justice and cultural freedom than to ensure that cultural conformity takes place. So individuals who fear that "our culture" (read Anglo-Celtic, or French) will be significantly changed through, for example, Sikh South Asians walking around with daggers, or becoming a significant proportion of our police force, need not worry for the forces of conformity will ensure that it does not materialize.

However, despite what might be said of the conforming aspect of Canada's multiculturalism policy and practices, there are clear signs that it has served Canada well, particularly in terms of public relations abroad and at home. The following comments from Jenny, an immigrant from Hong Kong, suggest that she earnestly believes that her choice of Canada as a country to immigrate to is a good one, for cultural freedom and tolerance exist here. She perceives that she and her family will prove to be "worthy members of society" while they seek to maintain their Chinese language, customs, beliefs, values and cultural celebrations. To what extent will Jenny and her family, some years hence, retain their customs and ideas and feel the same way?

Jenny: *"We have chosen Canada because it is a free country and it tolerates multiculturalism."*

My family came to Canada from Hong Kong as landed immigrants two years ago. We are Chinese, born and raised in Hong Kong. Our parents were born in China, but they went to Hong Kong in 1949 when the Communists took over mainland China. We decided to leave before the Communists took political control of Hong Kong. We have chosen Canada because it is a free country and it tolerates multiculturalism.

We are adapting to the Canadian culture. However, in no way do we want to give up our own identity as a distinct ethnic group. We are proud of our ethnic heritage, and we want our children to learn and uphold it. On the other hand, we are aware that it is important to learn the values of Canadians in order to integrate into the mainstream of the society. We feel ourselves to be at a crossroads, trying to find a good balance between the two value systems—the one we were brought up with, and the one we are confronted with at the moment.

The majority of Canadians are Anglo-white, and we are a Chinese-yellow minority. We know that no amount of cultural adaptation can completely eradicate our racial distinction. We find that being a minority means we are in a disadvantaged position in political, economic and social standing. Nevertheless, we want to be good citizens here, and we want to prove that we are worthy members of society.

I am writing this essay as an individual and as a parent. My racial and ethnic origins have bearing on my values and attitudes and are manifested in my behaviour in terms of what I do, what I plan for my children and what I expect from them.

It is a common view among the Chinese parents here that they do not want their children to be like "bananas"—yellow-skinned, yet white inside. I am a supporter of this viewpoint. I believe that it is important to retain our own ethnic identity through the maintenance of the Chinese language, familiarization with the Chinese history, celebration of the Chinese festivals and linkage with the Chinese community:

Maintenance of the Chinese Language. Language is an important means of differentiation for it distinguishes us from other ethnic groups. At home, we talk to our children in Chinese and expect them to answer in the same language. We ensure that they can read and write Chinese by sending them to heritage school every Saturday.

Familiarization with Chinese History. China is an ancient country with thousands of years of cultural heritage. We want our children to be familiar with the roots of our culture. We expose them to story books and videos about the deeds of the great men and women in Chinese history, and explain to them what we can learn from these celebrated people.

Celebration of the Chinese Festivals. The Chinese festivals, for example, the Chinese New Year, the Mid-Autumn Festival, and the Winter Solstice, have special meaning because they bring all members of the family together and promote kinship and common bonds. We value these celebrations and encourage our children to participate.

Linking with the Chinese Community. By visiting Chinatown, attending events organized by the Chinese community, reading Chinese newspapers and magazines and communicating with relatives and friends back in Hong Kong, we keep ourselves informed of the happenings in the Chinese community, and we expose our children to these aspects of the Chinese culture to supplement what we teach at home.

The Value of Learning from Confucius' Teaching

Here, in Canada, we find that at the grassroots level there is a general lack of seriousness towards work. At school, there is a liberal attitude towards students' academic achievement, and at home, there is little respect for parents and grandparents compared to that which exists in Chinese families. We would feel threatened if our children were to pick up these attitudes. To counteract them, we find it useful to emphasize the teaching of the great Chinese teacher and philosopher Confucius. Specifically, these values are spelled out as follows: (1) the virtue of filial piety—the love and respect for a parent; (2) the virtue of industry—the need to excel through hard work; (3) the virtue of being an all-round educated person—the need to be trained in the mind and the body, for education is the foundation of a future career.

The Value of Learning the Canadian Culture

Being in Canada, I believe that it is equally important to learn the Canadian culture in order to live a meaningful life. At the moment, I believe in the importance of mastering the English language, learning Canadian sports, celebrating Canadian festivals and enjoying family life.

The Importance of Learning the Language. I will continue to polish my English so that I can communicate well with people in the workplace; we want our children to learn both English and French so that they can do well in school.

The Importance of Learning Canadian Sports. Sports have become part of the Canadian way of life and a topic for conversation. We are learning how these sport games are played, and we want our children to be able to play hockey, baseball and soccer and learn skating, skiing and swimming.

Celebration of the Canadian Festivals. We celebrate the Canadian festivals such as Easter, Thanksgiving, Halloween and Christmas like other Canadians. I think this is important, as we want our children to be able to share and talk about the joy of these festivals with their friends at school.

The Importance of Family Life. I observe that most Canadians put a lot of emphasis on family life. Sunday is regarded as an important day for family gathering and religious worship, and the issue of Sunday shopping is attacked vigorously. Having been here for two years, I am used to the idea of going to church on Sunday morning and spending the rest of the day with my family.

I observe that, in one way or another, I am changing my behaviours and lifestyle. Though striving to uphold some of the values I have brought from my mother country, I am gradually assimilating the values of the Canadian culture. I am sure that in a few years I will subconsciously pick up more of the predominant values of the Canadian society.

SUMMARY

Each member of Canadian society participates in a culture. Cultures are dynamic, complex, contradictory and conflictive; and are influenced by the social and physical contexts in which they exist. The cultural practices and customs of the Italian, African, Scottish, Portuguese, Asian or South Asian groups in Canada differ from those in the countries in which they comprise the dominant group. With Canada's multiculturalism notion of integration, ethnic and racial minority group members are expected to conform to the norms, values and expectations of the society, which are largely informed by the dominant ethno-cultural group. The variations that are found among groups and individuals are a reflection of social stratification, inequalities and the socialization process, which are influenced by such characteristics as ethnicity, race, religion, citizenship, social class, gender, dis/abilities and so on. Agents of socialization, such as the family, school, work and peers, are expected to ensure that individuals acquire what they need to function in the society with a minimum of disruption to the established social, cultural, economic and political structures.

One signature aspect of Canadian culture is the institutionalization of two "official languages"–French and English. This has resulted in a duality of institutions and demonstrates the recognition given to the role of language as an integral part of culture. While communicating in the English or French language is understood to be important and crucial to the cultural identity and cultural retention of these two groups, the same argument is not made for other language groups. They are expected to retain their culture while communicating in the two official languages. Is cultural retention possible? What, in fact, does retention mean?

Driedger (1989) suggests that those ethnic groups that are closer in appearance and cultural practices to the dominant Anglo-Saxon ethnic group will adjust much more readily to the Canadian cultural and social context. Specifically, Northern Europeans, Driedger argues, have considerable cultural affinity with the Anglo-Saxon culture and, being white, they are subjected to little racial prejudice and discrimination. They have some level of influence and control over their situation in the society. They voluntarily integrate into the culture of the society by adopting the language, as well as by conforming and accommodating themselves. This has enabled them to compete quite well economically.

The perceived culture of respective ethnic groups, their population size, history, perceived role in the building of Canada and level of commitment towards maintaining their ancestral culture, all will help to determine how their cultural values, norms and aspirations are articulated in Canada. It can be expected, given the dynamism of culture, that elements of the culture of respective groups will be evident in the general Canadian culture. In cases where a group's cultural practices are not in conflict with the dominant cultural norms and values of the society, these cultural practices may persist over time and eventually elements of them will become absorbed into Canadian cultural norms.[7] But where conflicting cultural values and practices exist, and depending on the outcome of conformity pressures, cultural norms and values will emerge.

Tension and conflict are often found within culturally diverse societies. They are sometimes a result of differences in political perspectives, lack of recognition of respective differences, lack of access to political and economic resources and the society's inability to manage and accommodate these differences. Canada is not unique in the difficulties it experiences between the various ethno-cultural groups. The French-English issue is an example of the tension that exists in culturally diverse societies such as ours. Similar tension and conflict can be observed in other nations. How we address these issues and tensions reflects how we understand and accept our cultural diversity and cultural differences, as well as how we accommodate our minority population.

Before leaving the discussion of multiculturalism, it is important to reflect on multicultural education policies and practices and the extent to which they are likely to ensure education equity for minority students, as well as continue to promote misconceptions and misinformation to the school population.[8]

Scholars have argued that multicultural education, premised on the multiculturalism policy, does nothing to challenge the structural barriers such as racism, sexism, classism. These operate as barriers to the educational participation and success of minority students (James, 1998; Roman and Stanley, 1997; Dei, 1994; Lee, 1996). The promise that multicultural education can provide equal opportunity, address educational underachievement and improve individuals' self-image (Mansfield and Kehoe, 1994) will not be realized within the current context that ignores the hegemonic nature of the dominant culture, based as it is on compounded privileges accrued from class, race and gender.

Mazurek points out that the promises of multicultural education have turned out to be an "illusion." Multiculturalism, as practised in Canada, has not made "schools the fair, objective and unbiased institutions that they must become if the promise of equality of opportunity is to be fulfilled. The

---

[7] For example, most Canadians have had "Chinese" dinners and pizza, which we tend to assume were brought here by the Chinese and Italians respectively. Also, signs in languages other than English or French are common in many areas of Canada. Institutions, including governments, communicate to members of communities in languages other than French and English.

[8] What follows is an adapted portion of my article "Multicultural and Anti-racism Education in Canada." In *Race, Gender & Class: An Interdisciplinary & Multicultural Journal* 2, no. 3 (1995): 43-4.

meritocratic myth is just that–a myth" (1987: 152). On the idea of celebrating diversity, Lee (1994: 24) writes that

> one can organize a unity and diversity club and deal with cultural holidays and host a Multicultural Week and yet not deal with racism. These events may present some information about cultural groups and focus on the exotic and leave many people with a nice feeling but do nothing to address the schools' response or lack of response to the languages and faiths of students of colour. They may leave intact the Eurocentric curriculum that students consume daily.

Any approach to education that intends to provide students with the opportunity to succeed in our society must acknowledge the inherent structural inequalities that operate as barriers to participation and the role of institutions, such as schools, in perpetuating those inequalities. Insofar as the multicultural approach to education does not interrogate the cultural values and norms upon which the school system operates, then it will be ineffective in addressing the educational barriers to success for minorities. Further, as long as "cultural groups" are constructed as "other" Canadians with no regard to intra-cultural differences, then the particular issues of, for example, female, immigrant, working-class students, will be overlooked. This pre-packaged approach to learning about ethnic groups does little to ensure that students understand the particularities and inter-connections of inequality (Troyna 1987; Gillborn, 1995).

In order to provide an equitable education that values diversity while addressing the needs and interests of all students, our education system must provide opportunities for students to actively participate in their educational process. They must learn about the Canadian social structure so that they can come to understand the forces that affect their lives and those of others, and they must be encouraged to use their education as an agency for social change. Educators have a responsibility to acknowledge, not only the student's cultural perspective, but that of their own, which will influence the teaching-learning process (see Henry, 1998; Ahlquist, 1992; Sleeter, 1994, 1992; Delpit, 1988).

To ensure the equality of educational opportunities and outcomes in our diverse society, education curricula must address inequalities within the education system as well as in the society as a whole. The curriculum informed by critical theories, through its content, perspective and delivery, can be expected to recognize inequalities (Henry, 1998; Dei, 1996; Perry and Fraser, 1993) while seeking to engage students in critical analyses that will lead to informed collective action and a culturally and racially democratic society. In the current social context, in which multiculturalism policies and practices purport to remove barriers to participation and ensure full participation in society regardless of "cultural" group membership, Canadians have a false perception of equality of opportunity and outcome. The tendency for educators to assimilate anti-racism into an already ineffective multicultural framework is a reflection of the philosophy of equity and democracy of multiculturalism to which Canadians subscribe. The challenge for anti-racism educators, therefore, is to help students to re-conceptualize multiculturalism so that they understand the complex, unstable and hegemonic nature of culture and how their educational and occupational opportunities are structured and affected by characteristics such as class, gender, ethnicity and race. Ultimately, the success of the students will be determined by the extent to which the school environment, the curriculum content and school practices reflect and acknowledge the diverse cultural backgrounds represented within their classes and society as a whole.

SUGGESTIONS FOR DISCUSSION

1. How would you describe Canadian cultural identity?
2. Identify some of the sanctions imposed on immigrants and refugees to conform. How do they operate?
3. Account for the fact that Aboriginal peoples are not identified more prominently in national cultural policies.
4. The following scenario was produced by a group of class participants who had interviewed a French Canadian woman, and it is based on her experiences. Discuss the scenario and identify the relevance of Canadian multiculturalism to this French Canadian.

   Imagine that you grew up in a French neighbourhood in Sudbury. Although you always spoke French at home and all your friends were French, you can't remember a time when you didn't know English. Movies, music and most of the television and radio programs were in English. Therefore, you grew up switching naturally between the two languages: French at home; English at your part-time job; French at church. You used both languages at school, depending on where you were and to whom you're talking, and even on what you're talking about.

   After high school, you wanted to get away from small-town life and go to university, so you headed for Southern Ontario. Suddenly, everyone around you spoke English. There were no French newspapers, television or radio programs. You found a small group of other people from Sudbury and you all stuck together. You didn't really notice that even among your own group you spoke French less and less.

   After graduation, you got a job teaching in Ontario. The nearest Franco-Ontarian community was too far away to participate in. The other French teachers at the high school where you worked were all English, so you didn't speak French to them. Suddenly it seemed that the only time you spoke French was when you were teaching it.

   After a few years, you were engaged to be married. Your fiancé was English, but he knew a little French. Still, when you went home to Sudbury you spoke English so he wouldn't feel excluded.

   You got married in a Catholic church—an English service. The year you turned twenty-five you had your first baby. Your first child understood you when you used French words but your husband didn't. You had two more children.

   Now when you visit Sudbury you feel ashamed. Your French is rusty and you keep using English words. Your first child is nearly ten and the others are seven and five. They know only a few words of your language. They will probably never know more. In the span of one generation, your language has been lost and, with it, your culture.

Photo: Dick Hemingway

CHAPTER 8

Equity Programs

Ignoring differences and refusing to accommodate them is denial of equal access and opportunity. It is discrimination. To reduce discrimination, we must create and maintain barrier-free environments so that individuals can have genuine access free from arbitrary obstructions to demonstrate and exercise their full potential (Judge Rosalie Abella, A Royal Commission Report, *Equality in Employment* [Ottawa, November 1984], 3).

In recent years, equity programs pertaining to access to employment and education have generated much debate. These debates have centred on issues of merit; the disenfranchisement of whites (and white males, in particular); quotas as a factor in accessing job and/or university spaces; and the qualification of Aboriginals, racial minorities, people with disabilities and women for particular jobs and educational opportunities. Some tend to identity whites as the victims of employment and educational policies and programs that make it possible for "less qualified minorities" to gain access to post-secondary education and employment.

This chapter examines the ideas and issues surrounding the debates around employment and educational equity.[1] Specifically, in the essays that follow, we will examine the extent to which those who debate the merits of equity programs understand and take into account the historical context. Do they recognize that educational and employment structures are inherently unequal and consequently have built-in barriers to access[2] that have systematically excluded minorities from these opportunities? Or do they perceive opportunities as being accessible to everyone, irrespective of race, language, social class, gender, ethnicity, disability and so on, and it is therefore up to individuals to prepare themselves and take advantage of the opportunities?

We will begin with an essay on employment equity and discuss some of the salient points that are raised. As will be noted, the issue of "reverse racism/discrimination" is repeatedly raised as something that is limiting opportunities for whites, for young white males in particular. In the section entitled "Reverse Racism," I attempt to respond to this concern, with a challenge for us to think about the meaning of the term within the context of structural inequalities.

---

1 Here educational equity refers to access programs developed by universities and community colleges to address the concerns, needs and aspirations of marginalized applicants who, because of their experiences, have been unable to need the traditional entry expectations.

2 Access for me means, not only getting into a place of employment or education, but having "got in," or having gained *access*, the person will encounter conditions enabling him or her to participate effectively and without constraint.

Tribunal Ruling in Favour of Employment Equity

Summary: The Supreme Court of Canada unanimously reverses a decision of the Federal Court of Appeal and reinstates an order of a tribunal requiring Canadian National Railway to hire one woman in every four new hires into unskilled blue-collar jobs.

A Canadian Human Rights Tribunal ruled that Canadian National Railway had discriminated against women in the St. Lawrence region who were seeking employment in non-traditional blue-collar jobs. Women held only 0.7% of blue-collar jobs in the region, and the Tribunal found that CN Rail's recruitment, hiring and promotion policies prevented and discouraged women from working in blue-collar jobs. As part of a comprehensive remedial order, the Tribunal ordered CN Rail to hire one woman in every four new hires into blue-collar positions until the representation of women reached 13% which is the national percentage for women working in equivalent jobs.

CN Rail appealed this decision to the Federal Court of Appeal which ruled that the Tribunal did not have authority to impose a hiring quota on CN Rail because section 41 (2)(a) allows the Tribunal to prescribe measures which will prevent discriminatory practices from occurring in future, but not to remedy the consequences of past discrimination.

The Supreme Court of Canada overturns this decision of the Federal Court, ruling that the Tribunal was within its jurisdiction under section 41(2)(a) of the Act in making the order it did. Under this section, the Tribunal may order the adoption of a special program designed "to prevent the same or a similar (discriminatory) practice occurring in the future." The measures ordered by the Tribunal including the hiring quota were designed to break a continuing cycle of systemic discrimination against women. The goal is not to compensate pass inactions or even to provide new opportunities for specific individuals who have been unfairly refused jobs or promotion in the past. Rather, an employment equity program, much as the one ordered by the Tribunal in the present case, is an attempt to ensure that future applicants and workers from the affected group will not face the same insidious barriers that blocked their forebears. When confronted with systemic discrimination, the type of order issued by the Tribunal is the only means by which the purpose of the Canadian Human Rights Act can be met. In any program of employment equity, there simply cannot be a radical dissociation of "remedy" and "prevention," since there is no prevention without some form of remedy (*Canadian Human Rights* 8, 664 [1987], 4210).

EMPLOYMENT EQUITY

Jim: *"This new equity system ... is unbelievable."*

This new equity system they are going to put into place is unbelievable. I don't agree with it at all. I don't feel that all of the people are qualified for the jobs. You can't tell me that we, the white people, are getting treated fairly in this system. But there are some plus and minus points about this system of hiring.

Jim is referring here to the employment equity program initiated in Canada in the mid-1980s. We could consider the term *employment equity* to be uniquely Canadian. It was coined by the 1984 Royal Commission on Equality in Employment (Judge Rosalie Abella). It is used to "describe programs designed to improve the situation of individuals who, because of who they are or can be identified as being in a particular group, find themselves adversely affected by certainly systems or practices in the workplace" (Moreau, 1994: 147). The four groups identified as disadvantaged because of their labour force participation, unemployment rates, levels of income and persistent occupational segregation are: women, Aboriginal people, "visible" minorities and people with disabilities (Moreau, 1994: 147; see also Stephenson, 1996). Today, this program informs, not only government and business equity programs, but educational programs as well. Like Jim, most of the class participants found this difficult to accept.

Randy: *"It's a form of reverse discrimination."*

In almost every conversation about employment opportunities, you can bet the topic of employment equity will come up. This seems to be on a lot of people's minds, especially those who are interested in the police force or in fire-fighting employment.

It doesn't really matter how these agencies wish to carry out their hiring procedures, because in the end they are all under close supervision. By whom? By the NDP government, that's who. Bob Rae, the party leader, has implemented employment equity legislation. The rules were sent down to the agencies, and it was explained that they were to hire a certain percentage of women and minorities within a given time period. This is good, because it forces police and fire-fighting agencies to open their doors to the prescribed groups that have been discriminated against in the past. On the other hand, it's also kind of bad.

Being a member of the "white male" group, I am now up against an annoying obstacle. Because of this new employment equity legislation, the police forces are trying to increase the enrolment numbers of women, minority and disabled groups in order to meet Mr. Rae's requirements.

I think the phrase "employment equity" should be changed to "employment inequity." According to *Webster's New World Dictionary*, equity means "fairness and impartiality." The same dictionary defines the word *equal* as meaning "of the same value, having the same rights, to be equal to." Perhaps Mr. Rae's definitions come from a different dictionary.

The majority of the population should realize that women, minorities and the disabled have been, and in many cases still are, discriminated against. Most people might not admit it, but they know it's true. If this is the case, why turn everything upside down by trying to make amends with these prescribed groups over such a short time? Why turn the white male into the minority? What is happening is that the white male is being discriminated against for something beyond his control; it's a form of reverse discrimination. The police forces actually tell us (the white applicants), that our chances of getting hired are slim until the employment equity numbers balance out. This is where I start to get my back up. Equality should mean that everyone has the same chance of being hired. If the top ten applicants are Black, they should be hired; if they are white males, they should be hired; if they are female, the same. Forget about balancing the numbers. Give the job to the person who best deserves it. That's equal!

Employment equity has played a minor role in my personal life. A couple of years back, when this legislation came into effect, I applied to the Toronto Police along with a East Indian friend of mine. I received a higher mark than he on the physical testing, and we were close on the written. After these tests the Toronto Police declared a hiring freeze, and I was asked to re-apply at a later date. Two weeks after this, my friend received a phone call from the Toronto Police, asking him to come in for an interview. Toronto pushed him through the hiring process in less than two months and signed him up to go to police college the following month. On average, the normal hiring procedure takes roughly six to twelve months from start to finish. The main difference between our applications was that mine said "white male" and his said "visible minority." I'm sure there were more differences, but this stuck out and bothered me. From that point on, I knew I had to make myself a more attractive applicant to recruiters because the competition had just became tougher.

I'm a firm believer in the saying "Two wrongs don't make a right," but this is what's happening now with employment equity. I truly wish I had a solution to offer that would rectify the situation and make it fair for everyone.

Will employment equity benefit society as a whole? I don't think so. If anything it has created greater tension between the white applicants and the prescribed groups. It has brought our society into a state of disrepute. When employment equity has eventually succeeded, society as a whole may be better off, but then again I'm not sure. Even the minorities state that they want to be hired because they are the best, not because they are a minority. On the other hand, if some recruiter told me I was wanted because I was white and they were short of whites, I wouldn't think twice about the so-called "equity."

Competition is very tough in the job market these days and spreads b yond the police and fire-fighting professions. It's very common for som one to make an excuse or to blame someone else for his own problem For example, the fisherman always has ten reasons why the "big one" got away. Well, for some, not being hired on a police force or fire department brings about a similar set of excuses, such as "I didn't get hired because some minority took my spot" and various other reasons. Being in a Police Education class, I hear too many of these excuses every day, and it's usually before people even go to write their exam. In my opinion these people are probably not qualified. They are preparing themselves for defeat and, in turn, using the minorities as their scapegoats. In the long run all employment equity is doing is making the competition that much more stiff. Therefore, if you want the opportunity, you have to go and get it because it's not going to come to you. That's the bottom line.

Roger: *"The prime qualification has become skin colour."*

I come from an Irish-English family (75 percent/25 percent mix), and was raised in a white, middle-class household. My family has never been overly rich, but we have never starved. I was born in Toronto, but raised in the suburbs, so in essence I have lived a rather sheltered life.

Even though I grew up in a good, financially stable home, I don't consider this fact to be an advantage created by my race or ethnicity. Through school and social clubs, I've had many friends from different races and ethnic backgrounds from homes of equal to greater financial stability. Like those of many others, my parents are both fairly uneducated by today's standards. Yet, through hard work and determination, they have managed to make a success of themselves.

While talking with other people, I've been trying to think of an instance where my race or my ethnicity has been an advantage to me, and I haven't been able to think of one. Sure, there is the fact that I come from a stable home, but this has nothing to do with my race. It has to do with loving parents who have shown genuine concern with what I do. The fact that I am fairly well-educated could be considered an advantage, but my race didn't put me through school. My parents' guidance, my own drive to better myself and a desire to reach a certain goal are what completed my education. Perhaps my always having money in my pocket could be considered to be an advantage, but even this fact is not a result of my race; I have always had a part-time job and work hard to earn the money.

So even after listening to other people's stories and points of view, I have found no situation where my being white is an advantage. I have always been a believer in the human spirit. I believe that what a person is, not what a person looks like, determines his or her future.

Just as I have not been able to think of a past experience or incident in which my race or ethnicity has been an advantage, I am not able to think of an incident in which my race or ethnicity has been a disadvantage. That is, until recently.

As my graduation quickly approaches, I am becoming more and more frustrated by the tough, uphill battle I will have to undertake. My future goal is to become a police officer, a profession that has been drastically affected by special interest groups, pathetic government policies and government-appointed "overseers," such as the infamous Susan Eng. Through the media and schools, we are constantly bombarded with messages and slogans denouncing racism and discrimination. We are told that these will no longer be tolerated by society, and they will be slashed through government policies and public awareness. In our tireless search for racism and discrimination, two very interesting and disturbing phenomena have appeared: everything has become a "racial issue"; and "reverse discrimination."

This government's employment equity program and Multicultural Act have in essence turned my race and my ethnicity into a disadvantage. The fact that I am a high school and college graduate no longer carries any significant merit when I apply to a police force or any other government agency. The prime qualification has become skin colour.

Although many "experts" and government officials will deny the existence of reverse discrimination and hiring quotas, professionals within the affected fields will give you a completely different story. The agencies' personnel tell horror stories about the government-imposed, "hiring-of-minorities-at-all-costs" tactics. Their stories do little to give me optimism about my future career.

Many people talk about instances when they have been denied jobs because of their race. Well, in the near future, I too will be able to relate to these people. The only difference is that I will have been affected by a government-endorsed policy.

The next question is, how does this make me feel? Quite simply put, nauseous. The fact that I am qualified and possess more than sufficient skills to perform my job has little to no bearing. I may now be forced to sit back and watch less qualified and less educated persons pass by me in line because they are members of a race targeted by the government.

I have very mixed emotions about the employment equity program. The concept behind the program is good; it prevents employers from denying people positions within companies or agencies because of their colour or religion. The problem lies in how the government has implemented the program. In government agencies and in the public service sector, this program has made it extremely difficult (to almost impossible) for a white person, especially a white male, to find employment. In the business world, competition is not restricted to the boundaries of business transactions—the whole application process is also a competition. If a person is more qualified because of English skills, education and experience, he or she should get the job. This is not necessarily true with the implementation of employment equity.

An example of how the government has gone overboard with this program is an incident that took place during the summer. I had to go to the OHIP building to straighten out a problem I had with my health card. As soon as I entered the office, I was taken aback. Not only was I the only white in the office, I was the only one capable of speaking English at an understandable level. After approximately ten minutes of trying to understand what the OHIP employee was saying to me, the supervisor finally showed up (just returning from her lunch break). I was relieved to find out that the lady was not only capable of speaking English, but that she was also very understandable (and yes, she was also of a visible minority group). My point here is that, if these jobs are posted publicly, there would have to be applicants for them who possess good English skills. Did these people just not show up during the interviews for these jobs? In these economic times, I find that very hard to believe. Also, if the purpose of employment equity is to show an equal representation of the community, someone obviously made a mistake.

Eugene: *"It is hard to see past the fact that I am losing out."*

What I feel has affected me the most while in this class are the topics of reverse discrimination and of the whites of this generation "paying" for the mistakes and ignorance of our forefathers. The latter topic affected me in particular, because my background is both Chinese and white. Is it necessary, then, to split myself in half so that my white half may be condemned and my Chinese half may receive retribution? What also affected me were the ignorant and extremely racist attitudes that were displayed by certain classmates. These really appalled, shocked, dismayed and insulted me. Having people like this in my class really made the issue of racism hit close to home.

The topic of reverse discrimination basically made me realize that, even though I am willing to make an effort to understand, it does not mean that those I encounter will feel similarly. And I cannot allow these people to make me lose sight of what I feel is right, nor let them weaken my determination.

The topic of the whites of this generation paying for the mistakes of their forefathers also affects me greatly. I realize that this is a course of events that must inevitably come about, but it is hard to see past the fact that I am losing out. I guess where you stand on this topic depends on whether you feel that your present life is more important than the future or vice versa.

Photo: Dick Hemingway

Education for diversity. Daycare centres and schools can facilitate the learning about diversity and difference by promoting social participation and acceptance.

Radcliffe: *"Employment equity is a necessary hiring practice...."*

I believe that Employment Equity is a necessary hiring practice that needs to stay in effect until an acceptable balance in employment is achieved.

When I first learned of the employment equity program, I felt that it was reverse discrimination. I thought that minorities would have an unfair advantage over those who had more experience in their field. Now I understand that equity means giving people a fair chance at getting hired. Equity means that other factors will be taken into consideration when hiring. A man who has worked just as hard as another man and who has been hindered by prejudice and unfair hiring practices should be credited for what he has endured in order to enter the job market.

As children we learn through example. While growing up in our society, members of minorities are socialized by the cultural bias and unequal representation in their curriculum. If at a young age they are taught that positions of power are open to all people and yet are told that no minority has occupied such positions, they will not see themselves as being "good" enough for the job. Common sense dictates that, if there were equitable hiring practices in effect, there would be people of all races occupying such power positions. For example, a young Black female has never seen a Black female police officer. Therefore she does not take the steps necessary to reach that position. With the employment equity program in place, disadvantaged youth are given merit for enduring a culturally biased educational system. Now, when a young black girl sees someone like herself in such a power position, she will take the necessary steps to become a police officer, and she can get the job regardless of whether or not employment equity exists. When equal representation of cultures is met within the police force, or any other profession for that matter, the employment equity program should be discontinued. As the demographics of the surrounding area fluctuate, employment equity should be able to go with those changes.

CHALLENGING THE PERCEPTION OF EQUITY

> The new forms of white racism are "couched in expressions of unfairness and reverse discrimination" (Sleeter, 1994).

> "New racism" is expressed in a language of innocence which disguises its insidious intent by framing its message in a way that endorses 'folk' values of egalitarianism, social justice, and common sense. Racism, in effect, is ideological, transformed in ways that disavow, diminish or distract from its actuality in a democratic society" (Baker, 1981; cited in Kallen, 1995: 30)

"Equality should mean that everyone has the same chance of being hired" (Randy). This statement is correct, but first we must first establish what we mean by "the same chance." Equity can only be attained if "the same chance" involves taking differences into account–differences related to racial, ethnic, linguistic and gender experiences that speak not only to the individual experiences of applicants, but also to those of the diverse Canadian society that is to be represented and served within all organizations or institutions. Further, a "fair" chance requires that we recognize the barriers to educational opportunities–barriers related to racism, classism, sexism–that have traditionally operated to limit access to employment opportunities. Such recognition would mean that an individual's outcome or attainment is not merely a result of his or her failings, but is related to structural barriers over which he or she has little or no control. The fact that such individuals are now qualified to apply for jobs is representative of, not only their motivation, determination and capacity to work against the odds, but also a particular perspective that should be a valuable resource.

The experience that marginalized individuals bring to the job is often overlooked. Here, "the same chance" would mean valuing the differences that are evident in the experiences and perspectives of marginalized individuals and treating them differently in order to treat them equally. It would mean recognizing that obtaining a job or obtaining a particular level of education cannot be the "same" when race, gender, class, ethnicity and other factors operate in structural or systemic ways to limit opportunities.

"I don't feel that all of the people are qualified for the jobs" (Jim). When the argument of "the same chance" is challenged, this response quickly follows. Of course, being "qualified" for a job depends on many factors, all of which, in Randy's case, are subjective and contextually based. For

Table 10: Canadian Visible Minority Population, 1996 (20% Sample Data)

Total Population	**28,528,125**
Total visible minority[1] population[2]	3,197,480
Chinese	860,150
South Asian	670,590
Black	573,860
Arab/West Asian	244,665
Filipino	234,195
Southeast Asian	172,765
Latin American	176,970
Japanese	68,135
Korean	64,835
Visible minority, n.i.e. [3]	69,745
Multiple visible minority [4]	61,575
All others[5]	25,330,645

1 This table provides counts of the visible minority population as defined for employment equity purposes. The 1996 Census was the first census to ask a direct question to provide data on visible minorities. The data included in this table are obtained from the population group question (Question 19).The *Employment Equity Act* defines visible minorities as *"persons, other than Aboriginal peoples, who are non-Caucasian in race or non-white in colour"*. The mark-in groups, other than "White", listed in the population group question are those that are likely to be members of a visible minority group.

2 Includes respondents who have been identified as members of a visible minority group, based on employment equity definitions.

3 Includes respondents who reported a single write-in response indicating a Pacific Islander group (for example "Fijian" or "Polynesian") or another single write-in response likely to be a visible minority group (for example "Guyanese", "Mauritian", "South American" or "West Indian").

4 Includes respondents who reported more than one visible minority group by checking two or more mark-in circles, for example "Black and South Asian".

5 Includes respondents who reported "Yes" to Question 18 (Aboriginal Identity, known in the 1996 Census Dictionary as Aboriginal Self-reporting), as well as respondents who were not considered to be members of a visible minority group.

Source: Statistics Canada, 1996 Census, *Nation* tables.

instance, Randy claims to have done better than his "East Indian friend" on the test for the Toronto Police Force and yet was not invited for an interview. He needs to put the whole hiring process in which he was engaged into a historical context and also analyze what requirements the Police Force had of new recruits. What were they looking for? What were the differences between what he and his friend had to offer?

"I may now be forced to watch less qualified and less educated persons pass me by in line because they are members of a race targeted by the government" (Roger). It cannot be that race, or as Roger said, "skin colour," has become the "prime qualification" for a job. Contrary to Roger's statement, the OHIP office where he was "the only white," and "the only one capable of speaking English at an understandable level," could not have been staffed by "unqualified" individuals; and skin colour could not be the only reason for them being employed. What about the other skills they brought to the job? While the government did indicate that particular groups should be targeted under the equity program, nowhere was it said that the ability to competently execute the job would be compromised. If such a compromise takes place, then we need to question the objectives of those who did the hiring and the situation into which minority employees have been brought. Perhaps the situation does not afford them the opportunity to function at their potential and effectively carry out their tasks. [3]

"You can't tell me that we, the white people, are getting treated fairly in this system" (Jim). How is it that issues of fairness and qualification are raised when minorities are perceived to be entering areas of employment to which they have been traditionally excluded?[4] How do we explain employment situations that have been exclusively or largely homogeneously white for many years? Indeed, as Radcliffe quite correctly points out, "if there were equitable hiring practices in effect, there would be people of all races occupying power positions." Certainly minorities have long been "qualified" for many of the jobs for which they have applied. However, they have been excluded because of the recruiters' subjective interpretation of who is "best qualified."

Consider what studies have shown about contemporary employment practices and the experiences of racial and ethnic minorities. In a survey of employers in Toronto, Billingsley and Muzynski (1985) found that most employers relied on informal employee and friendship networks to recruit

---

[3] Obviously, the situation in which individuals are employed ought to enable them to perform their tasks effectively. Anything less might indeed lead to, as Roger indicates, horror stories resulting from what may be perceived as resistance to "government-imposed, 'hiring-of-minorities-at-all-costs' tactics" (Roger). While individuals might be "well qualified" for the job, their effectiveness at and success in the job is very much dependent on the support they receive from employers and colleagues.

[4] Why now, as Randy suggests, when equity programs are making competition for employment "much more stiff" and "tougher," are we hearing complaints about unfair practices and lack of qualifications?

and fill job positions. Therefore, it is more difficult for minorities to gain access to jobs in which they are not yet represented. Moreover, a survey of 672 corporate recruiters, hiring managers and agency recruiters conducted by Canadian Recruiters Guild in 1989 showed that 87 percent of corporate and 100 percent of agency recruiters surveyed received direct discriminatory requests. Nearly three-quarters of corporate and 94 percent of agency recruiters complied with these requests. The survey also showed that out of 6,720 available positions, only four target group members were placed by the recruiting agencies (*Currents*, 1989: 19-20).

In their 1985 Toronto study "Who Gets the Work: A Test of Racial Discrimination in Employment," Henry and Ginzberg found that, in cases where job applicants had similar resumes, white applicants were far more likely to be offered a position than non-whites. The study, which used two white and two Black actors (male and female) found that "Black job seekers face not only discrimination in the sense of receiving fewer job offers than Whites but also a considerable amount of abusive treatment while job hunting" (p. 306). In the part of the study where job seekers made telephone calls "to phone numbers listed in the classified employment section of the newspaper," the findings revealed that the "White-majority Canadian" with "no discernible accent" was "never screened," while the "Slavic or Italian accented" callers were screened "5 percent of the time" and the "Jamaican accented" and "Indo-Pakistani accented" callers received "three times as much screening as the White" (p.308). The result was that 65 percent of the jobs were open to "White" callers, 52 percent to "Jamaican-accented" callers and 47.3 percent to "Indo-Pakistani accented" callers (Henry and Ginzberg, 1985: 51). The researchers concluded that

> there is a very substantial racial discrimination affecting the ability of members of racial minorities to find employment even when they are well qualified and eager to find work.... Once an applicant is employed, discrimination can still affect opportunities for advancement, job retention, and level of earnings, to say nothing of the question of the quality of work and the relationship with co-workers (Henry and Ginzberg, 1993: 308).

In a seven-year, follow-up study I conducted with twenty young Black Canadians about their employment experiences, respondents reported that racism and discrimination were "challenges" with which they had to contend, both in terms of obtaining a job and while they were on the job. They suggested that "who you know" is even more important than education, "particularly in competition against a white person for a job." As one respondent stated, "while education can help, I have seen that who you know gets you further" (James, 1993: 10).

"In our tireless search for racism and discrimination, two very interesting and disturbing phenomena have appeared: everything has become a 'racial issue'; and 'reverse discrimination'" (Roger). If it is not because of racial discrimination,

how can we explain the employment opportunities and experiences of racial minorities in the studies cited above and in others to which we have referred throughout this book? Racism and discrimination are not new to Canada. We do not have to "search" for them. It has been established that race and racism have long characterized how "racialized" people in Canada have been subjected to the "racial issue" and discrimination. Take for example, the enslavement, extermination and control of Aboriginal peoples; the trading in Africans as slaves since 1628, and the existence of slavery in Canada until it was abolished in 1824; the Chinese "Head Tax"; the internment of Canadians of Japanese ethnic background; the systematic exclusion of non-white immigrants and the discriminatory treatment of non-white Canadians throughout the years. Roger's comment, therefore, reflects an ignorance of Canadian history and the treatment of racial minorities. George Elliott Clarke writes about this in his essay "White Like Canada."

> A 1995 poll conducted by the Canadian Civil Liberties Association found that 83 percent of Canadian adults did not know that slavery was practised in pre-Confederation Canada until 1834, when Britain abolished the institution throughout its empire. You would most likely find a similar ignorance regarding the existence, as recently as the 1950s, of school segregation in Ontario and Nova Scotia; the $500 head tax that the Canadian government once slapped on all Chinese immigrants; and the numerous "Black Codes" enacted by various levels of government to control where Chinese, Japanese, Native, and African citizens could work, live, be buried, and even, in some cases, vote. During the Second World War, Canada interned its Japanese (but not its Germans) and refused entry to Jews fleeing Nazi persecution....
>
> These incidents pale in comparison to the sustained maltreatment of Canada's aboriginal peoples. Though much of the country was never ceded by treaty, First Nations people were nevertheless sequestered on tiny reservations that grew smaller as monied interests claimed oil and mineral deposits on the land. Centuries-old colonial policies have decimated aboriginal populations–or wiped them out altogether, as in the case of the Beothuk of Newfoundland (1998: 103).

"The white male is being discriminated against for something beyond his control; it's a form of reverse discrimination" (Randy). We have all inherited the history of racism and discrimination and, with it, the consequences. These consequences constitute barriers to employment opportunities for some. For others, these constitute the privilege of access to employment, a benefit of the very barriers that are disadvantageous to others. It is this inherited race privilege that makes it possible for Roger not to notice instances where his "race or ethnicity has been an advantage." The hard work and determination of both he and his parents, as well as the guidance he received from them, have not been mediated by the racism that racial minorities experience in their drive to educational and employment opportunities and success. And the "human spirit" that Roger is convinced is critical to success exists in raced, classed, abled and gendered bodies and, as such, is

subject to the social, political, economic and cultural contestations in society. Just as the earned and unearned privileges (McIntosh, 1995) are accepted, so too must be the responsibility for how those privileges were acquired in the first place.

"Why turn the white male into a minority?" (Randy). What is Randy saying here? Is he suggesting that it is okay for "minorities," people other than white males, to experience "discrimination" in accessing employment? And in saying that these "amends" should not take place over "a short time" period, is he suggesting that minorities are able, compared to white males, to tolerate or accept the disadvantages they experience? Indeed, Randy goes on to say that "two wrongs don't make a right." While he can accept that minorities have been "wronged," he rejects any situation that allows equal access to employment because, for him, this means that white males will be "wronged." However, as Fish (1993) argues in his essay "Reverse Racism or How the Pot Got To Call the Kettle Black," the disenfranchisement that white males may experience as a result of such equity programs is "only a by-product" of attempts to remove the barriers to employment. Equity programs are attempts to make access to employment possible for those who otherwise might be rejected and not even get a chance to demonstrate what they know at an interview (see Stephenson, 1996).

"Where you stand on this topic depends on whether you feel your present life is more important than the future" (Eugene). This statement is quite true. But while we should be concerned about the future and therefore construct a present that ensures equitable opportunities for all Canadians, how individuals see their current situation will influence how they participate in constructing the present. So while Eugene feels that this "course of events," that is, equity programs, are "inevitable," Randy seems adamant that these programs will not "benefit society as a whole" but instead have "created greater tensions between the white applicants and the prescribed groups." This Randy believes "has brought our society into a state of disrepute." It is this sense of "disrepute" that appears to make Roger angry when he refers to his chances of becoming a police officer. Specifically, Roger writes that the "profession has been drastically affected by special interest groups,[5] pathetic government policies and government-appointed 'overseers.'" It is reactions such as Roger's that concern Eugene, causing him to state, "I cannot allow these people to make me lose sight of what I feel is right, nor let

[5] It is always important to note who is constructed as "special interest groups." Are those who lobby for the elimination of employment equity considered "special interest groups"? What descriptors would we then use for those who advocate for lower taxes?

Photo: Dick Hemingway

Parents help to set the stage for the appreciation and acceptance of diversity and difference in society.

them weaken my determination." Radcliffe concurs. He agrees that employment equity is a "necessary" program. He reasons that a "man who has worked just as hard as another man and who has been hindered by prejudice and unfair hiring practices should be credited for what he has endured in order to enter the job market."

Myths, misinformation and half-truths characterize much of the discussion about employment equity, as with that of immigration, immigrants and multiculturalism. These myths are based, on the one hand, on a lack of acknowledgment of the inherent economic and social inequities within our society, a fear of social change and an anticipated loss of political, economic, and social power and privilege. On the other hand, the multicultural, meritocratic ideology of Canada has so structured the ideas of individuals that they have difficulty in critically reflecting on the issues before them or in seeing the myths. More to the point, these protestations by students are possibly the "new racism" to which Kallen (1995) refers. With reference to Baker (1981), Kallen points out that "the 'new racism' has been conceptualized as an 'ideological gambit,' employed by majority authorities in a democratic society to maintain the *status quo* of racial and ethnic inequality in the face of espoused democratic ideals of anti-racism and egalitarianism" (p.30). Little wonder, therefore, that individuals might fail to see the role played by prejudices, stereotypes and racism as they are directed towards the groups who are characterized as the benefactors of equity programs. If we are to build a democratic and equitable society in

Laws and policies do not automatically guarantee equitable practices but, once enforced, they can provide a basis for equal opportunities, access and participation.

Canada, then we must be critically reflexive, prepared for social change and play a part in initiating and fighting for that change.

It is indeed inevitable that, in the words of one participant, "corrective measures" in the form of equity programs must be taken if equal employment and educational opportunities are to be realized. And while it seems simplistic to say, as did one participant, that such programs "would definitely help" because having co-workers from "all racial backgrounds can and will benefit a multicultural society," it is something worth striving for. The issue of "qualification" is important. Understandably, tradition has played a significant role in the determination of qualification. However, in contexts where equity is an important objective, qualification cannot be governed merely by tradition. Qualification will have to be relative and take into account the contemporary diverse and changing contexts in which individuals perform their duties. For this reason, diverse ideas, skills, values and expectations cannot be governed by one set of historical norms.

Unfortunately, individuals such as Jim, Randy and Roger need not be "dismayed," for as long as equity programs are not accompanied by systemic changes, where structures (e.g., legislation, policies, procedures and practices) that have traditionally operated as barriers to educational and employment opportunities are dismantled, then these so-called equity programs will remain ineffective. After all, the Conservative government of Ontario, in dismantling the employment equity program, has argued and indeed shown that such programs are not needed for individuals "should" be able to access jobs by their own effort. It does not acknowledge the systemic barriers that minority job applicants face. Nevertheless, there is a need for equity programs if we are to address the educational and employment situation of those citizens who are, and have been in the past, disadvantaged by structural inequalities. If not now, when?

SUMMARY DISCUSSION: "REVERSE RACISM"[6]

> Our commitment to address racism must not paralyze us. We should not be afraid to question, to make mistakes, and above all to learn. We should all commit ourselves to rights literacy for ourselves, our families, and our clients.... The process of naming racism is not an indictment. It is an opportunity for change (Joanne St. Lewis, 1996: 119).

During class discussion on the issue of equity and access for women and racial minorities, it was argued that too many jobs today are closed to white males because of the employment equity law in Ontario. Indeed, a number of job advertisements routinely state the organization's commitment to employment equity. For instance, advertisements might state: "[Organization] is committed to employment equity and encourages applicants from all qualified candidates, including Aboriginal peoples, persons with disabilities, visible minorities (or people of colour) and women."

For some, this statement represents "discrimination against white males." They perceive it to be "unfair" and "wrong," and it does not make sense to them as a way of achieving equity. The students argue that such advertisements are problematic in the case of governments, which are supposed to operate in the interest of all residents. It is further seen as a violation of the "merit principle," which has been replaced by hiring based on "racial quotas." So why do programs that have been initiated to address the systemic barriers to equity and access for First Nation peoples, women, racial minorities and persons with disabilities incite such negative reactions? Why do students, and white males in particular, react to equity and access programs in such a negative way? Why are the programs seen as "reverse racism"? What is racism and how does is it different from "reverse racism"? What is the role of educators in assisting students to address the issues of equity in today's multiracial classrooms?

In this discussion we will explore some of the ways in which white male college and university students have been grappling with the issues of race, racism and equity at a critical juncture of their lives and in a culturally and racially diverse and changing society, and how the notions of merit and privilege feature in their discussions. Many of the ideas and issues presented are informed by the foregoing essays and discussions. It is important to examine the reactions of young white male students to issues of equity in

---

[6] This essay appears under the title "Reverse racism: Students reponse to equity programs" in the *Journal of Professional Studies* 3, no. 1 (fall/winter, 1995): 48-54. Reprinted with permission.

order to understand their perception of equity programs as barriers to the realization of their goals.

Racism is more than acts of discrimination. It is not something that is experienced by all racial groups in the same way. We must "take into account the effects of unequal power" relations in our society (Neufield, 1992, B7). Hence, racism is understood in terms of the collective–how individuals, because of their membership in a particular racial group, are privileged or disadvantaged by the structural and cultural factors in society. Compared to prejudice, which is found within all groups, racism is associated with those who have "the power to enforce and act on their prejudices" (Dobbins and Skillings, 1991: 41).

Racism must be constructed in terms of historical and structural factors if current equity programs are to be seen as valid and appropriate. Challenges and criticism raised by individuals about equity and access policies, practices and programs that target race, gender and/or disability are justified only if racism is seen in terms of the attitudes and actions of individuals against other individuals, based on individual ignorance. We know, however, that rather than being perceived as the attitudes and behaviours of individuals, racism must be perceived in terms of policies and practices that have been the prevailing norm of institutions that have operated for years in favour of those by whom and for whom they have been constructed in the first place. And as Henry and Ginzberg (1985) found in their study of racial discrimination in employment in Toronto, "White Canadians have greater opportunities to set up job interviews and are subject to less pre-interview screening" (p.49) while racial minorities "must work harder and longer to gain access to potential opportunities even though they have equal educational and employment experience with Whites" (p.50). According to Fish (1993),

> If the mastery of the requirements for entry depends upon immersion in the cultural experiences of the mainstream majority, if the skills that make for success are nurtured by institutions and cultural practices from which the disadvantaged minority has been systematically excluded, if the language and ways of comporting oneself that identify a player as "one of us" are alien to the lives minorities are forced to live, then words like "fair" and "equal" are cruel jokes, for what they promote and celebrate is institutionalized unfairness and a perpetuated inequality (p.132).

More than individual attitudes

Racism involves more than the effects of individual attitudes. It implies a structural and cultural fact. That some students see equity programs as "reverse racism" raises questions about their understanding of racism. It is not racism when Aboriginal and racial minority Canadians are "targeted" under equity programs for equality of access and equality of opportunity; or when racial minorities demand that they be treated differently from whites in order to be treated equitably. Measures aimed at re-dressing inequities can only be perceived as racism or as a contravention of legitimate notions of universal equity when the desires and actions of oppressed groups are detached from the historical conditions of their reality (Fish, 1993), or when the reality of privileged groups is detached from their historical relations to unearned benefits from power (McIntosh, 1995; Sleeter, 1994). Racism is a cultural and historical fact that structures the norms and values of societies, and it is evident in the policies and practices of institutions. The effects are sufficiently great to warrant the attention of both governments and institutions.

As discussed in Chapter 4, racism is an ideology promoting the uncritical acceptance and negative social definitions of a group often identified by physical features (e.g., skin colour); and is premised on the belief in the cultural and biological superiority of a particular racial group over others. Insofar as racism is supported by a system of inequality and oppression constructed within a society, it is more than individual; it is structural and institutional. A key component of racism is power–structural and institutional power. This power is more than the "ordinary" influence an individual might have over another; it is the support of that influence by economic, political and ideological conditions. Often this power is an "invisible," regular and continuous part of everyday human existence, sustained by established laws, regulations and/or policies or by accepted conventions and customs. As sociologist C. Wright Mills (1956) explains, "No one can be truly powerful unless he [*sic*] has access to the command of major institutions, for it is over these institutional means of power that the truly powerful are, in the first instance, powerful" (p.9).

In the case of Canadian society, Ng (1993) states that

> white European men, especially those of British and French descent, are seen to be superior to women and to people from other racial and ethnic origins. Systems of ideas and practices have been developed over time to justify and support his notion of superiority. These ideas become the premise on which societal norms and values are based, and the practices become the "normal" way of doing things (p.52).

Ng goes on to say that racism could be treated as a "common sense" way of thinking. This refers to the "norms and forms of action that have become ordinary ways of doing things, of which we have little consciousness, so that certain things … 'disappear from the social surface'" (p.52).

If historical and social patterns have normalized the economic, political and ideological power of white males, can equity and access programs "discriminate" against white males in the same way in which racial minorities have been discriminated against? This is unlikely, for as Stanley Fish argues in his essay "Reverse Racism or How the Pot Got To Call The Kettle Black," such programs are "not intended to disenfranchise white males" (Fish, 1993: 136). Rather they are meant to remove barriers that have traditionally advantaged some groups and disadvantaged others. Further, such programs seek to address the impact of practices that have operated on the basis of white males' norms. For this reason, equity and access programs will include such things as minority representation and an acknowledgment of the factors that have historically and systematically operated as barriers to their participation in all sectors of our society. To this notion, many students respond, "Two wrongs don't make a right; if it is unfair to discriminate against Blacks, it is just as unfair to discriminate against whites." This position is premised on the notion that everyone should be treated the same, and dismisses the reality that not everyone has been or is the same. It is a dismissal of and a disregard for the power differences that advantage some and disadvantage others. Fairness cannot be evaluated independent of the histories of the respective groups to which individuals belong.

Equity programs must be seen as attempts to undo the effects of arbitrary and racist policies and practices that have operated historically as barriers to access and opportunities. And as Judge Abella (1984) states in her report, *Equity in Employment,*

> formerly we thought that equity only meant sameness and that treating persons as equals meant treating everyone the same. We now know that to treat everyone the same may be to offend the notions of equality.... To create opportunity we have to do different things for different people.... The process in an exercise in redistributive justice (p.3).

The difference between equity programs and the ways in which individuals have traditionally gained access to educational and occupational opportunities is "not in the outcome but in the ways of thinking that led up to the outcome. It is the difference between an unfairness that befalls one as an unintended effect of a policy rationally conceived and an unfairness that is pursued as an end in itself" (Fish, 1993: 136). Stated differently, equity programs as they are intentionally conceived are not intended to prevent males or whites from employment opportunities (as in the case of minorities), but to remove structural barriers that have been limiting minority participation.

The critical juncture

The critical juncture involves white students and equity programs. As they prepare for the world of work, many young white males hope that their post-secondary education and grades will "give them the edge" in their job search. They perceive employment equity programs as a challenge to their optimism and to any "edge" they might have had in realizing their occupational goals. Therefore, we can expect them to be concerned about the job market and the employment opportunities that await them. For this reason, many become quite frustrated and even angry. For instance, a class discussion on employment equity with reference to women and racial minorities led to a heated debate. Dominic, one of the two males in a class of thirty students, stated the following in a very angry voice:

> I am tired of all this racism bullshit. I've never been handed anything on a sliver platter.... This is fuckin' scary. You're not good enough to get in like others.... What about meritocracy? What about the esteem of people? You'd be seen as an equity quota, as a number. [Employment equity] undermines what has been accomplished.... It creates animosity and downright hatred. This means I'll be two years out of a job. I'm fed up of the bullshit. Is this what we call progress?

This student is also expressing anger because of what he sees as the compromise of his "inalienable right" and the thwarting of his career attainment by programs that give minorities an "unfair advantage over those who have more experience in their field." Not only is this young man's anger representative of a number of today's young white male students, but the same anger and arguments are being expressed by males in the corporate world.

In their cover story "White, Male and Worried," *Business Week* (Galen and Palmer, 1994) reports that today's white men must compete against racial minorities–people whom "they may not have taken all that seriously as rivals." So, "for the first time in their lives they are worrying about their future opportunities because of widespread layoff, corporate restructuring" and employment equity initiatives (White, 1994: 51). But, as the *Business Week* article adds, "At the heart of the issue for many white males is a question of merit–that in the rush for a more diverse workplace, they will lose out to less qualified workers" (p.52).

The question of merit

In a letter to *The Burlington Post* of December 29, 1993, a young man writes:

> I graduated from a local high school as an Ontario Scholar in 1987 and received my honours Bachelor of Arts in 1992 from a highly reputable university in south-western Ontario.... In the spring of 1992 I applied for 25 entry-level positions through the province's want ads.... With eight months' work experience in the Ministry of Treasury and Economics, my university degree, and my ability to save the province money, my white skin and gender couldn't possibly prevent me from at least getting an interview, right? Wrong! I did not get any interviews. Clearly, the new legislation assumes that the best person for the job is automatically either a non-white or female, despite qualifications.... Anti-white male (a.w.m. for short) discrimination has permeated institutions of higher learning.... In case you consider me to be sexist or a bigot, I assure you I'm not. I would truly like to see the most qualified person for any particular job regardless of color, creed, gender or any other non-performance-related factor, employed in that given position. Individual cases of discrimination should be dealt with on an individual basis, not by institutionalized reverse discrimination (p.14).

This young man and others believe that taking race into consideration in the equity programs is a violation of the principle of meritocracy and individualism. Their education has taught them that our society is democratic, that everyone has the same opportunities and chances and that everyone can succeed once they have the ability and skill and apply themselves. Hence, it is the individual's efforts and abilities, and not systemic factors, that determine achievement. A common belief is, "If you want something bad enough, you will get it; you just have to apply yourself." It is because of this belief that many insist, "If you work hard, you can get whatever you want." Within this middle-class context, education is often seen as the mechanism through which individuals are able to achieve their goals. Moreover, they argue, as education is free and accessible, all one needs to do is to "take advantage of the educational opportunities that are available to them." In terms of financial support for post-secondary education, they further argue that "OSAP [Ontario Students' Assistance Program] is available to everyone, especially those who have an economic need."

This belief in democracy and meritocracy has a powerful effect on how the students perceive their own opportunities and the opportunities of racial minorities in our society. After all, throughout their schooling they have been taught the lessons of equity and fairness. Therefore, it is logical that they would believe that race never operated in the first place to influence an individual's outcome and, in particular, to provide them with privilege. When educators and institutions challenge these traditional ideas of meritocracy, it raises doubt in the students' minds and shakes their confidence in the system. This can turn into frustration and anger, for they expect to hear from educators, and observe in institutional practices, the principles of meritocracy at work. Therefore, they must search for new meanings and interpretations of the values and principles on which they have come to rely.

While attempting to maintain confidence in a system they have been socialized to see as fair, equitable and accessible to all Canadians, young people must simultaneously find explanations for why the same system (specifically, state and private institutions) is now challenging the very ideals it taught them to embrace. In their search for answers to questions (e.g., "Why me? Why now?" "Why should I have to pay for the past? I didn't do anything wrong. It is not my fault."), they invent some interesting rationalizations. For example, in a class discussion on employment equity, after a very heated debate, one student made the point that "the reason why the police force has to hire so many Black officers is because they have to make the force representative of the criminal population." The speaker, a young white male of about twenty years of age, went on to say that Blacks commit most of the crimes in Metropolitan Toronto. When asked for the source of his data, he referred to the media, his instructors and his own experience. One week later, in order to further prove his point, he brought into class a copy of a local community newspaper. A front-page article reported that a young Black male was arrested for snatching the purse from a young female student. In another article in the same newspaper, a Black male was being sought for break-ins into a number of homes in the neighbourhood. For this student, these reports proved his point and indicated that Blacks contributed to the high crime rates in our country. The government was seen as being soft on "these minority groups who were pressuring the government because they want to change things." Other students claimed that the "power was shifting," that immigrants and racial minorities were getting the government to do what they want. One reason for these rationalizations is that, from within their framework, these students are unable or refuse to account for the inequities the "meritocratic" system has meted out to Aboriginal peoples, racial minorities, women and people with disabilities.

White privilege

How can it be that white males are being discriminated against? In her article "'The Silent Dialogue': Power and Pedagogy in Educating Other People's Children," Lisa Delpit (1988) points out that "those with power are frequently least aware of–or least willing to acknowledge–its existence. Those with less power are often most aware of its existence" (p.282). As this is the case, the white male students are unlikely to see, much less acknowledge, their power and privilege. Writing of her experience as a white woman, Peggy McIntosh (1995) proposes a reason for this "power ignorance."

> My schooling gave me no training in seeing myself as an oppressor, as an unfairly advantaged person, or as a participant in a damaged culture. I was taught to see myself as an individual whose moral state depended on her individual moral will. At school, we were not taught about slavery in any depth; we were not taught to see slave holders as damaged people.... Whites are taught to think of their lives as morally neutral, normative, and average and also ideal, so that when we work to benefit others, this is seen as work that will allow "them" to be like "us" (p.78).

According to social norms, it is not prudent for individuals to acknowledge their power and privilege openly. This, then, might be part of the denial we hear from these young males. The denial of their power and privileges might also reflect their reluctance to take responsibility for the historical conditions that have resulted in their privileges, or rather maintain their belief that in today's society, individual successes and failures are a result of individual efforts. Further, to acknowledge power and privilege, they will also have to agree that the opposite is true–that racial minorities have been disadvantaged by the same system that has benefited whites. The converse of this, that is, an acknowledgment of others' disadvantages without the acknowledgment of how these relate to their own advantages, is more often held. As a group that has been taught to uphold the principles of democracy and fairness, young white men must also take responsibility for rectifying and changing the historical conditions they have inherited.

The first step in doing this is admitting that their race, ethnicity, and gender play a role in their lives as Canadians. When confronted with this challenge, many young people often claim that racial minorities, women and adults in general, "just want them to feel guilty for a situation for which they are not responsible and which they have no interest in perpetuating." But in order for the students to understand the value of equity programs, they have to acknowledge the role that demographic characteristics play in providing access and opportunities to people in our society. They need to admit, like the following student, that their privilege–"being racially white"–allows them to escape the negative impact of racism.

> **Lyn**: It is white culture that I experience day to day, and the very fact that discrimination is rarely an issue for me personally results in my own racial identity becoming an invisible thing. The powerful people within my experience, directly or indirectly—the politician, the employer, the teacher, the social worker—are invariably white. I know that my race will not be an issue with most of the people I must deal with.... Neither will I expect my values or behaviour to be an issue because I fit into the "norm." It is in the idea of the "norm" that racial and ethnic cultures mesh to form a powerful image of what is accepted or expected (Chapter 2).

Addressing the issues

Essentially, the phrase "reverse racism" seems oxymoronic. It negates the inherent inequalities in resources and power among groups positioned by racial categorization in our society. It is a phrase that is important for young white males, for it gives political weight to their feelings of powerlessness and loss of privilege. For them, the term conveys the feeling that they too are oppressed, and that, like racial minorities, they are victims of a system over which they have very little or no control. Within this context, the phrase conveys the mistaken idea that racism is based on individual attitudes and ideologies and the individual exercise of power. It fails to construct power in structural and historical terms, which would explain the cultural capital that they possess because of their membership in a particular racial group. Inherent in their conceptualization of racism is the lack of acknowledgment of their own power and privilege and, with it, the lack of recognition that their own power is rooted in the historical and cultural conditions upon which this society has been built. By not recognizing the structural roots of racism and their white privilege, they are denying their own racism, the benefit they derive from its existence and their responsibility for participating in changing it (hooks, 1988; Roman, 1993).

Educators have an important role to play in engaging students in discussions about racism and equity. Evidently some students will resist such engagement. Nevertheless, as Tatum (1992) points out, as students learn from these discussions and become comfortable with the issues, "they take their friends with them" (p.22). Our aim must be to provide an educational climate where difficult issues can be brought up and all students can voice how they see the issues that affect their aspirations. The curriculum, assigned readings, class presentations and discussions should provide students with a critical awareness of how structural inequality, and racism in particular, influence individuals' educational and occupational opportunities and outcomes. Such an awareness must alert them to the need to act consciously to address and remove barriers that are inherent in the existing social structure (Dei, 1996; hooks, 1988). Hence, students will come to understand that barriers to employment and educational opportunities must necessarily be addressed through programs that deal with the social structure. Leslie Roman (1993) suggests that white educators have a responsibility to challenge and work with racially privileged students to help them understand that their (our) attempts to assume the positions of the racially oppressed are also the result of our contradictory desires to misrecognize and recognize the collective shame of facing those who have been effaced in the dominant texts of culture, history, and curricular knowledge (p.84).

In a socially stratified society such as ours, it is necessary that racism and equity are discussed in our classrooms. Providing opportunities for such discussions, according to Tatum (1992), "may be the most proactive learning opportunities an institution can provide" (p.23). Classroom forums can help students gain a critical understanding of the issues of equity and produce the needed paradigm shift to counter the racial tension and resentment underlying some student's negative reactions to employment equity programs.

SUGGESTIONS FOR DISCUSSION

1. Discuss the historical significance of immigration and immigrants to the economic, social, political and technological development of Canada. How will immigration play a role in the future development of Canada?

2. What is meant by the term "hyphenated Canadian"? What role does the population in general play in maintaining the "hyphen" in some Canadians' lives?

3. Is there such a thing as "reverse racism"? Do multiculturalism and employment equity contribute to reverse racism and discrimination in Canada?

Photo: Gary Gellert

CHAPTER 9

Seeing Ourselves and Others

Hugh: We cannot be held responsible for what society taught us … but we should be held responsible for educating ourselves.

Joanne: Although I realize I cannot change the attitudes, beliefs and values of society overnight, I can work to change them over time. In an earlier essay I said that I did not believe I had the ability to change society's attitudes. However, if no one tries to change them, we will never grow past the racial discrimination we experience today. If I can change the views of the people around me and try to get them to see past the racial discrimination, at least it will be a start. I feel that in order to understand something, you first have to educate yourself on the subject. If we educate ourselves about our own culture and come to an understanding of that, maybe it will be easier to look at another person's culture objectively. We all live on the same planet, and it is time that we realized that no one ethnic group is better than another. We are all equal. We are all just human beings.

In the above quotation, Joanne captures the sentiments of many of the participants in this project. Their essays document the crucial role that they felt sensitivity, awareness and education play in both their personal and career development. For these students, education means going beyond academic requirements to include awareness and knowledge of self and of others. Indeed, this education should include, as Britzman (1993) has said, "persistent self and social reflexivity, a double vision of seeing one's own identity through the eyes of others and looking again at others with lenses that are not one's own" (p.28).

In their comments, many of which appear in this chapter, participants express the need to understand the significance of culture in people's lives, the process involved in overcoming ignorance about racism, prejudice and ethnocentrism and the importance of accepting the diversity of our society. As Joanne states (above), substantive societal attitude changes are too much to expect. However, even those participants who admitted an absence of change in their attitudes confessed to an increase in their level of awareness. For other participants, the course meant "discovering the true meaning of racism," and finding that it applied to themselves. In reading the essays, it is instructive to observe how participants reflect on the process of learning and self-discovery.

The chapter opens with a series of excerpts from essays written by Paul. In each, he articulates his response to course assignments and informs us of his understanding of the issues. Over the thirteen weeks of the course, Paul wrote four essays rather than simply meeting the course requirement of three. He was invited to further consider some of the ideas he expressed in his third essay, identified here as his diary entry of March 27. In his final essay, or diary entry of April 10, one week later, Paul reconsiders his understanding of racism.

Paul's essays are instructive as they alert us to how the class activities, i.e., the reflective essays and the interview, enabled Paul to think through his sense of identity, his taken-for-granted privileges, his relationships with family, friends and neighbours, his growing-up years and his attempts at, and probable resistance to, confronting the "difficult knowledge" (Britzman, 1997) with which he must live. How well did Paul do in terms of recognizing his privileges and confronting the difficult knowledge of his racism? Can a thirteen-week course of three hours per week, based on these assignments, discussions and supportive readings, really help to bring about the changes in ideas, attitudes and ideologies that we would like to see in individuals like Paul? While using Paul as a case in point, the same questions could be asked of all the participants whose essays are presented here.

In the "Concluding Reflections" section, other class participants reflect on their course experience. We conclude with an essay by a racial minority participant who, in looking at her experiences in the class and in society generally, contemplates what it would be like to be unaware of inequity.

PAUL: CONSTRUCTING IDENTITY

"The biggest influence in my life now is me."

I was born and raised in Toronto. In our neighbourhood, if a new kid moved in and he was white and he didn't have an accent, and he didn't let on in any other way that he had immigrated from another country, he could be accepted as one of the gang. This was provisional on whether he could perform admirably on the field of sport and he and his parents didn't tell anyone where they were from until after he was accepted. Then it was, "You're from South Africa? Neat!"

To be accepted at the public school I went to, located at the heart of a wealthy Toronto community, you had to be white, Protestant, very well off and, above all, good at more than one of the accepted sports of the time: hockey (both ice and road), soccer, baseball or any of the track and field events.

Today, as a result of the events that have shaped my life, I am a bigot and a hypocrite. Don't get me wrong—I don't fancy myself as a red-neck who goes around killing Blacks à la the KKK, nor do I participate in gay bashing or any other type of physical outburst aimed at any particular race or ethnic group. Where I am prejudiced is through all the stereotypes. Women and Chinese people can't drive. Pakistanis smell bad. Blacks are thieves and smell bad. Italians either build houses or kill people for a living.

Most of these stereotypes were fed to me over the years by my parents and my older brother. I didn't know what the word stereotype meant then. I took these "phrases of wisdom" as truths, and they altered my view of people. Prejudice is learned, not instinctive. I will quote a song we often used to sing, written about my great-grandmother, Mrs. Murphy: "Who put the overalls in Mrs. Murphy's chowder? / No one spoke up, so she hollared all the louder / 'It's a dirty, rotten trick and I could lick a Mick' / Who put the overalls in Mrs. Murphy's Chowwwwwwwwder?"

I remember asking my father what a Mick was. He replied, "A Roman Catholic." No further explanation was required, as I knew they were the ones who didn't go to my school. At that point in my life, being Canadian was being white and playing hockey.

When I graduated, I went to a junior high school. It was very different from what I had been accustomed to. At the end of my first day, my father asked me how it went. I said the school was "full of Niggers and Wops." I was not scolded for or corrected in my use of derogatory remarks. It was then that my Dad wanted me to go to an exclusive all-boys' school, but one thing kept me at the junior high—the girls started getting breasts. Besides, thank God, I still belonged to the clique that had graduated with me from public school.

My friends and I got into a lot of fights in Grade 7—ones that weren't our fault, we'd say. Looking back, I can truthfully say it was as much the fault of society as it was ours. There had not been one non-white person at my public school nor one white person at our rival school. Junior high is where the two cultures clashed. I'm sure that there had been as much racial discrimination going on at the other public school as there had been in ours. Clearly there should have been some cultural integration.

In high school I met, and became friends with, a guy named Chris. We got along famously. The fact that he was Black didn't matter, except to my parents. They didn't like him. When pressed as to what they had against him, they couldn't, or wouldn't, reply. The fact that he was at the top of the class in nearly every subject and worked at school harder than anyone I'd ever met mattered little to them. It was then, at age sixteen, that I realized what bigots my parents were, and I increased my rebellion against them. I grew my hair long, very long. I drank with my other friends, my white friends. I had my ear pierced. I was tattooed. I quit high school. I won't say that this was all due to my parents' view of Chris, but that's what sparked it.

If rebellions can be won or lost, then chalk one up for the kids. My parents came to really like Chris. Through the two years of my rebellion, Chris was the one friend who stuck by me through it all. The day arrived when they looked past the Black and saw the person.

You can probably tell from the content of this paper that my youth and upbringing have been the major influences in my life. I am still very much confused about what the Canadian culture is. As for my morals and values, I try to give everyone and everything a fair chance before passing judgment. The prejudices I have are not without basis. They are based on fact, life experiences, or are a convenient way to blow off steam. When I say women can't drive, I am drawing a conclusion based on the number of times that I have witnessed driving infractions and seen which gender has committed them.

I have very few biases any more. The biggest influence in my life now is me. I no longer listen to others' opinions as if they were gospel and now have a clear-cut sense of where my values lie. Culturally, I do, and enjoy, all the things that are typically Canadian: play hockey; eat salt and vinegar chips; and try to belong and socialize within all the other cultures that make up our society. I am a Canadian and very proud of it.

PAUL: MAKING COMPARISONS

"I was, and for the most part still am, politely racist."

White Canadians versus Black Canadians: an interesting title for an essay. The idea came about in some part through my interviews with some Black Canadians. It mostly came from the person within me. Someone who has never shown his face on paper before. Someone I am ashamed to have as a part of me. That someone is a bigot.

This paper is supposed to show the differences and similarities that I as a white Canadian share with my Black Canadian counterparts. What makes white Canadians different from Black Canadians? Well, I think there is a problem with that question. Why should there be any difference, other than the colour of one's skin? The simple fact is that there is. So, let me also ask why they are different.

When told that we would be researching Black Canadians, I can't say that I was overly enthusiastic about the whole idea. I was, and for the most part still am, politely racist. When interviewing them, I found them to be polite and eager to help but at the same time they were very non-committal. Maybe I'm being paranoid or maybe I'm superimposing my own faults onto those Black Canadians, but I couldn't help but think that those I was interviewing were hiding something from me. I felt the tension in their voices, and they seemed to be very careful in the words they chose when speaking.

I interviewed a man named Trevor who was originally from South Africa. Trevor and I are very different. First and foremost, he is very dark black and I am very white. Aside from our obvious physical differences, his whole life (his schooling, the way he was brought up, the foods he eats, the clothes he wears) has been nothing like my own. Trevor is a computer programmer, as am I. The more we talked, the more I came to realize that we are alike in many ways too. The ways in which we are alike aren't as superficial as what kind of clothes we wear or how we grew up, but on a deeper plane. Our goals, for instance, are very similar. Career advancement, buying a home, getting married to someone; but aren't these the goals of most Canadians, regardless of race, creed or colour? Of course they are, and that's what I came to realize.

While I came upon my revelation, I learned a few things about myself that I didn't really want to know. First, that I think I am a bigot, and second, that I am probably a white supremacist too. Strong words indeed, but not without basis. Don't get me wrong: I am definitely not proud of my last comment. It is just something I have to admit.

If I hold a prejudice against a racial group, I am a bigot, says *The Oxford Dictionary.* It goes on to say that a stereotype is an idea or character that is standardized in a conventional form without individuality. If I laugh at a joke that uses a Black for its punch line, because I associate a stereotype with what has been said, I am a bigot. For example, "What do you call a Black guy in a new car? A thief." Funny, eh? No, the joke itself is not funny, but it makes reference to a stereotype about Blacks all being thieves, which I do find funny. Does bigotry come in varying degrees? I think it must. Although I would chuckle on the inside at the preceding joke, I find it hard to say anything bad about Black Canadians in public, and stick up for them when comments are made that are in particularly bad taste. An example of this is when, not too long ago, a co-worker recited this joke: "What do you call a busload of Blacks going over a cliff with one empty seat? A crying shame." That kind of joke is not funny. It does not point out a funny stereotype of a certain race *à la* Newfie jokes. It is pure malice and cruelty against a specific group. The fact that it was about Blacks mattered little. Am I a bigot? I don't know what I am any more.

Am I a white supremacist, though? I think so, sometimes. During my interview with Trevor, he pointed out ways in which prejudice had been used against him since he came to Canada. His difficulties are shared by most Black Canadians: finding suitable housing, finding a truly non-discriminatory workplace and striving for equality in almost every aspect of everyday life. For some reason, though, I secretly found happiness in the fact that he had had trouble finding a job. I had found a way in which I was superior to him, because I felt that I could find another job at any time without much difficulty. Knowing how society is, I felt that if it came down to a choice between him or me for a job, I would be certain to get the job. By the same token, I am a very competitive person. I often seek out other people's faults and use them to my advantage when I can. I often make my job appear to be more challenging when comparing it to someone else's position, and I can always fall back on my large salary to help me dominate over another. I often lie to make a point, and I don't hesitate to point out faults in others to improve my position over them. This is not a confession, but a statement to alleviate me from thinking I'm a white supremacist. So have I done a good job? Do I still think I'm a white supremacist? I really don't know what to think any more.

Trevor and I talked a lot about the ways in which he had been prejudiced against and by whom. As the conversation progressed, some hostility came into his voice as he spoke about certain groups, including whites. This automatically put me on the defensive, and I started increasingly to defend the white person's position. He made me feel as though I donned a white cape and mask on the weekends or something. He was obviously upset about the way he had at times been treated, but I didn't know whether he was mad at me because I had been born white, at himself because he had been born Black or at society because it mattered. I chose the latter. As for myself, I am happy that I was born white, but I don't feel I should be prejudiced against just because I was. I now see that this is how Trevor feels as well. So, this is not a Black Canadian's point of view, but one shared by all humans.

There is no reason whatsoever that anyone in Canada should be a victim of prejudice. I think I find fault in others to make myself seem a little bit better than they are. I think this competitive spirit within me is human nature and will not stop. I think discrimination against others based on their sex, race, creed or colour is something that is superimposed on us by authority figures and the media while we are young.

After talking with Trevor, I felt guilty for thinking that we were different or should be treated differently by society. I am confused about how I am supposed to feel about someone of another race. If I use a stereotype to describe them, how accurate am I being? I mean, women still can't drive, but are all Blacks thieves, and is this in good taste? I don't understand my role in society any more and am almost embarrassed about my whiteness when not in a white majority situation.

I think white Canadians and Black Canadians are very similar in almost all regards. We eat alike, we dress much the same, our tastes in music are not all that different. We even suffer from the same identity crises that society has caused, only in opposite corners.

PAUL: RE-DEFINING RACISM

March 27

In earlier essays, I used such words as bigoted, racist, prejudiced and white supremacist to describe myself, my ideals and my upbringing. Certainly those are strong words, but they are not entirely untrue. To a certain degree, I know that I will put on one of those masks in order to deal with or to explain away any given situation. Am I a racist because I think that white people as a whole are better drivers than Oriental people? I can back up my theory with statistics, such as the number of accidents caused by Chinese people as compared with white people, or with the number of times I've been cut off and who has committed the offence, or even the fact that you would be hard pressed to find even one Oriental involved in the professional driving circuit. But these facts wouldn't sway me either. The simple fact is that I grew up with the "knowledge" that Orientals cannot drive, and now I believe that to be a truth. I admit to my prejudice.

Does that make me a racist ? I do not believe so. I think that there is a hidden boundary that separates a racist from a normal human who holds prejudices that don't affect how he looks at the person behind their ethnic origins. As soon as you take malicious action against someone based strictly on his ethnic origin, or hold prejudice against him in such a manner as to cause him emotional or physical harm, you have crossed the line. True, I have given my own definition for racism, but I think it is a fair one that takes into consideration the fact that we are all human and therefore susceptible to beliefs bestowed upon us. I can honestly say that I have never crossed this line, as my best friend is an Oriental and I rented the upper two-thirds of my townhouse to a Black family. In both cases, I looked beyond the origin of these persons and saw them for what they were; human, just like me. Well, I've done it. I've absolved myself of any guilt for possibly being a racist by giving it my own definition.

April 10

So, you again ask if I am a racist? I want to believe that deep down in my heart I am not. I'm a nice guy who gives to charity and helps old ladies cross the street. I'm the first person to give up my seat on the bus for a blind person and have more than once helped a distraught mother carry her groceries. I have never gone gay bashing or burned any crosses on lawns, nor do I want to. That makes me not a racist, right? Wrong. The person who has been my best friend for more than six years, with whom I have shared all of life's ups and downs, is an Oriental. This must mean I am not a racist, right? No. I rented the top half of my house to a Black family. Doesn't that prove that I'm not a racist? No, no, no. I do sound like a helluva nice guy though, don't I? So, am I a racist? Yes.

How did I come to that conclusion? Well, first I looked up the meaning of the word *racism* in *The Oxford Dictionary*. The definition reads: "belief in

> the superiority of a particular race." That is what the classified definition is. I defined it in a different way. I thought it meant when one person takes malicious action against another person based strictly on the colour of skin or on religious beliefs. One racial slur here and there doesn't a racist make, does it? I mean, okay, as a rule I think that Oriental people can't drive. And, if the truth be known, I do sort of feel superior to Black people. Deep down I don't believe I'm any better than they are, but because Black people are highly discriminated against in today's society, I feel I have an advantage over them because I enjoy a relatively discrimination-free lifestyle. This course has caused me to find something out about myself that I didn't necessarily want to find out. It has made me realize that I am a racist. Yes, my best friend is Oriental, but I take the ethnicity out of him. I don't take him for the Oriental that he is, I take him for the white person I have made him. I enjoy knowing that Black people are discriminated against because it gives me a decisive edge over them. As I said before, maybe I am not a demonstrative racist, but a rose by any other name is ...
>
> I guess the saddest part of all is knowing that I will not change. I am probably worse than those who run about actively showing their racism. If nothing else, they are up-front about it. I lobby for equal rights for minority groups knowing full well they will never get them. I give them my charity because it makes me feel good; makes me feel like I'm not a racist.

It would be too much to expect significant changes in Paul's ideas between his first and final essay. In relating his story about growing up, Paul points out how his parents and friends helped to socialize him into his admittedly racist ideas. But quite significant is his understanding of racism as an individual attitude held particularly by "red-neck" people "à la KKK," who are likely to go about hating, injuring or killing non-whites, gays and women. Since these actions are not a part of his repertoire, he does not consider himself to be a racist, no matter the stereotypes he holds of groups (how could he be when his best friend in high school, Chris, was Black, a person with whom his parents did not want him to associate; when he rented his townhouse to a Black South African while he lived in the basement; when his best friend was Chinese?). Paul argues that he might be prejudiced, but he is not a racist. This is based on his own definition of racism.

When invited to re-examine his ideas about racism, Paul makes it clear that he will accept the fact that he is racist. He goes further and says that he might be "worse that those who run about actively showing their racism" for "at least they are up-front about it." What can we say about Paul and his so-called new consciousness or awareness, particularly when he says that he is prepared to act to maintain his privileges? Paul demonstrates that he understands racism, both in its individual and structural forms, but he is not willing to make the investment, or what he might consider sacrifices, to bring about the changes that might be needed, at least at this time. One might therefore ask what the value is of such a course as this for people like Paul.

CONCLUDING REFLECTIONS

> Is intolerance, non-acceptance, racism and prejudice based on ignorance? Lack of knowledge? Lack of objectivity? Close-mindedness? Will interaction with "others," knowing "others" and having "others" as friends bring about acceptance? Remove ignorance? Cause us to show humanity? Bring compassion? Develop objectivity?

After weeks of exploring issues related to cultural identity, ethnicity, race, racism, prejudice and discrimination, both old and new questions and much confusion are much in evidence. Although attempts were made to address many questions and concerns, in many cases participants were for the first time confronting the complex, contradictory, transitory and conflicting nature of many of the issues. Participants were also asked to think about racism, prejudice and discrimination, not only in individual terms, but also in structural terms. As the following essay excerpts show, after weeks of discussion and reading, many participants still perceived the issues to be reflections of solely individual attitudes and behaviours, rather than of structural. But should we expect otherwise?

Robin: *"Lack of knowledge breeds discrimination and stereotypes."*

Interaction during our group assignments and personal interaction with people of other racial and ethnic origins have had a positive effect on me. It is lack of knowledge that breeds discrimination and stereotypes. Without personal contact with members of other racial and/or ethnic groups, it is understandable that a person might fall prey to accepting stereotypes of people they know very little about. This interaction gives you a foundation on which to base relations with other groups, and enables the people involved to see the similarities and differences in culture and background. From here a relationship of understanding and compromise can evolve.

The most important step in understanding other people is first understanding yourself. This includes your own background, culture and personal biases. If you can objectively assess these traits, then a more understanding relationship is possible with people of different ethnic or racial origins. This seems to be a problem for some Canadians, including me. My ethnic origin has become somewhat uncertain as generations have gone by. It wasn't until this course that I became interested in my ethnic origin, for before the course I was told that I was Canadian, and that whites such as myself are real Canadians. Yet many other races have been here since the formation of Canada. This is a fact very few are aware of, which adds to the belief that

Canada is a "white country." This makes me better understand just how institutionalized racism is in Canada.

The lack of history taught about Canadians of non-white origin is harmful to these people as it makes it seem as though they don't belong. The taking away of their roots in Canada takes away the foundation on which these people can base their pride in their country. This creates a feeling of alienation from their own country. From this I became aware of the need for multicultural programs, both at the federal level and the community level. Programs like employment equity are needed to attempt to balance the scales of power. These programs can open the doors of opportunity for minority groups. Ethnic associations are especially important now, as they provide people with a forum in which to share with others of the same culture and background. They also provide historical information, which is not taught in the public school system. This lack of cultural history may cause the minority student to lose interest in school and thus drop out, continuing the cycle initially created by racism. The student who does drop out may turn to crime, which is exploited by the media. The media's portrayal of the minority groups further reinforces the stereotypes in the minds of both minority and majority group members.

An awareness of the differences among people of various ethnic and/or racial origins is valuable to the person who is considering a career in human services. A person in this field encounters various people on the job, and how he handles the situation is key. If the person is equipped to deal with people of various ethnic and/or racial origins, this can affect the outcome of situations. This idea is based on an individual level of relating, but if more individuals are better equipped to deal with people, then relations between the various communities can be improved.

Doreen: *"Prejudice is based upon ignorance."*

My research on ethnic and racial groups brought me to the conclusion that prejudice is based on ignorance. I also believe that knowledge forces a person to confront his or her beliefs with the facts. I believe that, if more people were exposed to knowledge about other cultures in our society, much of the prejudice that exists would surely diminish.

We must become aware that our race, as well as cultural and ethnic background, affects our attitudes and behaviours towards others who are both similar and different based on these factors. When we become aware of this, we are well on our way to understanding our prejudices. Anything that is unknown or strange to us is susceptible to discrimination on the basis of our fear…

I cannot say that my prejudices have diminished, as they have not. But I now understand that these factors do exist. I find that, to a certain degree, I am able to stop myself when I am about to discriminate against others by reminding myself that my prejudices are based on ignorance and fear of the unknown…

I feel that, in order for my prejudices to diminish, I must confront them directly, and also understand why I have these feelings towards people who are ethnically, racially and culturally different from me.

Lorna: *"Ignorance—not having the chance to experience another's suffering."*

I am now more aware of how much my Ukrainian background has affected my view of the world and of other ethnic groups. I learned that I am indeed ethnocentric with respect to immigrants not learning English. All my life I have heard, "When my grandparents and parents came to Canada, they didn't know a word of English, but they learned it. Therefore, all should learn English." I do not think I am as rigid on this point now, as I realize that there are some who just can't learn another language despite making the effort.

I think about the people I consider ignorant. How can I blame someone for being ignorant if she or he has not had the chance to experience or to have empathy for another's suffering?

Pat: *"Know people intimately."*

Every one of us sees other cultures through our own set of glasses. We see what we want to see and no more. This is sad but true. If people say that all their biases and prejudices were laid to rest after learning about another culture, I think they are being untruthful with themselves. We have all been influenced by our parents, siblings, peers and significant others, and these influences have shaped our behaviours into what we are today. We are taught to be prejudiced. We don't teach ourselves, but others teach us. We are influenced by what is said in ethnic jokes, by what our family has encountered and even by what we encounter in day-to-day life. We may have learned about different cultures in general, but unless we know people intimately we can never get over our prejudices about people who are different from ourselves …

Tina: *"I can more deeply question the culture that is part of me."*

In an earlier essay, I had the opportunity to think through some of the assumptions I hold about my culture. Its familiarity and power so often disguises the fact that it is only one culture among many. I could see clearly how success, for example, can be defined culturally. I could see how the priorities of this society are reflections of white English Canadian culture. And I could see myself as a product of that culture—how it could trap me. I could see that much can be understood only if you step outside and look back in.

From this course, I have learned about how culture is internalized. Although I often feel at odds with my culture, I can perhaps see more clearly now how my individual identity will always be rooted to some extent in my whiteness and my Englishness. But to some degree, as a result of seeing myself in those terms, I can also more deeply question the culture that is part of me. In doing so, I hope I will be less afraid of my own inevitable ignorance and that I will be more open to other ways of life. I hope I will also be more determined to challenge my own view of the world and the assumptions that lie within it as well as those of the society in which I live.

Hugh: *"Be open-minded and educated."*

I found that my open-mindedness was not all that was required in order to gain a better understanding of people of different racial and ethnic backgrounds. Although I realized that I should not always accept other people's opinions and stereotypes as true or accept media "statistics" as 100 percent factual, when this is all you have to base your opinions on, your feelings are affected by them. This is why being open-minded must be combined with education. When people have knowledge about a subject, they are less likely to assume things and less likely to be swayed by the "opinions" of others. I don't profess to be totally void of prejudice and possibly racist thoughts, but I do make an effort to dissolve the stereotypes and feelings that have built up within me for twenty-two years now. I constantly make an effort to give all people the opportunity to impress me with the merit of who they are as a person and not with what they are.

This is difficult at times because our present social system unknowingly or knowingly promotes segregation, prejudice, racism and ostracism. We are "brainwashed" by what is around us throughout our lives, and we cannot be held responsible for what society taught us as we grew up. But we can and should be held responsible for educating ourselves and learning the difference between what is wrong and what is right. Whether we like it or not, we are all human, and we all possess one very important human ability—the ability to feel compassion. No matter what differences we have, we will always be bonded by a far greater number of similarities. Whatever good we have, we can find in others; whatever bad we see in others, we will find within ourselves.

Shelagh: *"Is it that we really do not see what is happening?"*

Any course that requires us to re-think our values and beliefs is bound to be interesting and of some merit. Sometimes it can even turn into a heated internal debate. Anything that requires us to question our validity and goodness is bound to raise our emotional level a little, for some more than others. Having to think about what we think about others when we have never had to think about it before is also difficult. We may even question the sanity of the teacher that stands before us. We may even dislike the course because we are not able to see where it is leading us.

I hated seeing the discrimination that actually does happen from day to day in front of our very eyes. Is it that we really do not see what is happening or is it that we just believe our way is right? I watched a program about a white supremacist group a few weeks ago. My curiosity had been piqued by this course, and I was disgusted to discover that they were average people, the kind of people you might meet in the grocery store or at church. What was even worse was that these people actually believe deep in their hearts that they are supreme. They do not think they are doing anything wrong.

So then I had to sit down and think about my brother and my father. Here we are, immigrants to Canada. They think they have the right to the same opportunities as every other Canadian, yet they do not think that other immigrants have that right.

I had to stop and consider what the difference was between them and the white supremacists. All the difference is, is a matter of degree. My brother and father wouldn't kill another immigrant for taking a job they had applied for, yet I believe a white supremacist might. Then I had to stop and think again about which was better: letting them know you hate them or spreading vicious remarks about them as a group? In one of the class presentations, the presenters said that the group they had studied had wanted to know up-front where they stood. At least then they could deal with it.

Then I had to think about myself. No, I could never be a bigot, or could I? Having to sit down and reassess who I was and what I believed was very hard for me because I have always considered myself to be an open-minded person. But then who ever admits to being close-minded? That was when I discovered that I did not personally know anyone from another race. I thought immediately that this meant that I was a bigot. I condemned myself then and there.

But so what if I did not know anyone of another race? It was not because I am a bigot, it was because I came from a town where there are only white people. I had not been exposed to other groups until now. Besides, which is better, admitting that you do not have any culturally different friends or going out in search of that "token Black" or "token Jew"? I feel strongly that I do have an open mind and that, if the opportunity arises where I do come in contact with another person of a different race that I happen to get along with, things will be fine.

After thinking this, I was feeling pretty okay about myself. I was not that bad. And then up came the question, "Why am I still tied to Scotland if I am happy here?" Does this mean that I think of myself as not fully Canadian, as different from those out there who drink beer, eat potato chips and say, "Eh"? It was only after my research projects, the question of the conversion law in Israel, and my meeting with Mehul (the subject of my second essay) that I discovered what it was that made me so anxious to keep my Scottish roots and the path to Scotland open. There is a certain security in knowing who you are and where you come from, and there is an even bigger sense of belonging in knowing that you can return at any time.

To be told that I would never be able to return to Scotland because I had come to Canada or that I would no longer be able to consider myself Scottish would be devastating. But I have only just recently discovered why that is. My history is there; it is part of me, no matter what. Yes, I am Canadian and I love Canada, but I was not born here. I was born in Scotland. It holds my heart even though I cannot remember what it looks like. It is me, and if you try to take it away, you destroy a part of me.

Throughout this course, we have been asked to analyze ourselves, to look deep into ourselves to see if there were faults. If faults were present, we needed to ask what to do about them. We have been made to see the discrimination around us and to become aware of other cultures and what they might have to offer us. The best part for me was testing myself and believing that I passed. The worst part was finding out that there are others who will fail, because it is easier to hide and to not change than it is to challenge yourself and come into the light. A faith never tested does not constitute a complete faith. A person who does not test himself is also not a complete person.

Paula: *"Why did I not categorize my friend in a stereotypical way?"*

When I started this course in September, I thought, "Oh good, this should be interesting. I'll get to learn about different cultural groups and how to deal with them when I eventually come across them as clients. I am not a prejudiced person and I have been to many different and diverse countries in the world and so this course should be easy for me. I'll probably be able to contribute to the class discussions more than the other students because of my knowledge of different cultures."

What a shock I received when I realized that this self-assured and narrow-minded attitude was being torn apart by my own discoveries during the course. There is no handbook for social service workers that can effectively teach you how to deal with East Indians, Blacks, Italians or any other race, colour or culture. That was just my own stereotypical view of people that I hoped would make my job easier. To believe that we can treat all people of one culture in a certain way would be a disastrous mistake.

I was also sure that I had no prejudices. Many of us in the course said that we had none. We backed this up by saying that we couldn't be prejudiced because we had friends who were Black, Vietnamese, Italian or East Indian (these were my examples of friends I had that proved that I was not prejudiced). When I looked at my relationships with these friends objectively, I realized that I had put their differences from me out of my mind. My Vietnamese friend was so like me that I unconsciously considered him to be Canadian. When I think of the Vietnamese people as a whole group, my immediate thoughts are of those people with large, poor families who used to spend most of their time in the learning centre at high school because of their difficulties with the language. I hate to admit it, but this stereotype still comes to mind when I think of them as a group. Why then did I not categorize my friend in this stereotypical way? Because I had seen him as the person he was, a wonderful, extremely intelligent man who would do anything for anybody. However, I had taken away his culture. Had I not known him personally, would I have categorized him with the group as a whole? I hate to admit it, but I think I would have, and, even more frightening with my new awareness, maybe I still would. My East Indian friend was a wonderful girl who was killed on the Air India jet that exploded and took so many lives. I was saddened by her death (she was only twenty-one and so pretty that she was in the preliminary stages of becoming a model). Had I taken away her ethnicity too?

To say that we are not prejudiced is a lie, and it's one that I too am guilty of. I loathe the idea of the Ku Klux Klan and other groups that display their prejudice so openly and with such hatred, but at least they are honest. To say that you are not prejudiced while holding ideas that are stereotypical is just as dangerous, only in a more subtle way.

An aspect of the course that I found most interesting was the difficulty we all had in examining Canadian culture. What was strange was that during class discussions I found myself saying things like "When immigrants come to our country they..." and yet I am an immigrant too. Would an East Indian say that, or have I mentally grouped myself with Canadians because I am white and speak English? I fit in so easily, but an East Indian that is born in Canada and is a Canadian would be questioned if he were to say the same thing. No one questioned me, despite the fact that I had openly admitted to being an immigrant. As a class we may have been showing our racism without even realizing it.

I can at least recognize the mistakes I have made and am still making. To be critical of myself I must answer the question, "Have I come to these conclusions because I want to pass the course and I want to think that I am objective, or do I truly believe this?" The real test for me will come when the course is over. Will I continue to apply this knowledge and question my thoughts and feelings when I am no longer forced to do so? I don't know the answer. I hope it is yes, as this course has made me challenge my own ideas and opinions. I hope this is a new habit that has just begun. I feel that this course is just the beginning, that my concepts must be analyzed and challenged on an ongoing basis, but at least I have made a start.

Shelley: *"I should not be ignorant of these differences."*

It is obvious that a person's race and cultural and ethnic background play a large part in establishing a set of values or in explaining an individual's behaviour pattern ...

When a person recognizes that these factors do indeed exist, he or she is on the way to understanding better and appreciating, not only themselves, but other people as well—people who might previously have been seen as strange and unknown, who appeared threatening and were to be avoided at all costs. In an ever-changing world, the word *understanding* is often not only misused but abused. For if a person cannot understand himself, how can he understand others?

It is very obvious to me that many ethnic or cultural groups react with surprise, anger and frustration when their values are threatened. They make assumptions and take things at face value as if in fear of examining them further, for it may mean changing. Human beings are funny creatures. Many of us have a hard time admitting when we are wrong. No one likes to admit they might have jumped to false conclusions. It makes people feel insecure and unsure of their judgment—or at least that's what it does to me.

Similarly, when cultural groups feel that they are not being listened to or that people are trying to change their ways, there is an initial shock. They ask themselves, "Why us? What did we do?" Once they have established where they stand and how they feel about it, they usually establish some sort of goal to work towards so that they can begin to change what they are unhappy with. This is unavoidable; it is a natural problem-solving process that is used in most situations that arise. However, this is often a slow and painful process, especially when one is attempting to change or adapt one's personal values and belief system, as I did with my fellow students. Many groups meet with more discrimination and stronger feelings as they begin to implement this process. Educating both parties about their differences and their similarities is a difficult process; however, if we could do this, the rewards would be immeasurable.

When examining my cultural group and while watching other presentations, I realized, as a relatively intelligent, educated Canadian citizen, how little I know. As was stated many times, you cannot really understand a culture unless you spend some time with the people and begin to see how they view the world. So much of how they have been treated historically influences where they stand and/or what they currently experience. Again, gathering all the information that is accessible to you is so important.

Learning about racial and ethnic groups may or may not directly reflect the nature of a specific program of study; however, it deals with developing an important skill that is essential in my field and, as I interact with others, especially those who are different.

I have come to realize the importance of learning about racial and ethnic groups as it pertains to my career as a social worker and also to me as a Black Canadian. I used to think that it didn't matter what ethnicity, colour or culture a person is, that all people should be treated equally. This is true to an extent, but it is also questionable. I now realize that I must not only treat every individual with respect and as an equal, but I should also be aware of the individual's differences in terms of their ethnicity, culture and colour. I should not be ignorant of these differences, but I should be able to understand them in order to better cater to their needs as an individual.

William: *"Canadian culture is a mixture of many cultures."*

Cultural differences will always be present in Canada but the acceptance of these differences will become less of a barrier when people can handle the fact that there is not just one way to live within this country. They must accept that "Canadian culture" is a mixture of many cultures combined together.

Everybody, including myself, seems to dwell on the "unique" aspects of cultures. Indeed, all cultures are unique in some ways, just as individuals are; but all these cultures reside in Canada and are therefore part of our Canadian culture. I think that comparing cultures would shed a great deal more light on the similarities between people. We could learn more about ourselves in the process.

Kathy: *"I have been reminded that Canada is a multicultural country ..."*

I am ashamed to admit what a prejudiced and ethnocentric person I am. I had thought I viewed and treated all ethnic groups with equality in relation to my ethnicity, but I do not. Now certainly there are individual people of ethnic backgrounds different from my own whom I respect and admire for their accomplishments. However, I do not regard ethnic groups in general on an equal basis. I have also come to realize that minority groups of a different colour stand a lesser chance of achieving equality than those who are white. For some reason I possess the deep-rooted notion that white English people are superior. Their colour is a ticket to success. If I were asked to categorize all minorities, the bottom of the file would consist of the coloureds, leading up to those who are white but have a foreign accent.

My only consolation is that I am now more aware of my biases, and with luck the impact will create a positive change. I can realistically admit that a thirteen-week course cannot change twenty-eight years of prejudice.

However, I do feel I have acquired a new appreciation for all ethnic groups and feel confident that my outlook has been altered enough to approach them with more understanding and tolerance. I have once again been reminded that Canada is a multicultural country, and I should not allow the difference of skin colour to set the standards of superiority.

We all have different backgrounds, which will assuredly lead to differences in many areas, but I feel confident that I will now approach these differences as such and avoid the urge to criticize and view others through ethnocentric eyes.

During the first class we were asked about our prejudices. Our general response was that we had none. Some said they viewed everyone as equal, be they black, white or purple, and if I recall correctly, one student ventured to say that there were absolutely no prejudices in his family. I would guess that our response reflected our naïveté. Physical features such as skin colour and shape of eyes cannot be hidden, and I find it difficult to believe that someone could look at, for example, a white person and a Black person at the same time and view them in the same way. I feel quite sure that I would have viewed the instructor differently if he had not been Black. In fact, the moment he walked into the classroom on the first day, I thought to myself, "Oh, he's Black. This course will be right up his alley."

Corey: *"It is people like me who are the most dangerous in our society."*

During this course I have become aware of my racism, and I must now make a conscious effort to change my way of thinking. I honestly believe that it is people like me who are the most dangerous in our society: smart enough to know better, sly enough to keep it hidden and naïve enough to convince myself that I am not a racist. Whether or not we choose to admit it, we are all racist in one way or another. Some, like me, are able to hide it much better than others when we walk down the street, interview someone for a job or look at our neighbours. It is perfectly acceptable to criticize, compare and take care of one's self in our society at the expense of others. Children are conditioned from their first days at school to follow these rules. We believe this teaching to be an innocent lesson on the facts of life, but the underlying reality is that we are teaching racism and discrimination.

It amazes me how we can be so blind to our own actions. I always find ways of justifying what I say and how I say it. I have perfected this to a fine performing art. I can cover up anything I want if I have to. The thing that amazes me most is that if you lie to yourself for long enough you actually start to believe it.

I have a responsibility as a Canadian and as a person to be fair and honest. Yet I want so desperately to fit into society and get ahead that I ignore those around me, abusing them in the process. I have been taught that this is what life is all about and that it is okay because I am white and middle class. Anything less than the best for me, I am told, is unacceptable and I am entitled to so much more.

SUMMARY

According to the participants, stereotyping, prejudice, racism and discrimination are based on ignorance about others, a lack of awareness of differences, which in turn breeds "fear" based on the strangeness of others. There is also the belief that "not having the chance to experience another person's suffering" makes it difficult for people to develop empathy, which is perceived to be an aspect of sensitivity and awareness. Therefore, as Lorna argues, we cannot "blame someone for being ignorant if she or he has not had the chance to experience or to have empathy for another's suffering."

Given the participants' logic that the lack of knowledge, historical information, and exposure to issues is what breeds prejudices, stereotyping, racism, and discrimination, it is understandable that participants would suggest that if individuals get to know each other, in some cases "intimately," develop an open mind, educate themselves, try not to stereotype and become aware of differences, then people would live more amicably. Also, if individuals remember or realize that Canada "is a mixture of cultures," in other words "a multicultural country," then "understanding and tolerance" will become realities.

Rather than reflecting an understanding of the structural and systemic character of prejudice, racism and discrimination, these essays express the view that prejudice and discrimination indeed exist in our society and are largely due to individual attitudes and actions. One might suspect that these class participants were unable to understand structural influence, yet there is evidence of the more sophisticated "new" form of racism (e.g., Paul; Corey) (Kallen 1995; Sleeter, 1993) in their reluctance to confront the myths they have been taught and by which they have lived. And, as Corey indicates, it is difficult to be self-critical, honest and non-abusive to others, particularly when an individual wants desperately to fit into society and "get ahead." So, it is highly likely that participants do understand that attitudes and actions are indeed nurtured by the social system and are not solely a product of an individual's fancies.

The empathy that some participants believe is necessary for cultural understanding might be a reflection of what Roman (1997) terms *redemption discourse.* She points out that this occurs in cases where "it is felt that loving identification with, and caring for, the 'racial other' partially overcomes and appreciates what the racially privileged are not able to know (consciously) from their own direct experiences–that is, the concrete experiences of racism" (Roman, 1997: 274).

It is not that participants cannot or do not recognize their privileges; or that racism is a factor in everybody's life; or that their efforts are insufficient to bring about respect, acceptance, understanding and fairness. Rather, it is the conflict they now experience, knowing that the very stereotyping, (mis)understandings and intolerance that they claim can be eradicated through individual effort are built into the social values, norms and morals of the society, into the things in which they have believed. Further, it is likely that participants have difficulty in accepting the larger effort and more critical role they have to play in bringing about the needed structural changes that will produce acceptance and justice for all Canadians. And as Dorne, in the following and concluding essay, so passionately writes, acceptance and justice must come soon.

Dorne: *"What would it be like to be unaware?"*

A young boy of nine or ten, while walking down the street, encountered a car full of people of a different cultural group. Something caused him to behave out of the ordinary. He stuck his middle finger up at the three female passengers, scowled and resumed strutting as if nothing else were required. Shock and fear registered on his face as the car swerved into the driveway not three feet from where he stood. As it dawned on him that his actions might bring consequences, he was spurned to run. With his arrogance gone, he fled the situation, yet he was unable to escape the pursuit of his victims. He was brought up short, face to face with the youngest of the three. He had no response, no reason, no explanation when faced with the meanness of his racism. The young girl returned to the car, turning her back on yet another dirty incident.

As the driver of that vehicle, a Black female aged twenty-six years at the time, I was once again disappointed with the white youth of today.

Racism exists, and it is ugly. It has damaged countless individuals through the ages, and it has damaged me. Throughout this course, I have been given the opportunity to consider reasons not to succumb to bitterness.

People are generally motivated to act due to various forces, both external and internal. One such factor is fear. Fear causes many individuals to react contrary to the principles and morals driven into them by their civilization. Fear of the unknown, fear of change, fear of the loss of status, fear of losing control; all can lead a person to regrettable action. Police officers shoot Black youths before giving them an opportunity to vindicate themselves. Government officials unjustly put countless Sikh men and women behind bars to satisfy the public's need for a scapegoat in the Air India flight disaster of June 1985. Hong Kong policies deter the immigration of non-Asian groups into their country. Such actions have no credible long-term benefits without necessitating apologies or under-the-table pay-offs.

We are forced to act, not only out of a primitive response to fear, but to the cobweb-like tug of insecurity. I am shocked that my sister's teacher actively prevents non-white students from studying autobiographies of their own cultural heroes in an assignment where they are given supposedly free reign in reviewing figures of historical portent. Teachers who inadvertently colour history to suit their own agenda influence the minds of our children. I grew up in basic ignorance of the major contribution my race has made, not only to Canada, but the world. I am ashamed that it is only recently that I have had even the slightest interest in peering out from under my perpetual shell of belief that racially I am inferior, unsuitable, not worthy of seeking equality. I had grown as accustomed to the thought, "I am Black; I cannot rate what the white race rates," as to the thought, "I am female; I cannot rate what the male rates."

With the recognition of having been duped came rage. I deliberately recalled what my mother had told me growing up. "Don't trust the white man," she said. "They will friend you up, then use you." I looked at everything they did and said as having a double meaning. I became so absorbed with what had been done to my race in the past that I lost sight of my personal goals for the future. No cultural group can afford to spend all their time looking back at the ravages of time.

With the fading of rage comes resolve. As a *female* member of a *minority* race, I have much to offer this world. My impact will be left on the friends I have chosen and acquaintances both casual and fleeting. My past, both racially and individually, is mine. No group or individual can diminish my experiences. I am determined that my skills and abilities will receive the nurturing they need to develop. That means relating with my society fully. The power group might not be of my ethnicity, but they cannot exist without mine and every other minority group in this country. As we discover the power we each hold in the unity of our individual groups, we will create our own history for future generations to look back on. I am as proud of my heritage as the Jews are of theirs, the Greeks, theirs, the Asians, theirs. It is our very hardships that have made us as resilient as we are. We are more alike than we are willing to admit.

I am still disappointed at the imbalance of global power, even a little envious. What would it be like, I ask myself, not to be aware of inequality because it is to my benefit? What would it be like if my only concern with a job interview were really my credentials? What would it be like to raise teenage sons and not worry that the police may mistake them for troublemakers or drug addicts? What would it be like to apply for a bank loan and not have the additional worry of racial distinction being applied? What, I ask myself, would it be like?

Because I have no answers for these questions, I cannot relinquish the nagging tendrils of mistrust. It would be foolish for me to do so, for would I not protect these "benefits" if they were truly mine? Maybe the only place they exist is in my homeland, but even there the power group's hand can be felt. Maybe with all the inter-marriages taking place, we will escape white dominance or any distinct group dominance for that matter. Then again, maybe not. As mentioned earlier, people have done and will do unnatural deeds in order to maintain their "natural balance."

As it stands, we can learn to live with the current balance or we can develop a new balance. Either way we will have to do away with ignorant, non-educated assumptions about other groups. We are truly different, as different as the seasons, as the flowers that bloom and the animals that roam this planet. And yet, we are more alike than we care to admit. We are humans. Isn't that worth celebrating together? What potential such a concept would hold for this world's future!

SUGGESTIONS FOR DISCUSSION

1. To what extent is it possible for you to interpret another person's ideas and actions completely independent of your own worldview?
2. What does "seeing ourselves" mean to you? What can be gained in terms of human relationships and interaction through self-reflectivity?
3. To what extent do you believe education and social interaction are able to bring about acceptance of difference and diversity?

Photo: Dick Hemingway

POSTSCRIPT

A Final Note

> [T]he most important learning experience that could happen in our classroom was that students would learn to think critically and analytically, not just about the required books, but about the world they live in. Education for critical consciousness that encourages all students–privileged or non-privileged–who are seeking an entry into class privilege rather than providing a sense of freedom and release, invites critique of conventional expectations and desires. They may find such an experience terribly threatening. And even though they may approach the situation with great openness, it may still be difficult, and even painful (hooks 1988: 102).

With this volume I have attempted to build a further understanding of culture, race, ethnicity, prejudice and racism and to expand the issues in and the range of perspectives on the dialogue that currently exists in this field. The comments and essays that appear provide insight into how students, within the critical discussions about these issues, locate their experiences and how the issues in turn affect the students. This educational process is premised on, as stated by bell hooks in the above quotation, "education for critical consciousness." hooks (1988) argues that such an approach to pedagogy needs to be taken if we are to prepare students to live and act more fully in the world–if they are to develop an awareness of themselves and the existing social structures so that they may be active participants in the movement for social change.

I do not believe that these essays reflect only the ideas and opinions of the writers. Surely these views, interpretations and analyses have the consensual support of ourselves and/or others we know. However, these writers have expressed on paper what many of us might say only privately, or might think but dare not articulate publicly. While some essays reflect an awareness and a sensitivity that we would wish all Canadians to hold, they also contain many unsettling comments from which we might like to disassociate ourselves. We should not dismiss these negative comments and disturbing perspectives as being those of a mere minority of Canadians, for they too have an impact on defining our social relations.

We have discussed culture as a dynamic, contradictory and conflictive force that has an impact upon everyone and upon which everyone has an impact. To understand culture one is required to recognize its colonizing effects and the role that the mechanisms of racism, stereotyping, prejudice, sexism, classism and other factors play in defining, maintaining and perpetuating culture. Individual and group resistance to the effects of cultural hegemony or colonization (in the case of Canada, Anglo-conformity) produce tension and conflicts that give meaning to race and ethnicity within the Canadian context. Our identities, then, insofar as they are of social and not only of individual production, are related to the social construction of race and ethnicity in Canada. We are a part of the dynamic production and reproduction of culture, inclusive of our race, ethnicity, gender, class and so on. For instance, while I may have cultural practices that are sometimes attributed to my racial group (Black), they are not independent of Canadian culture; rather, they are part of it. My various identities (immigrant, male, middle class, parent, partner) and behaviours are just as much Canadian as those of any other Canadian person, for I am a product of, and I respond to, the Canadian social structure. My behaviours are in part informed by my understanding of, and interaction with, the institutions of Canada and the values and norms that have been communicated to me. My behaviours are also related to how I perceive my situation contextually in terms of power and privilege in the society, and are influenced by my capacity to participate and influence social, political and economic structures and events.

This educational process is political (Freire, 1968; hooks, 1988). It provides insights into the structures that determine the relationships between racial and ethnic groups, between the dominant and subordinate, and between individuals. As a result, we can expect participants to react in both positive and negative ways, and it is understandable that many of them express that they have been affected by this learning experience. We might conclude that the discussion of race, ethnicity and culture initiated the development of the understanding and sensitivity necessary to confront the issues. This includes the participants' engagement in self-criticism and the admission of their own negative qualities. However, this is only the beginning of what will be, for many, a long and painful lesson in race and ethnic relations. And without nurturing, coaching and encouragement, these initial insights, and the commitment and determination to take up the challenge, might be lost.

Despite awareness, sensitivity and understanding, there are some issues that we as individuals still find difficult to discuss. Racism is such an issue. However, if we are to discuss meaningfully prejudices based on race, and the power factor that accompanies racial prejudices, then we must talk of racism and all its related painful and negative conditions. This talk will include its history and its colonial construction. To attribute the problems of racism and its inherent tensions and conflicts to our individual experiences with cultural differences is to misrepresent difference. Difference is not what contributes to tension and conflict in diverse settings; rather, it is the value, understanding and interpretations of difference and how we, in turn, use these to inform our actions.

It is to be hoped that, through these essays, we have brought into focus many of the issues that must be discussed if we are to move to a more equitable society. It is time for a more critical approach to education, for the multicultural and cross-cultural approaches have not helped to alleviate the social and educational problems we are experiencing today. The issues we currently identify as being rooted in cultural differences, due to a large minority population comprised largely of "immigrants," will still be here in the first decade of the new millennium. By then, many more members of racial minorities in Canada will have been born, socialized or have reached adulthood. Moreover, estimates indicate that by the second decade, the 2010's, Canada's racial minority population will have grown to more than 15 percent of the total, with a greater concentration in large urban centres. In Metropolitan Toronto, the racial minority population will be more than 35 percent (Samuel, 1992).

As emphasized in the following points, we need to equip ourselves now for working and living in a multiracial and multicultural society where social justice and equity are actively sought.

1. We must begin with our education system. Curricula and materials must reflect our diverse population and present all groups as Canadian. We must rid education of its Euro-centric approach and include the contributions that all groups have made to the historical, political, economic, social and cultural development of Canada today. We must strive to inculcate in students the critical thinking and analytical skills that are necessary for living in a diverse society.

2. We need to commit to understanding ourselves, as understanding ourselves is an important part of the process of coming to understand others. We must recognize that we are all cultural, racial and ethnic beings (just as we are gendered, classed, sexual and ability beings); we produce and reproduce culture, and are affected by culture. As Canadians, the "differences" between us are based on interpretations related to our various social locations in society and the social conditions under which we exist.

3. Racism and discrimination, as social mechanisms that are rooted in our Canadian history, must be acknowledged and addressed directly. We are all affected by them. Issues and situations that are racist and discriminatory must be identified explicitly as such. They must be named, and we must use language that names the issues and events. We need to use language that allows us to act together while recognizing each other's individuality. As Steinem (1983) writes, there can be no big social change "without words and phrases that first create a dream of change in our heads" (p.2).

4. With the appropriate awareness, knowledge, skills and language, we must proceed to engage in advocacy and action for social change. Engaging in social change activities means accepting that we all have varying degrees and sources of power. When combined, they can be used to transform the system that provides advantages or privileges to some and disadvantages to others.

The individuals who shared their work with us and allowed us insight into their thinking, attitudes and the process of change in which they were involved admit that this was only the beginning of a long journey of self-discovery and social awareness. Both self-discovery and social awareness are necessary if we are to gain an understanding of each other. Only then can we work towards building a society where all members have equality of opportunity and access.

CONCLUSION

I wish to end by sharing part of a conversation I had with a friend and colleague, Carol Geddis, who had commented on a draft copy of the revised edition (1995) of this book. She had also read and commented on the earlier version of the book some years ago.

C.G. You talk about things like self-awareness and increased understanding of others (in fact, largely, the Other) as being central and important to any kind of individual change as well as social change, over time, towards a more equitable society. Why do you believe that? Why do you think that, if I understand myself better and increase my understanding of people who are racially and culturally different, somehow that will all accrue to the good?

C.J. I don't think that it *necessarily* follows that because I am more aware of myself I will be much more active in social change. But I do think that personal awareness is a critical and crucial aspect in the whole issue of social change. If you are going to be involved in social change, you have to understand yourself–and understanding yourself involves understanding how structures have impacted on you; how they have affected your life; and consequently how you can influence the structures in order to bring about change. So personal awareness is an important starting point in the process of social change.

C.G. It seems to me that something more than self-knowledge and understanding of others is required in order for substantive change to come about. Or do you believe, in your heart of hearts, in the "perfectibility of human kind"? That you can take anyone from anywhere, teach them some things, and this will turn them around?

C.J. I believe, like you do, that more than self-knowledge is required. It is a matter of how we move people towards collective action. We can move towards collective action if we have a common understanding of the forces that shape all our lives. These forces impact on racial minorities differently from the racial majority. In knowing that, a person–either racial minority or racial majority–will understand the role she or he will have to play individually and collectively in bringing about change.

C.G. Whether or not they accept that role is another thing, though, isn't it?

C.J. Oh, yes. But some will accept the role and others will reject it.

C.G. Yes, that is true. You did not answer my question directly. I asked you if you believe in the perfectibility of human kind. I think that at some level you must, if you believe what you are saying to me now.

Let me respond to you as a white person. If I accept the fact that racism as we know it in Canada is a white problem, given the historical forces such as colonialism that have helped to shape this society, then, as a white person, I also need to clarify my responsibility–or the role that I could be playing to help make society more equitable. When I interact with other white people around that issue, it seems to me that it comes down to the big question of power and privilege. I am too often left with the question of what it will take to have white people share, relinquish or somehow modify our power and privilege. Or even to have us realize that we have such things as power and privilege. Even when there is recognition of white power and privilege, then the issue often becomes one of, once I know that I have it, why should I give it up? It seems to me that it is not only a matter of us white folk holding tight to our power and privilege because it is to our advantage to do so, but sometimes it is also a matter of risk and fear. I have had white people say to me, for example, that if they challenge racism among family or friends by defining it as an expression of white power, they are putting themselves in some jeopardy. By this they mean that they run the risk of damaging their relationships by setting themselves apart from their group. That is a powerful combination–self-interest in wanting to maintain power and privilege, on the one hand, and not wanting to pull away from the group, on the other. I would like to know what is it going to take to get us beyond those major road blocks.

C.J. It is going to take a lot of efforts and struggle. While you were talking, I was thinking about the students whose experiences are documented in this book. Most are white and are twenty-one, twenty-two, and up to twenty-four years of age. Their understanding of their own power and privilege, and of the impact of social structures on individuals and groups, is limited. They seem to believe that they don't have any power. For example, when employment equity was being discussed, the assumption was that racial minorities have all the power now and are taking over. So much work remains to be done in terms of bringing people to an understanding of their power and privilege. There is nothing wrong in recognizing one's personal power. One has it because of his or her skin colour and because of the meaning given to such things by our society. Understanding the structural aspect of power would hopefully lead to an understanding of how one can use her or his power for social change.

C.G. I think the employment equity issue moves the discussion of power, and the recognition and acceptance of differential power as part of the problem, past the academic level of discussion. It is true that the notion of unearned power and the part it plays in advantaging the lives of those that have it is a complex and difficult issue for some people to come to grips with. Not only twenty-years-olds but also forty- and fifty-year-olds find the notion of power difficult to understand. They have trouble perceiving of themselves as having power, of understanding power as a factor of how things are structured, as something that works in some people's favour and to the disadvantage of others. They have difficulty relating this understanding of power to their own experience. My concern is that, as we try to lead people through this type of analysis of power, too often the discussion remains academic. Employment equity is going to take it beyond the academic. People, for the first time, are going to experience what it feels like to have a system or structure that does not automatically work in their favour. Employment equity is going to be a "test case" for this society and for those of us who see ourselves as agents of change.

C.J. Yes. I wonder about those people who participated in the course and who expressed a growth in their level of awareness. I wonder what changes I would see in them if I met them ten years from now. The changes they write about in their essays will be evident only then, through their sustained effort. There is only so much that can be done in the course of thirteen or so weeks in terms of getting people to seriously understand that they have a role to play in social change.

C.G. I could not help but think, as I read the words of the students, that there were varying degrees of growth around the understanding of the issues. In some cases, it seemed superficial. In other cases, it was quite profound–the degree of personal insight and so on that the writers were gaining. I must also admit that the insights, understanding and emotions that I found most telling were in the writings of minority group members. I am reminded of the woman who put herself in the place of a majority group person and asked the sort of questions that a majority group person should ask about issues such as power. She asked what it must feel like to be able to do A, B and C without reservation or restriction. She also asked what it must it feel like to be expected to give up some things. She admitted, did she not, that she was not sure if she would be able to if she herself were in such a situation? This woman demonstrated a level of insight and empathy that was not in evidence in the writing of other students.

C.J. Sometimes that kind of awareness produces empathy. Sometimes it produces anger and frustration. It is also possible that some people do the exercise merely to fulfil course requirements–and then simply leave it behind them when the course is over. One of the challenges of this type of course is to have people see it as more than an academic exercise–that it can be a combination of intellectual insight and insights into the structural operation of society.

C.G. It also shows the danger of the path we take when we open up these issues in a classroom setting. Some people can approach it academically and just walk away. For others, it is like the continuous bleeding of an open wound. As the person facilitating such discussions, how does one manage it so that there are not deeper scars left from what is supposed to be an enlightening experience?

C.J. A sense of guilt also emerges as a result of such discussions.

C.G. I am less patient with guilt than I used to be. I find it is self-defeating; and too often it can become a ploy to prevent people from getting beyond a certain point to a deeper analysis and, ultimately, to action.

C.J. Guilt is not a productive consequence of these exercises. It is important to present this kind of material and manage these kinds of discussions in a way that does not produce feelings that are counter-productive in terms of moving towards action.

C.G. You mentioned that many of the students you worked with were in their early twenties. Presumably many of them have gone through the school system here, up to the college and university levels. The fact that they approached the course material as if it were the first time they had been exposed to the issues is, for me, an indictment of the school system in general. One should not have to wait until the post-secondary level before one is given the opportunity to contend with the major issues that are central to the health of this society.

C.J. Yes. And as our society becomes even more multiracial, multifaith and multicultural, we are going to have to do a better job in the schools to prepare students to live and work in our diverse society. If social change is going to take place, if education is to liberate and be meaningful to the students, then we must educate our students early about issues of classism, sexism, racism and other oppressive mechanisms.

C.G. You realize that you are talking about a big change?

C.J. Certainly; and a re-education of the teachers who are responsible for educating the students.

C.G. Yes, re-education of existing teachers and a re-conceiving of teacher training programs.

References

Abella, Irving, and Troper, Harold. 1982. *None Is Too Many.* Toronto: Lester & Orpen Dennys Publishers.

Abella, Rosalie. 1984. *Equality in Employment: A Royal Commission Report.* Ottawa: Ministry of Supply and Services.

Adams, Howard. 1989. *Prison of Grass: Canada from a Native Point of View.* Saskatchewan: Fifth House.

Adhopia, Ajit. 1988. Prejudice and Pride. *Mississauga Magazine,* premier issue (July).

Adler, Peter S. 1977. Beyond Cultural Identity: Reflections upon Cultural and Multicultural Man. In *Cultural Learning,* edited by R.W. Brislin. Honolulu: East-West Center.

Agocs, Carol. 1987. Ethnic Group Relations. In *Basic Sociology,* edited by J.J. Teevan. Scarborough: Prentice-Hall.

Ahlquist, Roberta. 1992. Manifestations of Inequality: Overcoming Resistance in a Multicultural Foundations Course. In *Research and Multicultural Education: From the Margins to the Mainstream,* edited by C.A. Grant. New York: Falmer.

Allport, Gordon. 1958. *The Nature of Prejudice.* New York: Doubleday Anchor.

Anderson, Alan B., and James S. Frideres. 1981. *Ethnicity in Canada: Theoretical Perspectives.* Toronto: Butterworth.

Anderson, G.L., Kathryn Herr, and Ann S. Nihlen. 1994 *Studying Your Own School: An Educator's Guide to Qualitative Practitioner Research.* California: Corwin Press, Inc.

Angus Reid Group Inc. 1989. *Immigration to Canada: Aspects of Public Opinion.* Ottawa: Employment and Immigration Canada. October.

Anisef, Paul. 1975. Consequences of Ethnicity for Educational Plans among Grade 12 Students. In *Education of Immigrant Students: Issues and Answers,* edited by A. Wolgang. Toronto: Ontario Institute for Studies in Education.

Anisef, Paul, Paul Axelrod, Etta Baichman, Carl James, and Anton Turrittin. Forthcoming. *Opportunity and Uncertainty: Life Course Experience of the Class of '73.* Toronto: York University.

Apple, M. 1993. Constructing the "Other": Rightist Reconstructions of Common Sense. In *Race, Identity and Representation in Education,* edited by Cameron McCarthy and Warren Crichlow. New York: Routledge.

———. 1993. Introduction. In *Race, Identity and Representation in Education,* edited by Cameron McCarthy and Warren Crichlow. New York: Routledge.

Arnold, Rick, B. Burke, C. James, D. Martin, and B. Thomas. 1991. *Educating for a Change.* Toronto: Between the Lines.

Ashworth, Mary. 1988. *Blessed with Bilingual Brain.* Vancouver: Pacific Educational Press.

Avison, William R., and John Kunkel. 1987. Socialization. In *Basic Sociology,* edited by J.J. Teevan. Scarborough: Prentice-Hall.

Bannerji, Hamani. 1997. Geography Lessons: On Being an Insider/Outsider to the Canadian Nation. In *Dangerous Territories: Struggles for Difference and Equality in Education,* edited by L.G. Roman and L. Eyre. New York: Routledge.

Banton, M. 1987. *Racial Theories.* Cambridge: Cambridge University Press.

Barlund, Dean C. 1988. Communication in a Global Village. In *Intercultural Communication: A Reader,* edited by L.A. Samovar and R.E. Porter. New York: Wadsworth.

Bedassigae-Pheasant, Valerie. 1996. Manufacturing Racism: The Two Faces of Canadian Develpment. In *Perspectives on Racism and the Human Service Sector: A Case for Change,* edited by C.E. James. Toronto: University of Toronto Press.

Benedict, Ruth. 1983. *Race and Racism.* London: Routledge.

Berry, Brewton. 1958. *Race and Ethnic Relations.* Boston: Houghton Mifflin.

Billingsley, Brenda, and Leon Muszynski. 1985. *No Discrimination Here! Toronto Employers and the Multi-Racial Workforce.* Toronto: Social Planning Council of Metropolitan Toronto, May.

Bolaria, B. Singh, and Peter Li, eds. 1988. *Racial Oppression in Canada.* Toronto: Garamond Press.

Bopp, Julie, Michael Bopp, Lee Brown, and Phil Lane. 1984. The Sacred Tree. Lethbridge, Alta.: Four Worlds Development Press.

Brathwaite, K., and C.E. James, eds. 1996. *Educating African Canadians.* Toronto: Our Schools/Our Selves, James Lorimer & Company Ltd., Publishers.

Brislin, Richard. 1993. *Understanding Culture's Influence on Behavior.* Orlando: Harcourt Brace Jovanovich.

Britzman, Deborah P. 1991. Decentering Discourses in Teacher Education; or, the Unleashing of Unpopular Things. *Journal of Education* 173, no. 3.

———. 1993. Beyond Rolling Models: Gender and Multicultural Education. In *Gender and Education: Ninety-Second Yearbook of the National Society for the Study of Education,* edited by S.K. Biklen and D. Pollard. Chicago: University of Chicago Press, 25-42.

Burnet, Jean. 1981. The Social and Historical Context of Ethnic Relations. In *A Canadian Social Psychology of Ethnic Relations*, edited by R.C. Gardener and R. Kalin. Toronto: Methuen.

———. 1984. Myths and Multiculturalism. In *Multiculturalism in Canada: Social and Educational Perspectives,* edited by R.J. Samuda, J.W. Berry and M. Laferriere. Toronto: Allyn and Bacon, Inc.

———, and Howard Palmer. 1989. *"Coming Canadians": An Introduction to a History of Canada's Peoples.* Ottawa: Ministry of Supply and Services.

Calliste, Agnes. 1994. "Race, Gender and Canadian Immigration Policy: Blacks from the Caribbean, 1900-1932." *Journal of Canadian Studies* 28, no. 4 (winter): 131-147.

Canada's Employment Discriminators. 1989. *Currents: Readings in Race Relations* 5, no. 4 (March).

Canadian Human Rights Act. 1987. Canadian National Railway Co. V. Canada (Canadian Human Rights Commission). *Federal/Employment/Sex: Supreme Court of Canada* 8, Decision 664. Canadian Human Rights Reporter.

Carnegie, Herbert H., O.Ont., O.M.C. 1997. *A Fly in a Pail of Milk: The Herb Carnegie Story.* Oakville, Ont.: Mosaic Press.

Carroll, Michael P. 1993. Culture. In *Basic Sociology: A Canadian Introduction,* edited by J.J. Teevan. Scarborough: Prentice-Hall Canada Inc.

Carter, Robert T. 1991. Cultural Values: A Review of Empirical Research and Implications for Counselling. *Journal of Counselling and Development* 70, no. 1: 164-73.

Christensen, Carole Pigler. 1992. Enhancing Cross-Cultural Understanding in Multicultural and Multiracial Educational Settings: A Perceptual Framework. In *Beyond Multicultural Education: International Perspective*, edited by K.A. Moodley. Calgary: Detselig.

Clarke, George Elliott. 1998. White Like Canada. *Transition*, no. 73: 98-109.

Cochran-Smith, Marilyn, and Susan L. Lytle. 1993. *Inside/Outside: Teacher Research and Knowledge.* New York: Teachers College Press.

Cryderman, Brian K., Chris N. O'Toole, and Augie Fleras. 1992. *Police, Race and Ethnicity: A Guide for Police Services.* Toronto: Butterworth.

Curtis, James, and Ronald D. Lambert. 1986. Culture. In *Sociology,* edited by R. Hagedorn. Toronto: Holt, Rinehart and Winston.

Das Gupta, Tania. 1996. *Racism and Paid Work.* Toronto: Garamond Press.

Dei, George J. Sefa. 1994. Reflections of an Anti-Racist Pedagogue. In *Sociology of Education in Canada: Critical Perspectives on Theory, Research and Practice*, edited by L. Erwin and D. MacLennan. Toronto: Copp Clark Longman.

———. 1996. *Anti-Racism Education Theory and Practice.* Halifax: Fernwood Publishing.

———. 1998. The Denial of Difference: Reframing Anti-Racist Praxis. *Race, Ethnicity, and Education* 1, no. 1.

Delpit, Lisa D. 1988. The Silent Dialogue: Power and Pedagogy in Educating Other People's Children. *Harvard Educational Review* 58, no. 3: 280-298.

Dobbins, James E., and Judith H. Skillings. 1991. The Utility of Race Labelling in Understanding Cultural Identity: A Conceptual Tool for the Social Science Practitioner. *Journal of Counselling and Development* 70, no. 1: 37-44.

Driedger, Leo. 1989. *The Ethnic Factor: Identity in Diversity.* Toronto: McGraw-Hill Ryerson Ltd.

DuCharme, Michèle. 1986. The Canadian Origins of South Africa Apartheid? *Perspectives* (summer): *2.*

Elliott, Jean L. and Augie Fleras. 1992. *Unequal Relations: An Introduction to Race and Ethnic Dynamics In Canada.* Scarborough: Prentice-Hall Canada.

Ellsworth, E. 1997. Double Binds of Whiteness. In *Off White: Readings on Race, Power and Society,* edited by Michelle Fine, Lois Weis, Linda Powell, and L. Mun Wong. New York: Routledge.

Fanon, Frantz. 1967. *Black Skin, White Masks.* New York: Grove Press.

Fine, M., L. Weis, L.C. Powell, and M. L. Wong, eds. 1997. *Off White: Readings on Race, Power and Society.* New York: Routledge.

Fish, Stanley. 1993. Reverse Racism or How the Pot Got to Call the Kettle Black. *The Atlantic Monthly,* November, 132-136.

Fleras, Augie and L. Elliott. 1992. *The Challenge of Diversity: Multiculturalism in Canada.* Scarborough: Nelson.

Frankenberg, Ruth. 1993. *White Women, Race Matters: The Social Construction of Whiteness.* Minneapolis: University of Minnesota Press.

Freire, Paulo. 1968. *Pedagogy of the Oppressed.* New York: Seabury.

Frideres, James S. 1993. *Native People in Canada: Contemporary Conflicts.* Scarborough: Prentice-Hall.

Gaine, Chris. 1995. *No Problem Here: A Practical Approach to Education and Race in White Schools.* London: Hutchinson Education.

Galen, Michele, and Ann Palmer. 1994. White, Male and Worried. *Business Week*, 31 January, 50-55.

Garvey, J., and N. Ignatiev. 1997. Toward a New Abilitionism: A Race Traitor Manifesto. In *Whiteness: A Critical Reader,* edited by Mike Hill. New York: New York University Press, 346-349.

Gates Jr., H.L., ed. 1986. *"Race," Writing, and Difference.* Chicago: Chicago University Press.

Gauthier, Pierre. 1994. Canada's Seniors. In *Canadian Social Trends,* Vol. 2. Toronto: Thompson Educational Publishing.

Gill, Dawn, and Les Levidow, eds. 1987. *Anti-Racist Science Teaching.* London: Free Association.

Gillborn, D. 1995. Antiracism and the Whole School. In *Racism and Antiracism in Real Schools: Theory, Policy, Practice.* Buckingham, Pa.: Open University Press.

Gilroy, Paul. 1993. *The Black Atlantic.* Cambridge, Mass.: Harvard University Press.

Giroux, Henry A. 1997. Rewriting the Discourse of Racial Identity: Towards a Pedagogy and Politics of Whiteness. *Harvard Educational Review* 67, no. 2 (summer): 285-320.

Globe and Mail. 1989. 50 Years Ago. *The Globe and Mail*, January 15, 15.

Goldberg, D.T. 1993. *Racist Culture.* Cambridge, Mass.: Blackwell Press.

Gruneau, Richard, and David Whitson. 1993. *Hockey Night in Canada: Sport, Identities and Cultural Politics.* Toronto: Garamond Press.

Haas, Jack, and William Shaffir. 1978. *Shaping Identity in Canadian Society.* Scarborough: Prentice-Hall.

Hagan, John. 1987. Finding and Defining Discrimination. In *Ethnic Canada: Identities and Inequalities*, edited by L. Driedger. Toronto: Copp Clark Pitman.

Haig-Brown, Celia. 1993. *Resistance and Renewal: Surviving the Indian Residential School.* Vancouver: Arsenal Pulp Press Ltd.

———. 1998. Warrior Mothers: Lessons and Possibilities. *Journal for Just and Caring Education* 4, no. 1 (January): 96-109.

———. In press. Moving into Difference (with Echo). In *Experiencing Difference: Encounters in Culture Language and Identity,* edited by C.E. James and A.Shadd. Halifax: Fernwood Publishing.

———, Kathy L. Hodgson-Smith, Robert Regnier, and Jo-ann Archibald. 1997. *Making the Spirit Dance within: Joe Duquette High School and an Aboriginal Community.* Toronto: Our Schools/Our Selves, James Lorimer & Co. Ltd., Publishers.

Hall, Stuart. 1991. Old and New Identities, Old and New Ethnicities. In *Culture Globalization and the World System: Contemporary Conditions for the Representation of Identity,* edited by D. King. London: Macmillan, 41-68.

Harris, Cheryl I. 1993. Whiteness as Property. *Harvard Law Review* 106: 1709-1791.

Head, Wilson. 1975. *The Black Presence in the Canadian Mosaic.* Toronto: Ontario Human Rights Commission.

Henry, Annette. 1998. *Taking Back Control: African Canadian Women Teachers' Lives and Practice.* Albany, N.Y.: State University of New York Press.

Henry, Frances. 1978. *The Dynamics of Racism in Toronto.* Research Report. Toronto: York University.

———. 1994. *The Caribbean Diaspora in Toronto: Learning to Live with Race.* Toronto: University of Toronto Press.

———, and Effie Ginzberg. 1985. *Who Gets the Work: A Test of Racial Discrimination in Employment.* Toronto: Social Planning Council.

———. 1993. Racial Discrimination in Employment. In *Social Inequalities in Canada: Patterns, Problems, Policies,* edited by J. Curtis, E. Crabb, N. Guppy, and S. Gilbert. Scarborough: Prentice-Hall.

Henry, Frances, Carol Tator, Winston Mattis, and Tim Rees, eds. 1995. *The Colour of Democracy: Racism in Canadian Society.* Toronto: Harcourt Brace & Company Canada, Ltd.

Hill, Mike, ed. 1997. *Whiteness: A Critical Reader.* New York: New York University Press.

hooks, bell. 1988. *Talking Back: Thinking Feminist, Thinking Black.* Toronto: Between the Lines.

———. 1992. *Black Looks: Race and Representation.* Toronto: Between the Lines.

Hoopes, David S. 1981. Intercultural Communication Concepts and the Psychology of Intercultural Experience. In *Multicultural Education*, edited by M. Pusch. Yarmount: Intercultural Press.

———, and Margaret D. Pusch. 1981. Definition of Terms. In *Multicultural Education*, edited by M. Pusch. Pittsburgh: Intercultural Network.

House of Commons Debates. 1947. Vol. 3, 2644-2647.

Hughes, David R., and Evelyn Kallen. 1974. *The Anatomy of Racism: Canadian Dimension.* Montreal: Harvest House.

Hutcheon, Linda, and Marion Richmond, eds. 1990. *Other Solitudes: Canadian Multicultural Fictions.* Toronto: Oxford University Press.

Igantiev, N. 1995. *How the Irish Became White.* New York: Routledge.

Immigration Canada. 1989. *Annual Report to Parliament on Future Immigration Levels.* Ottawa: Minister of Employment and Immigration.

Innis, Hugh R. 1973. *Bilingualism and Biculturalism: An Abridged Version of the Royal Commission Report.* Toronto: McClelland and Stewart Ltd.

Isajiw, Wsevolod W. 1977. Olga in Wonderland: Ethnicity in a Technological Society. *Canadian Ethnic Studies* 9, no. 1: 77-85.

Jackson, Anita P., and Ferguson B. Meadows. 1991. Getting to the Bottom to Understand the Top. *Journal of Counseling and Development* 70, no. 1: 72-76.

Jaenen, Cornelius J. 1977. Multiculturalism and Public Education. In *Precepts, Policy and Process: Perspectives on Contemporary Canadian Education,* edited by H. Stevenson and D. Wilson. London, Ont.: Alexander, Blake Associates, 77-95.

Jakubowski, Lisa Marie. 1997. *Immigration and the Legalization of Racism.* Halifax: Fernwood Publishing.

James, Carl E. 1990. *Making It: Black Youth, Racism and Career Aspirations in a Big City.* Oakville: Mosaic Press.

———. 1993. Getting There and Staying There: Blacks' Employment Experience. In *Transitions: Schooling and Employment in Canada,* edited by P. Anisef and P. Axelrod. Toronto: Thompson Educational Publishing.

———. 1995. "Reverse Racism": Students' Responses to Equity Programs. *Journal of Professional Studies* 3, no. 1: 48-54.

———, ed. 1996. Race, Culture, and Identity. In *Perspectives on Racism and the Human Services Sector: A Case for Change.* Toronto: University of Toronto Press.

———. 1997. The Distorted Images of African Canadians: Impact, Implications, and Responses. In *Globalization and Survival in the Black Diaspora: The New Urban Challenge,* edited by Charles Green. Albany: State University of New York Press.

———. 1998b. The Long Shot: Chasing the Dream through Basketball. In *Re/visioning: Canadian Perspectives on the Education of Africans in the Late 20th Century,* edited by Vincent R. D'Oyley and Carl E. James. Toronto: Captus Press Inc.

———. 1998a. Multiculturalism, Diversity and Education in the Canadian Context: The Search for an Inclusive Pedagogy. Paper presented at the 1998 American Educational Research Association (AERA) Annual Meeting. San Diego, April.

———, and Adrienne Shadd, eds. 1994. *Talking about Difference: Encounters, in Culture, Language and Identity.* Toronto: Between the Lines.

———, and Celia Haig-Brown. 1998. Opportunities and Possibilities: School Board/University Partnership as means of Enhancing the Educational Experiences of Immigrant and Refugee Students. Paper presented at the 19th Annual Ethnography in Education Research Forum. Philadelphia: University of Pennsylvania, March.

Jansen, Clifford J. 1981. Problems and Issues in Post-War Immigration to Canada and Their Effects on Origins and Characteristics of Immigrants. Paper presented at Meetings of The Canadian Population Society. Halifax: Dalhousie University, June.

———, and Anthony Richmond. 1990. Immigrant Settlement and Integration. Paper presented at the Symposium for Immigrant Settlement and Integration. Toronto, May 28-29.

———, Dwaine Plaza, Carl E. James. Forthcoming. *Despite the Odds: Upward Mobility among Second Generation Caribbeans Living in Toronto.* Toronto: York University.

Jones, James M. 1991. Psychological Models of Race: What Have They Been and What Should They Be. In *Psychological Perspectives on Human Diversity in America,* edited by J.D. Goodchilds and L. Garnets. Washington: American Psychological Association.

Kalbach, Warren E., and Wayne W. McVey. 1971. *The Demographic Bases of Canadian Society.* Toronto: McGraw-Hill Co., Ltd.

———, Ravi Verma, M.V. George, and S.Y. Dai. 1993. *Population Projections of Visible Minority Groups, Canada, Provinces and Regions, 1991-2016.* Ottawa: Statistics Canada, Interdepartmental Working Group on Employment Equity Data, December.

Kallen, Evelyn. 1982. *Ethnicity and Human Rights in Canada.* Toronto: Gage Publishing Ltd.

———. 1989. *Label Me Human: Minority Rights in Multicultural Canada.* Toronto: Garamond Press.

———. 1995. *Ethnicity and Human Rights in Canada,* Second Edition. Toronto: Oxford University Press.

Kalin, Rudolf. 1981. Ethnic Attitudes. In *A Canadian Social Psychology of Ethnic Relations,* edited by R.C. Gardner and R. Kalin. Toronto: Methuen.

Karapinski, Eva C., and Ian Lea, eds. 1993. *Pens of Colour: A Canadian Reader.* Toronto: Harcourt Brace Jovanovich.

Kinloch, Graham C. 1974. *The Dynamics of Race Relations: A Sociological Analysis.* Toronto: McGraw-Hill.

Kondo, Dorinne K. 1990. *Crafting Selves: Power, Gender, and Discourses of Identity in a Japanese Workplace.* Chicago: University of Chicago Press.

Kubat, Daniel, U. Merhlander, and E. Gehmacher. 1979. *The Politics of Migration Policies: The First World in the 1970's.* New York: Center for Migration Studies.

Lam, Larry. 1994. Immigrant Students. In *Learning and Sociological Profiles of Canadian High School Students: An Overview of 15 to 18 Year Olds and Educational Policy Implications for Dropouts, Exceptional Students, Employed Students, Immigrant Students and Native Youth,* edited by P. Anisef. Queenston, Ont.: Edwin Mellen Press, 121-130.

Larter, Sylvia, Maisy Cheng, S. Capps, and M. Lee. 1982. *Post Secondary Plans of Grade Eight Students and Related Variables 165. Toronto: The Board of Education for the City of Toronto.*

Lee, Enid. 1985. *Letters to Marcia: A Teacher's Guide to Anti-Racist Education.* Toronto: Cross Cultural Communication Centre.

———. 1994. Ant-Racist Education: Panacea or Palliative? *Orbit* 25, no. 2: 22-25.

Leslie, J., and R. Maguire, eds. 1978. *The Historical Development of the Indian Act.* Ottawa: Ministry of Indian Affairs.

Li, Peter S., ed. 1990. *Race and Ethnic Relations in Canada.* Toronto: Oxford University Press.

Logan, Ronald. 1991. Immigration during the 80s. *Canadian Social Trends.* Ottawa: Statistics Canada, Spring, 9-13.

Mackie, Marlene. 1986. Socialization. In *Sociology,* edited by R. Hagedorn. Toronto: Holt, Rinehart and Winston.

Mannette, Joy, ed. 1992. *Elusive Justice: Beyond the Marshall Inquiry.* Halifax: Fernwood Books.

Mansfield, E., and J.W. Kehoe. 1994. A Critical Examination of Anti-Racist Education. *Canadian Journal of Education* 19, no. 4: 419-430.

Martin, June Roland. 1994. Methodological Essentialism, False Difference, and Other Dangerous Traps. *Signs: Journal of Women In Culture and Society* 19, no. 3: 630-657.

Mazurek, Kas. 1987. Multiculturalism, Education, and Ideology of Meritocracy. In *The Political Economy of Canadian Schooling,* edited by T. Wotherspoon. Toronto: Methuen, 141-163.

McAndrew, Marie. 1991. Ethnicity, Multiculturalism, and Multicultural Education in Canada. In *Social Change and Education in Canada,* edited by R. Ghosh and D. Ray. Toronto: Harcourt Brace Jovanovich.

McCarthy, C., and W. Crichlow, eds. 1993. *Race, Identity and Representation in Education.* New York: Routledge.

McIntosh, Peggy. 1995. White Privilege and Male Privilege: A Personal Account of Coming to See Correspondences through Work in Women's Studies. In *Race, Class and Gender: An Anthology,* edited by M.L. Andersen and P. Hill Collins. Belmont, Calif.: Wadsworth, 70-81.

McNeill, J.L. 1974. Egerton Ryerson: Founder of Canadian (English-Speaking) Education. In *Profiles of Canadian Educators,* edited by R.S. Patterson, J.W. Chalmers, and J.W. Friesen. Toronto: D.C. Heath Canada.

Mills, C. Wright. 1956. *The Power Elite.* New York: Oxford University Press.

Miner, Horace. 1956. Body Rituals among the Nacirema. *American Anthropologist* 58.

Minister of Supply and Services Canada. 1991. *Multiculturalism: What Is It Really About?* Ottawa: Multiculturalism and Citizenship Canada.

Ministry of Employment and Immigration. 1978. *New Directions: A Look at Canada's Immigration Act and Regulations.* Ottawa: Ministry of Supply and Services.

———. 1992. *Background: The Immigration Management System.* Ottawa: Public Affairs Branch, Ministry of Supply and Services.

———. 1992. *Managing Immigration: A Framework for the 1990s.* Ottawa: Public Affairs Branch, Ministry of Supply and Services.

Monture-Angus, Patricia. 1995. *Thunder in My Soul: A Mohawk Woman Speaks.* Halifax: Fernwood Publishing.

Moreau, Joanne. 1994. Changing Faces: Visible Minorities In Toronto. In *Canadian Social Trends.* Vol. 2. Toronto: Thompson Educational Publishing.

Morrison, Toni. 1990. *Playing in the Dark: Whiteness and the Literary Imagination.* Cambridge: Howard University Press.

Mukherjee, Arun. 1993. *Sharing Our Experience.* Ottawa: Canadian Advisory Council for the Status of Women.

Multiculturalism Policy of Canada. 1988. Excerpts from the Canadian Multiculturalism Act (July).

Neufeld, Mark. 1992. Can an Entire Society Be Racist, or Just Individuals? *The Toronto Star,* 25 October, B7.

Ng, Roxana. 1993. Racism, Sexism, and Nation Building in Canada. In *Race, Identity and Representation in Education,* edited by M.L. Andersen and P. Hill Collins. New York: Routledge.

Office of the Prime Minister. 1971. Statement by the Prime Minister in the House of Commons. Press release, 8 October, Ottawa.

Omi, Michael, and Howard Winant. 1993. On the Theoretical Status of the Concept of Race. In *Race, Identity and Representation in Education,* edited by C. McCarthy and W. Crichlow. New York: Routledge.

Palmer, Howard. 1975. *Immigration and the Rise of Multiculturalism.* Vancouver: Copp Clark.

Perry, Theresa, and James W. Fraser. 1993. Reconstructing Schools as Multiracial and Multicultural Democracies: Toward a Theoretical Perspective. In *Freedom's Plow: Teaching in the Multicultural Classroom,* edited by T. Perry and J.W. Fraser. New York: Routledge.

Pettigrew, Thomas F., F.M. George, D.T. Knobel, N. Glazer, and R. Ueda. 1980. *Prejudice: Dimensions of Ethnicity.* Cambridge: Harvard University Press.

Pfeil, F. 1995. *White Guys: Studies in Postmodern Domination and Difference.* New York: Verso.

———. 1997. Sympathy for the Devil: Notes on Some White Guys in the Ridiculous Class War. In *Whiteness: A Critical Reader,* edited by Mike Hill. New York: New York University Press.

Philip, M. Nourbese. 1992. *Frontiers: Essays and Writings on Racism and Culture.* Stratford, Ont.: Mercury.

———. 1993. *Showing Grit: Showboating North of the 44th Parallel,* Second Edition. Toronto: Poui.

Phoenix, A. 1997. "I'm White! So What?" The Construction of Whiteness for Young Londoners. In *Off White: Readings on Race, Power, and Society,* edited by Michelle Fine, Lois Weis, Linda Powell, and L. Mun Wong. New York: Routledge.

Pinar, William. 1993. Notes on Understanding Curriculum as a Racial Text. In *Race, Identity and Representation in Education,* edited by C. McCarthy and W. Crichlow. New York: Routledge, 60-70.

Pleasant-Jétte, Corinne. 1996. Comments: Disturbing the Silence: Reflections on Racism and Aboriginal People. In *Perspectives on Racism and the Human Service Sector: A Case for Change,* edited by C.E. James. Toronto: University of Toronto Press, 36-44.

Porter, John. 1965. *The Vertical Mosaic: An Analysis of Social Class and Power in Canada.* Toronto: University of Toronto Press.

Price, John. 1978. *Native Studies: American and Canadian Indians.* Toronto: McGraw-Hill Ryerson Ltd.

Quamina, Odida T. 1991. Convenient Use of Race, Colour. *Share*, 10 October.

———. 1996. *All Things Considered Can We Live Together*? Toronto: Exile Editions.

Ramcharan, Subhas. 1975. Special Problems of Immigrant Children in the Toronto School System. In *Education of Immigrant Students,* edited by A. Wolfgang. Toronto: Ontario Institute of Education.

———. 1982. *Racism: Nonwhites in Canada.* Toronto: Butterworth.

Roman, Leslie G. 1993. White is a Color! White Defensiveness, Postmodernism, and Anti-Racism Pedagogy. In *Race, Identity and Representation in Education*, edited by C. McCarthy and W. Crichlow. New York: Routlege.

———. 1997. Denying (White) Racial Privilege: Redemption Discourses and the Uses of Fantacy. In *Off White: Readings on Race, Power and Society,* edited by M. Fine, L. Weis, L.C. Powell and L.M. Wong. New York: Routledge, 270-282.

———, and Timothy Stanley. 1997. Empires, Emigrants, and Aliens: Young People's Negotiations of Official and Popular Racism in Canada. In *Dangerous Territories: Struggles for Difference and Equality in Education,* edited by L.G. Roman and L. Eyre. New York: Routledge.

Rosaldo, Renato. 1993. *Culture & Truth: The Remaking of Social Analysis.* Boston, Mass.: Beacon Press.

Rosenberg, P. 1997. Underground Discourses: Exploring Whiteness in Teacher Education. In *Off White: Readings on Race, Power and Society,* edited by Michelle Fine, Lois Weis, Linda Powell and L. Mun Wong. New York: Routledge.

St. Lewis, Joanne. 1996. Race, Racism, and the Justice System. In *Perspectives on Racism and the Human Service Sector: A Case for Change,* edited by C.E. James. Toronto: University of Toronto Press.

Samuel, John T. 1989. Visible Minorities and Immigration. *Currents: Readings in Race Relations* 5, no. 2: 3-6.

———. 1992. Visible Minorities in Canada: A Projection. Ottawa: Carleton University (June).

Satzewich, V. 1991. Social Stratification: Class and Racial Inequality. In *Social Issues and Contradictions in Canadian Society,* edited by B.S. Bolaria. Toronto: Harcourt Brace Jovanovich.

———, ed. 1992 *Deconstructing a Nation: Immigration, Multiculturalism and Racism in 90's Canada.* Halifax: Fernwood Publishing.

———. 1998. *Racism & Social Inequality in Canada.* Toronto: Thompson Educational Publishing.

Schecter, Sandra R., Diane Sharken-Taboada, and Robert Bayley. 1996. Bilingual by Choice: Latino Parents' Rationales and Strategies for Raising Children with Two Languages. *The Bilingual Research Journal* 20, no.2 (spring).

Schoem, David, ed. 1991. *Inside Separate Worlds: Life Stories of Young Blacks, Jews, and Latinos.* Ann Arbor: University of Michigan Press.

Schuster, Charles I., and William V. Van Pelt, eds. 1992. *Speculations: Readings in Culture, Identity, and Values.* Englewood Cliffs, N.J.: Blair.

Seward, Shirley B., and Marc Tremblay. 1989. *Immigrants in the Canadian Labour Force: Their Role in Structural Change.* Ottawa: Institute for Research on Public Policy (September).

Shadd, Adrienne. 1994. Where Are You Really From? Notes of an "Immigrant" from North Buxton, Ontario. In *Talking about Difference: Encounters, in Culture, Language and Identity,* edited by C.E. James and A. Shadd. Toronto: Between the Lines.

Shepard, R. Bruce. 1991. Plain Racism: The Reaction against Oklahoma Black Immigration to the Canadian Plains. In *Racism in Canada*, edited by O. McKague. Saskatoon: Fifth House.

———. 1997. *Deemed Unsuitable: Blacks from Oklahoma Move to the Canadian Prairies in Search of Equality in the Early 20th Century Only to Find Racism in their New Home.* Toronto: Umbrella Press.

Silvera, Makeda. 1984. *Silenced: Talks with Working Class West Indian Women about Their Lives and Struggles as Domestic Workers in Canada.* Toronto: Sister Vision Press.

Simon, Roger. 1987. Being Ethnic/Doing Ethnicity: A Response to Corrigan. In *Breaking Identities in Canadian Schooling,* edited by J. Young. Toronto: Garamond.

Sleeter, Christine. 1993. How White Teachers Construct Race. In *Race Identity and Representation in Education*, edited by Cameron McCarthy and Warren Crichlow. New York: Routledge, 157-171.

———. 1994. White Racism. *Multicultural Education,* (spring).

Smith, Elsie J. 1991. Ethnic Identity Development: Toward the Development of a Theory within the Context of Minority/Majority Status. *Journal of Counselling and Development* 70, no. 1: 181-188.

Smith, Michael Peter. 1992. Postmodernism, Urban Ethnography, and the New Social Space of Ethnic Identity. *Theory and Society* 2: 493-531.

Smolicz, J.J. 1981. Culture, Ethnicity and Education: Multiculturalism in a Plural Society. In *World Yearbook of Education 1981: Education of Minorities.* London: Kegan Page Ltd.

Sodowsky, Gargi R., Edward W.M. Lai, and Barbara S. Plake. 1991. Moderating Effects of Sociocultural Variables on Acculturation Attitudes of Hispanic and Asian Americans. *Journal of Counselling and Development* 70, no. 1: 194-203.

Solomon, R. Patrick. 1992. *Black Resistance in High School: Forging a Separatist Culture.* Albany: State University of New York Press.

Special Committee on Visible Minorities. 1984. *Equality Now: Participation of Visible Minorities in Canadian Society.* Ottawa: Supply and Services.

Spivak, Gayatri. 1993. *Outside in the Teaching Machine.* New York: Routledge.

Spivey, Mike. 1998. Identity Politics of a Southern Tribe: A Critical Ethnography. Ph.D. Dissertation. Toronto: Department of Sociology, York University.

Standing Committee on Multiculturalism. 1987. *Multiculturism: Building the Canadian Mosaic.* Ottawa: Minister of Supply and Services.

Statistics Canada. 1994. Housing, Family and Social Statistics Division.

Stebbins, Robert A. 1989. *Sociology: The Study of Society.* New York: Harper & Row, Publishers.

Steinem, Gloria. 1983. *Outrageous Acts and Everyday Rebellions.* Scarborough: New American Library.

Stephen Leacock Collegiate Institute, History Department. 1994. *Our Roots 2: Personal and Family Histories from the OAC Stephen Leacock Black History Class, 1994.* Scarborough: Scarborough Board of Education.

Stephenson, Cynthia. 1996. The Nuts and Bolts of Employment Equity: A Quick Primer for Social Service Agencies. In *Perspectives on Racism and the Human Service Sector: A Case for Change,* edited by C.E. James. Toronto: University of Toronto Press.

Tatum, Beverly Daniel. 1992. Talking about Race, Learning about Racism: The Application of Racial Identity Development Theory in the Classroom. *Harvard Educational Review* 62, no. 1: 1-24.

Taylor, Donald M. 1981. Stereotypes and Intergroup Relations. In *A Canadian Social Psychology of Ethnic Relations,* edited by R. Gardner and R. Kalin. Toronto: Methuen.

Tedesco, Theresa. 1989. The Moneyed Class: Rich Immigrants Jump the Queue. *Maclean's* 102, no. 28, 10 July.

Todorov, T. 1993. *On Human Diversity: Nationalism, Racism, and Exoticism in French Thought.* Cambridge and London: Harvard University Press.

Tomkins, George. 1977. Traditions and Change in Canadian Education: Historical and Comtemporary Perspectives. In *Precepts, Policy and Process: Perspectives on Contemporary Canadian Education,* edited by H. Stevenson and D. Wilson. London, Ont.: Alexander, Blake Associates.

Torzyner, J., W. Boxhill, C. James and C. Muller. 1997. *Diversity, Mobility and Change: The Dynamics of Black Communities in Canada.* Montreal: McGill School of Social Work.

Toronto Star. 1990. Ethnic Stereotyping: What Does It Take to Be Canadian? Thursday, 7 June.

———. 1986. *A Minority Report.* Toronto.

Troyna, Barry. 1987. Beyond Multiculturalism: Toward the Enactment of Anti-Racist Education in Policy, Provision and Pedagogy. *Oxford Review of Education* 13, no. 3: 307-320.

Vallee, Frank G. 1983. Inequality and Identity in Multi-Ethnic Societies. In *Social Issues: Sociological Views of Canada,* edited by D. Forcese and S. Richer. Scarborough: Prentice-Hall.

van den Berghe, Pierre L. 1967. *Race and Racism: A Comparative Perspective.* New York: John Wiley & Sons.

Walcott, R. 1980. *History of Blacks in Canada. A Study Guide for Teachers and Parents.* Ottawa: Minister of State for Multiculturalism

———. 1997. *Black Like Who? Writing Black Canada.* Toronto: Insomniac Press.

Watson, Paul. 1991. Somalis Find Home in Etobicoke. *The Toronto Star,* 27 September, A11.

Weinfield, Morton. 1998. Immigration Facts. *Transition—Newcomers: Immigrant Families adapting to Life in Canada* (September).

———. 1990. Trends in Ethnic and Racial Inequality. In *Images of Canada: The Sociological Tradition,* edited by J. Curtis and L. Tepperman. Scarborough, Ont.: Prentice-Hall, Inc.

Weis, Lois, and Michelle Fine. 1996. Notes on "White as Race." *Race, Gender & Class: An Interdisciplinary and Multicultural Journal* 3, no. 3: 5-9.

———, A. Proweller, and C. Centrie. 1997. Reexamining "A Moment in History": Loss of Privilege Inside White Working-class Masculinity in the 1990s. In *Off White: Readings on Race, Power, and Society,* edited by Michelle Fine, Lois Weis, Linda Powell, and L. Mun Wong. New York: Routledge.

Williams, Raymond. 1983. *Keywords: A Vocabulary of Culture and Society.* London: Fontana Paperbacks.

Woodsworth, J.S. 1909. *Strangers within Our Gate.* Missionary Society of the Methodist Church. Cited in Porter, 1965.

Wotherspoon, Terry, and Vic Satzewich. 1993. *First Nations: Race, Class, and Gender Relations.* Scarborough: Nelson.

Yeboah, Samuel Kennedy. 1988. *The Ideology of Racism.* London: Hansils.

Yi, Sun-Kyung. 1992. An Immigrant's Split Personality. *The Globe and Mail,* 1 April, A20.

Yon, Dan. 1999. The Discursive Space of Schooling: On the Theories of Power and Enpowerment in Multiculturalism and Anti-Racism. In *The Anthropology of Power,* edited by A. Cheater. New York: Routledge.

Index